THE MINNESOTA

LIBRARY

ON AMERICAN WRITERS

LEONARD UNGER

AND GEORGE T. WRIGHT,

EDITORS

The seven essays which appear in this book were first published separately in the series of University of Minnesota Pamphlets on American Writers and, together with the other pamphlets in the series, are intended as introductions to authors who have helped to shape American culture over the years of our colonial and national existence. The editors of the pamphlet series have been Richard Foster, William Van O'Connor, Allen Tate, Leonard Unger, Robert Penn Warren, and George T. Wright. Many pamphlets, in addition to the seven represented here, are available from the University of Minnesota Press.

SEVEN
AMERICAN POETS
from MacLeish
to Nemerov
An Introduction

edited by Denis Donoghue

UNIVERSITY OF MINNESOTA PRESS
MINNEAPOLIS

Library of Congress Catalog Card Number: 74-22560

ISBN 0-8166-0739-7

Acknowledgment is gratefully made to those publishers, agents, and individuals who have permitted the use of the following materials in copyright.

"Archibald MacLeish": From *A Time to Speak: The Selected Prose of Archibald MacLeish,* copyright 1941 Archibald MacLeish, by permission of Houghton Mifflin Company. From *Actfive and Other Poems,* copyright 1948 Archibald MacLeish, by permission of Random House, Inc. From *Collected Poems 1917–1952,* copyright 1952 Archibald MacLeish, by permission of Houghton Mifflin Company. From *Songs for Eve,* copyright 1954 Archibald MacLeish, by permission of Houghton Mifflin Company. From *The Wild Old Wicked Man, and Other Poems,* copyright © 1968 Archibald MacLeish, by permission of Houghton Mifflin Company.

"Richard Eberhart": From Richard Eberhart, *Collected Poems 1930–1960,* copyright © 1960, by permission of Oxford University Press and Chatto and Windus Ltd. From *The Quarry,* copyright © 1964, by permission of Oxford University Press and Chatto and Windus Ltd. From *The Visionary Farms,* in *Collected Verse Plays,* copyright © 1962, by permission of the University of North Carolina Press. From *A Bravery of Earth,* copyright 1930, by permission of Mr. Eberhart.

"Theodore Roethke": From "The Feud," copyright 1935 Theodore Roethke; "The Heron," copyright 1937 Theodore Roethke; "The Light Comes Brighter," copyright 1938 Theodore Roethke; "Open House," copyright 1941 Theodore Roethke; "The Return," copyright 1946 Modern Poetry Association, Inc.; "The Lost Son," copyright 1947 Theodore Roethke; "Cuttings (later)," copyright 1948 Theodore Roethke; "Orchids," copyright 1948 Theodore Roethke; "I Cry, Love! Love!" "Praise to the End," and "Where Knock Is Open Wide," copyright 1950 Theodore Roethke; "Bring the Day" and "O Lull Me, Lull Me," copyright 1951 Theodore Roethke; "Frau Bauman, Frau Schmidt, and Frau Schwartze," copyright 1952 Theodore Roethke; "Four for Sir John Davies," copyright 1952 by The Atlantic Monthly Company; "Meditations of an Old Woman" and "Words for the Wind," copyright © 1955 Theodore Roethke; "The Dying Man," copyright © 1956 The Atlantic Monthly Company; "Meditation at Oyster River," copyright © 1960 Beatrice Roethke as administratrix of the estate of Theodore Roethke; "The Tree, The Bird," copyright © 1961 Beatrice Roethke as administratrix of the estate of Theodore Roethke; "Wish for a Young Wife" and "Infirmity," copyright © 1963 Beatrice Roethke as administratrix of the estate of Theodore Roethke. All these poems appear in the *Collected Poems of Theodore Roethke,* reprinted by permission of Doubleday & Company, Inc., and Faber and Faber Ltd. From "Once More, the Round," by Theodore Roethke, copyright © 1963 Hearst Corporation, by permission of *Harper's Bazaar.* From "The Minimal," by

Contents

SEVEN

AMERICAN POETS

from MacLeish

to Nemerov

Introduction

It is a relief, after years of critical asperity, to rank the poets in an order merely chronological, to say of poet A not that he is superior to poet B but that he is a year older. Every teacher knows that the first thing to say of Shakespeare's "That Time of Year" is that it is a sonnet: it is well to start with such a fact before marching into polemic. So I have been consulting the calendar of modern American poetry and noting, with occasional surprise, a few dates of birth. Begin with Frost, 1874, then Stevens, 1879, Williams, 1883, Pound, 1885, where all the ladders start. Marianne Moore, 1887, then Eliot, 1888, Ransom the same year: a poet who is born in the same year as Eliot probably feels that the gods have been severe with him. Jump a few years to MacLeish, 1892, Cummings, 1894, Hart Crane, 1899, and Allen Tate the same year. The calendar rushes into the new century, but we are not obliged to follow. A young poet looking for a master will find one among these names, unless he leaps over them altogether and runs back to Whitman, Emerson, Emily Dickinson. There are as many poets as he is likely to need, and more than he is likely to use. Faced with the range and diversity of modern American poetry, the young poet is nearly bound to say of his profession, as Yeats said of his companions who

3

gathered at the Cheshire Cheese, "the only thing certain about us is that we are too many."

The present book asks the reader to attend upon seven poets. I shall make a few notes upon each, bearing chiefly in mind that seven modern American poets demonstrate seven different ways of being an American. The poets begin with MacLeish, 1892, then Eberhart, 1904, Roethke, 1908, Jarrell, 1914, Berryman the same year, Lowell, 1917, and Nemerov, 1920. It is not my business, nor would it give me any pleasure, to comment on the difficulty of being an American poet: I am neither American nor poet. But it is my impression that American poets have become more skillful in the art of being themselves; poets born in 1920 or later have had the advantage of seeing a thousand ways in which the job has been done, and the encouragement of such examples. Each poet must still do the work for himself, but he has before him the pioneers from Poe and Whitman to Williams, and he knows by their example what it means to work in the American grain. Williams conducted a singlehanded and largely one-sided war against Eliot on the grounds that he fled the American scene, groveled before Europe and antiquity, and gave no help at all to American poets intent upon declaring their independence. Late in the evening, Williams came to terms with Eliot and — persuaded by Robert Lowell — forgave him. But the war, such as it was, is finished: young American poets know that Williams's side has won; they no longer feel intimidated by England or France. If there is still a war, it is a different war; England has nothing to do with it; France is a nuance, a possibility, but not a problem.

So much the better; it is pleasant to find a problem resolved or circumvented. When Archibald MacLeish published *Songs for a Summer's Day* in 1915, the problem still presented itself in the old terms; America and Europe, American English and English English, the relation between an individual talent and the old masters he was called upon to acknowledge. The singer of *Songs for a Summer's Day* found his head full of European sounds, his verse forms "hung with pleasing wraiths of former masteries," as Wil-

liams wrote of someone else's forms. It was difficult to speak out
boldly in one's own voice. MacLeish kept good company:

> Dos that saw the tyrants in the lime
> Ernest that saw the first snow in the
> fox's feather
> Stephen that saw his wife
> Cummings his quick fillies
> Eliot the caul between the ribs of life
> Pound — Pound cracking the eggs of a cock
> with the beautiful sword of Achilles.

But he had to discover his own voice, and make it audible against
former masteries. It is my impression that he became a "public
poet" not because he was a politician in poet's clothing but be-
cause he felt that an American voice would issue from American
themes. He had a taste for ancestral plangencies; even as a
young poet he loved the kind of poem that might be sung in the
streets. I sense in his poems a note of nostalgia for a time in
which the natural poetic form was the epic: the lines which stay
in my mind from his mature poems invariably sound as though
they were the only surviving fragments of a lost saga. Floating
free from their contexts, they make a broken poetry: "the horn
of Roland in the passages of Spain," "and garlic longed-for by
the eager dead," "and strange at Ecbatan the trees," "the dead
against the dead and on the silent ground / The silent slain,"
"and by what way shall I go back?" I do not know any poet who
so much loves the word *and*. MacLeish also loves to repeat his
words, as though the penury of each were to cause, upon repeti-
tion, a corresponding reverberation, a sense of desired relations,
fostered echoes: "Of sorrow of sorrow of sorrow her heart full,"
"And there, there overhead, there, there, hung over / Those
thousands of white faces, those dazed eyes," "O day that brings
the earth back bring again / That well-swept town those towers
and that island." MacLeish was content to think of the poem as
occupying "the space between ourselves on the one side and the
world on the other"; he did not press the metaphysics too hard;
the poet is a man speaking to men about a world in some meas-

ure shared. But he knew that a poet needs some force to mediate
between himself and the multiplicity of linguistic possibilities: if
everything is possible, nothing is prescribed. Yearning for epic
grandeur and the heroism of tragedy, he often went directly to
the Greeks, as in *Herakles*, or to the Old Testament, as in the Job
of *J. B.* When he wanted something of the same scale nearer
home, he went to Mexico for *Conquistador*. But he always came
back to Boston, Washington, and Mr. Rockefeller's City. He was
always a patriot, never an expatriate: he has been rebuked for
making his patriotism somewhat blatant. But he pointed to
Yeats's political poems to show that public themes, direct speech,
and poetry were not incompatible. He insisted upon being an
American in that way, while retaining the right to listen to Lu
Chi, Yeats, Rimbaud, Keats.

   Richard Eberhart has said of poetry that it is "like the mystery
of the world; it comes from secret wells, it is a fresh draft from
heaven, warmed in earth." It takes courage to speak of poetry in
these terms; the fashion has run the other way. But Eberhart has
refused to be intimidated; he lives in a free country and sees
every reason for exercising that freedom. Temperamentally, he
is a platonist in the sense that he construes poetry as divine rage,
an imperative vision of things, answerable to its intensity but to
no other criterion. "If I could only live at the pitch that is near
madness": why not? Or, if it is impossible, why not seize the few
moments in which it is possible and make them into poems?
Eberhart has expounded his preference by recourse to Will and
Psyche, but the idiom does not matter; it is only his way of saying
that poetry is inspiration. So he reads the spirit, meditates upon
death, ponders the four elements, chances a prophecy from
time to time, praises "the light beyond compare," listens to "an-
cient harmonies," and runs along by "the river of sweetness that
runs through the meadow of lies." His masters are Wordsworth
and Hopkins, to begin with — Wordsworth for his meditative
power, the voice ranging through the chances and choices of
experience; Hopkins for his language of seizure, the concentra-
tion and pressure which force an event to yield up its secret. But
Eberhart is his own man, he trusts his "summer intuition" more

than the arithmetic of reason, and I suspect he would rather be companioned with Blake and Smart than with Pope and Dryden. Perhaps he counts too much upon his intimacy with the big words: *beauty, mystery, humanity, vision, freedom, pride, spirit.* They are hard to manage, even for a platonist. Eberhart's best poems are not his high talk but poems in which he has found for the grand abstraction a domestic embodiment; it may be a casual event, a homely incident releasing the significance of a parable as in "Sea Burial from the Cruiser *Reve*" and "Am I My Neighbor's Keeper?" He is particularly good in praising the things which have offered themselves to his attention when he wants to praise the world. That is to say: he is unabashed.

The pitch that is near madness is Theodore Roethke's pitch, too, but in a different sense. While he professed himself interested in "the Platonic tradition," meaning Spinoza, Kant, Bergson, and Bradley, he was never a true platonist. If his poetry is written at the pitch that is near madness, it is because it testifies to his violence of feeling: the violence was acknowledged not for its own sake but because it was Roethke's way of driving himself beyond or beneath himself. To Babette Deutsch he wrote: "to go forward (as spiritual man) it is necessary first to go back." He meant not only back in time, in history, but down in feeling, as though he were to begin all over again in prerational stirrings and unconsciousness. Some of his poems he described as "poems that run back into the unconscious and depend upon associational rightness." We think of his work as occupying two areas of feeling: first, that of aboriginal experience, "a struggle out of the slime," featuring beginnings, roots, cuttings, the first twitching movements of organic life; second, Roethke's aspiration toward pure spirit, disembodied, aerial. There are poems of each kind. No modern poet is more sensitive to beginnings, to the zoology of feeling, to the primitive but rampant life of the greenhouse. Roethke is almost equally gifted at the other end of the scale of desire, the incorrigible urge to escape from the finite condition into pure being, not existence but essence. If there is a disability in his talent, it reveals itself in the middle ground of life, the experience of man in relation to society, other people,

other lives, the world of time and place. Roethke is a characteris-
tic American in feeling the appalling need to be himself and at
the same time to keep his innocence inviolate. He was afraid of
nothing he might come upon in the aboriginal world or in the
world of spirit; he feared nearly everything he might come upon
in the common world, the middle world of daily relationships,
the chances of Monday and Tuesday. He thought of the com-
mon world as he thought of money: a constant need, a necessary
evil, testifying to the venom of things. He fought for whatever
he needed in the common world, but it was alien to his poetry;
he released his spleen in the violence of his correspondence and
the acrimony of common relations. The poems speak to us most
powerfully when we want to start our lives again, going back to
first principles; or when we want to release ourselves from the
dead weight of history, convention, "the malady of the quo-
tidian," as Stevens called it.

Beside Roethke, Randall Jarrell seems almost genial, and
though the narrative of his later years is appalling, it is natural to
think of him as a golden boy to whom everything was possible.
America was promises to him more than to MacLeish, because
he had the gift of tongues, a native eloquence. More than half in
love with language, he was loved by language in return, and
received her gifts and graces. His themes were the perennial
concerns, childhood, exile, dream, loss ("the world we were"),
war, rage, pity, and tenderness: but mostly loss. No wonder he
loved Hardy's poems, where nearly everything is lost except the
voice, at once grave and mettlesome, in which the loss is con-
tained. Jarrell was a critic as much as a poet and a novelist, but I
think he took to criticism because he wanted to list and celebrate
the things he loved when he found them in books. Hardy was
crucial; but so also were Rilke, Goethe, Frost, Ransom, Marianne
Moore, Whitman, lots of people. A critical essay by Jarrell is a joy
to read because of the gaiety of its response to poetry. When a
poet delighted him, he listed the superior poems partly for the
pleasure of reciting them all over again, partly because the list
became a form of poetry, the titles going down the page like
verses. But I suppose his poems are the thing, after all. Robert

Lowell called him "the most heartbreaking English poet of his generation," and the only fault I find with that statement is "English." "Heartbreaking," yes: he could break your heart by turning a phrase against itself, by repeating a phrase that never expected itself to be repeated, by providing a setting in which a wife, looking at her husband, says to herself, "I'm old, you're old." Or by saying of a bomber pilot in "Eighth Air Force" "I find no fault in this just man." Jarrell's poems are heartrending because he asks so much of life and cannot help losing: so he writes of being a child in California, and therefore he cannot help writing of women, mothers, wives, grandmothers. And he takes chances: who but Jarrell would take the risk of writing, as he does in the poem "Woman," "But then, a woman never is a man's type"? Jarrell gets away with it because the whole poem is so moving we won't let one line unmove us, we'll do anything for this man, forgive him any excess or failure. I must not claim that Jarrell was impeccable in tone; sometimes he misjudged a situation, the smile turns into a giggle. Golden boys sometimes fall below the gold standard. But he got things right so often, wrote so eloquently and with such dash, that forgiveness is easy.

John Berryman thought Jarrell a cruel reviewer, though he acknowledged that his cruelty served a good cause, the elimination of inferior poetry. Better still: he acknowledged that at the end of the day it was Jarrell's praise that mattered. Perhaps he was excessive in praise; Berryman thought William Carlos Williams a good poet but not as good as Jarrell said he was. And so on. In the poem "Richard & Randall, & one who never did," Berryman recalls Blackmur, Jarrell, and Delmore Schwartz, "the three freaks in their different notes" discussing "our meaning to the Old World, theirs to us" before singing "the new forms in which ancient thought appears." Berryman's poetry deals in those appearances: the thoughts are ancient because they are always with us, clinging to perennial situations, love, lovelessness, fear, failure, joy at times. Berryman's aesthetic procedure was direct: let whatever is going to happen happen, then take the good or the harm out of it and put it in a poem. The poem should be eventful in terms of diction, syntax, and above all rhythm, because rhythm is the most intimate sign of a poet's presence. Many things happened to Berryman, including some that a wise man would have taken care to avoid; they all went into poems. Not, in every case, a good poem: Berryman had to write six poems so that one of them would succeed; the other five were vitiated by vanity, self-indulgence, high jinks. Now that the whole work is finished we can see that it makes an enormous autobiography. *Homage to Mistress Bradstreet* is a magnificent essay in self-discipline, and certainly one of the enduring poems of modern American literature, but it did not hold Berryman to the dramatic way of writing. In the *Dream Songs* and the later poems the elaborate routines played by Henry and Mr. Bones do not conceal the fact that, increasingly, the dramatic obliquity is breaking down into the direct narrative of Berryman's life and feeling. At the end, in the poems written in Dublin, for instance, Berryman hardly bothers to keep up the pretense that these are dramatic poems, separately construed and independent of their poet's history. They are personal lyrics, and their themes are mostly the predicaments shared by Berryman and his generation, the common joys and miseries of Randall, Delmore, Richard, Howard, *et al*. The last books came in a rush, and they sheltered the best and the worst of Berryman's talent. Maybe he knew that his number was up and that the next crisis would be the last, so he made those years a verse-machine, an anthology, heaping up the lines and knowing that posterity, a cruel critic, would retain some poems and throw away the rest. The penultimate poem in the ultimate book, *Delusions, Etc.*, ends:

> Let me be clear about this. It is plain to me
> *Christ* underwent man & treachery & socks
> & lashes, thirst, exhaustion, the bit, for
>   *my* pathetic & disgusting vices,
> to make this filthy fact of particular, long-after,
> faraway, five-foot-ten & moribund
> human being happy. Well, he has!
> I am so happy I could scream!
> It's *enough*! I can't BEAR ANY MORE.
> *Let this be it.*   I've *had* it.   I can't wait.

Shortly after that, Berryman brought the whole story to an end, jumped from the bridge. It is churlish of a reader to look too closely at final things or to prefer this poem to that in such a desperate setting. But I prefer Berryman's Act III to his Act V, mainly because I find the religious phase of his last years unconvincing and I value more than I can briefly say the poems in which he had all his talent under control. In "Filling her compact & delicious body," "Life, friends is boring," "There sat down, once, a thing on Henry's heart," and several other poems numerous enough to constitute a list, Berryman's imagination, making poetry, takes account of all the things in life that are not poetry and proceeds to its task, unabashed. Yeats spoke of holding reality and justice in a single thought. When Berryman's poems go off the rails it is because they run wild after reality without a care for justice or the saving continuity of life. The superb occasions in his poetry are those in which the wit, fluency, razzmatazz, Berryman's mischief making, and the rest are made to serve purposes higher than themselves. Posterity will have to be extraordinarily cruel if it (he, she) throws those occasions away.

It is hard to keep these names separate. Jarrell writes of Lowell, reviews his books. Lowell has at least two poems to Jarrell, one to Roethke, two to Berryman. Berryman fills his poems with Lowell, Jarrell, Schwartz. Lowell's *History* records, among several hundred exemplary narratives, "the swift vanishing of my older / generation — the deaths, suicide, madness / of Roethke, Berryman, Jarrell, Lowell." It is a powerful story, if it were not already twice-told. These poets, it may as well be said, are not, despite appearances, a mutual admiration society; they were held together as much by envy as by friendship. It is my impression that Lowell not only admires Jarrell's poems but envies the poet his flair and panache. When a poem by Jarrell goes well every gift of style is lavished upon it, the words seem to come so readily into the lines that we think the poet had only to reach out and catch them or lob them back and forth as in good tennis. Not so: it is hard to be fluent and intelligent at the same time.

But Jarrell's poems give an impression of nonchalance, and this, I believe, is what Lowell envies. Jarrell wrote as though he had only to throw language a smile and she smiled back. Lowell writes (often, not always) as though he and language were locked in enmity and only one of them could win. He is immensely gifted in language, but mostly in the language of collision and abrasion. Smiles are few: this poet has to put his life under interrogation and, if that doesn't yield the secrets, he puts it under torture, third degree. *Life Studies* was an attempt, heroic in its way, to bring a little urbanity to the situation lest it defeat the continuities of speech altogether. In the later books Lowell's poems are still as nervous as ever, but he has been trying to give them the air of conversation, however desperate: anything, so long as it is speech. But it is hard to keep the poetry strong without recourse to the old jagged language. Lowell's way for the past few years has been to place himself near the center of the moral history of his generation and to seize every day for what it is worth. Many of the recent poems seem to me practice shots, where failure doesn't matter: they are often brilliant, especially in single lines and phrases, but rarely definitive in the sense of achieving their own finality. An intention of appalling grandeur informs the work; it is a privilege to see books attempted on such a scale. But many of the individual poems strike me as occasional in the limiting sense; they help the poet to get through the day or to move from one point to another, but they do not stay in my mind except as transitional moments, chapters to be read for the sake of the whole story. Lowell's way of writing poems is certainly his way of being an American, even while he chooses to reside in England: by putting his entire life on the line, for the sake of the poetry. English poets choose more precisely the moments they wish to put on display. It is not my duty to award marks either way; besides, the proof is in the event, not the habit or the policy. But the American way appeals to our demand for a poetry as large as large lives, even if it sprawls and runs amuck. It doesn't always run amuck. Hasn't Lowell himself written classic poems, "Mr. Edwards and the Spider," "Skunk

Hour," "The Quaker Graveyard in Nantucket," "The Severed Head"? Any reader of modern poetry can extend the list.

Howard Nemerov, the youngest of our poets (but old enough to be, at fifty-four, the author of eleven books of poems), came into his own with the publication of *The Salt Garden*, his third, in 1955. His name comes in the last pages of nearly every anthology that concerns itself with American poetry up to 1950 or thereabouts. Thereafter, anthologists become rhetoricians and polemicists, party men fixing elections. In 1951 Richard Blackmur, employing Lord Tennyson's scissors on the poetry written between 1912 and 1950, found that Yeats, Eliot, and Pound by making form and substance possible made many poets possible, including Auden. Thinking of poets born between 1913 and 1918 (and listing for that generation Shapiro, Barker, Schwartz, Thomas, Berryman, Manifold, Lowell, Betjeman, Meredith, and Reed) Blackmur said: "I would not say that any of these men have managed the full creation, but they have the enormous advantage over their predecessors that there is an idiom ready for them to develop according to their own needs. . . . They have more than a chance — it is half done for them — to develop out of personality the most objective of all creations, the least arbitrary and spontaneous, a style." It must be said now that some of Blackmur's poets never managed anything like the full creation and did very little with the idiom available to them: presumably there are causes in each case. Some of the poets still have a chance. And then there are the poets, equally gifted, a few years younger than Blackmur's list and therefore ready to try again for that most objective of all creations, a style. I mean the poets, including Nemerov and Wilbur, born about 1920. The books Nemerov has published since *The Salt Garden* (he has now given his eleventh, *Gnomes and Occasions*) show what he has done with the available idiom. He has studied the masters, notably Yeats, Eliot, Stevens, and Ransom, not to warm his spirit at their fires but to admire what could be done and to discover that nearly anything can be done. That much settled, he has gone on to write his own poems and free his voice. It is my understand-

ing that the figure his poems make is indicated in "The Sanc-
tuary," where he describes the movement of the trout:

>   slow
> And so definite, like thoughts emerging
> Into a clear place in the mind, then going
>   back,
> Exchanging shape for shade.

It is a fair exchange, since there is always enough shade and
never enough shape. The figure is good enough for Nemerov's
aesthetic and his sense of life. I find it again in "The Human
Condition," this time along with Nemerov's wit, his delicacy of
touch:

> Once I saw world and thought exactly meet,
> But only in a picture by Magritte,
>
> A picture of a picture, by Magritte,
> Wherein a landscape on an easel stands
> Before a window opening on a land-
>   scape, and the pair of them a perfect fit,
> Silent and mad. You know right off, the room
> Before that scene was always an empty room.

One poem of twenty-four lines does not make a full creation, but
we can say this much of "The Human Condition," that its poet is
not short of means. If he fails to write a major poetry it will not
be because the idiom available to him was a blunt instrument or
that he was bewildered by former masteries.

It is not my purpose to make more than a general claim for
the modern poetry embodied in these seven poets: the poetry is,
at the least, interesting; at best, exemplary in its power to move.
We seem to have come a long way from MacLeish quarreling
with Malcolm Cowley about poetry, war, and propaganda; start-
ing out in the thirties, ending up in the seventies, is an experi-
ence to which I cannot testify — I know it only from books,
novels, poems. But a man would need to be dead to find the
whole story a bore. The book is still engrossing in the last chap-
ters, Nemerov's poems which are his own while implicating
other poems, other efforts to make sense of things. Is it not

splendid that a poem beginning with the picture-postcard legend "Wish you were here" ends with another legend, "Wish I were here"? And if we demand that our poems be relevant, can we ask for anything more relevant than a poem that begins "There used to be gods in everything, and now they've gone" and goes on to make something out of the situation: the something, a good poem.

GROVER SMITH

Archibald MacLeish

As a poet and man of letters, Archibald MacLeish has illuminated the most serious problems which the twentieth-century literary artist must face, and at the same time has shown how they may be solved. This is not to say that in his work MacLeish himself has completely solved them; but his achievement has been so generally adequate that his poetry seems likely to survive the present antipoetic age and become an inspiration to happier times. The problems are, of course, derived from that famous romantic alienation from the environment almost two centuries ago, a disorder now apparently aggravated out of all cure in an era of mass culture. They consist, on the one hand, in the poet's ethical need to maintain the traditional concern with craftsmanship and, on the other hand, in his equally great desire to communicate with the public — a desire which also is a need. Few successful poets of the present day manage without compromising the one or the other of these endeavors. To sacrifice craftsmanship is to submit to the tyranny of common values, produced by the demotic passion for *equality*; to sacrifice communication, though imaginably in the cause of *quality*, invites, and often with full justice, the charge of snobbishness. In the case of MacLeish, the love of craftsmanship is not snobbish

16

and the sympathy for the contemporary world is genuine. His poetry has avoided the animosity toward ordinary conditions of modern life which is shown, for example, in some of T. S. Eliot's work. At the same time it — or the best of it — is a poetry of ideas as well as emotions.

MacLeish was born in Glencoe, Illinois, on May 7, 1892. A good private secondary school, Hotchkiss, prepared him for Yale. At the university he was in most ways a thoroughly typical young man of his station (well-to-do middle class) and generation: he has spoken of how much more important it was, to him at Yale, that he played football than that he was enrolled in such and such academic courses. Yet he was elected to Phi Beta Kappa without, presumably, any enormous efforts as a student — a fact suggesting the appropriate commentary. Being graduated in 1915, and already planning to be married, he went to Harvard for the study of law. His marriage, to Ada Hitchcock, took place the following year. In 1917 he enlisted and served with the American army in France, where he attained the rank of captain. His brother Kenneth was killed in the war. MacLeish returned to Harvard and took the law degree in 1919; he stayed there as a teacher of government for a year, but from 1920 to 1923 practiced law in Boston.

He was already a published poet (and at Yale winner of a prize for poetry), and he continued to write, though without a strong sense of accomplishment. It was nevertheless for the sake of his poetry that he gave up his law office and took his wife and young children to Paris. He hoped, by devoting himself solely to poetry, to be able eventually to make it his vocation and means of support. He lived abroad for nearly six years and there matured as a poet. Those years have been called his expatriate period. Ernest Hemingway, John Dos Passos, F. Scott Fitzgerald, and the already long-uprooted Ezra Pound were among the wandering Americans whom MacLeish knew in Paris. Hemingway, who stayed with the MacLeishes for an extended time, remained one of his closest friends for the next decade. Pound, clearly, was on principle an expatriate; but as applied to himself and the others this term is distasteful to MacLeish, who is certainly correct about it: *expatriate* had better be reserved as a name for those who exiled themselves irrevocably.

MacLeish never had any intention of remaining in Paris for the rest of his life. In 1928 he came back to the United States, a recognized poet at last. Here he was to make his permanent home, although he traveled from time to time, for example to Mexico, where he gathered material for a poem about the expedition of Cortez (*Conquistador*, 1932). In the early years of the New Deal he diverted his energies into lucrative journalism, and for the magazine *Fortune* he wrote carefully researched articles on current social problems (see the bibliography at the end of this volume). He composed a stage play in verse, *Panic* (1935), and a series of verse plays for radio — these latter a notable contribution to a new genre already beginning to thrive in Britain but undeveloped in the United States.

Not only his journalistic but his poetic and especially his dramatic writings in the 1930s manifested the extroverted temperament which equipped MacLeish for the role of "communicator," or public spokesman. This was no new attribute: his poems of the 1920s and earlier could only have come from a man of this type, but in technique they resembled works of introspective writers, symbolists and impressionists, who were very different from MacLeish. In the 1940s he proved perhaps all too well extroverted, in the sense that his public duties left him less time for poetry. As curator of the Nieman journalism collection at Harvard (1938) and as a sympathizer with the Roosevelt administration he became a "target" for presidential appointment to the post of librarian of Congress, in which capacity he served from 1939 to 1944. In 1941–42 he was also director of the Office of Facts and Figures, a wartime information agency of the government; in 1942–43 he worked as assistant director of the Office of War Information, a full-scale propaganda bureau. In 1944–45 he was assistant secretary of state. In 1945 and 1946 he led official American participation in establishing UNESCO and starting its programs. It is clear that MacLeish was not only highly extroverted but patriotic — something not at all surprising. In World War I he had served with honor. Never truly expatriated, because neither an alienated intellectual nor an aesthete nor a communist, he had lived abroad as a poet in the 1920s when France was less expensive than America and Paris was the capital of the arts. In the 1930s he joined with millions in America who acclaimed Franklin D. Roosevelt first for economic reforms and then for the courage to arm against Hitler. And in the decade that followed, he stood among those who believed that the best hope for future peace lay in international cooperation through the United Nations. If MacLeish can be said to have had a mission as distinguished from a vocation, it has been to integrate the role of poet with that of public man.

Substantially MacLeish's poetic output of the 1940s was limited to the collection *Actfive and Other Poems* (1948). Apart from radio plays, the bulk of his publications in the decade was made up of prose pieces. The best of these, articles dating from the years after Hitler came to power in Germany, appeared in the 1941 volume *A Time to Speak*. In a companion volume of 1943, *A Time to Act*, was published a selection of wartime addresses. The latter are comparatively high-keyed and have now far less interest than the articles, which argued MacLeish's political convictions as these were sharpened in the context of current history. His beliefs, like many other people's in America during those years, underwent two phases: the one of response to the economic ideologies debated generally in the 1930s, the other of response to the Italians' and Germans' strategies of conquest. Since MacLeish has consistently opposed Marxism, and even though he was then a New Dealer with affinities for the native revolutionary tradition as celebrated, for example, by Carl Sandburg, his response in the first phase took a civil-libertarian rather than a socialistic character. It thus was, as in retrospect it appears, irrelevant in fact to the main social issues of the period, when an altered balance of economic power was being brought about between capital and government. His response in the second phase, beginning about the time of the Spanish Civil War, was antifascist and, because libertarian, anti-Marxist still; in 1937 he could use the phrase *common front* in referring to

enemies of the fascists, but he rejected the popular-front frenzy
and stood ready with a half-Jeffersonian, half-populist
definition of American national principles as the United States
prepared for war (*The American Cause*, 1941). This time his re-
sponse was clearly in the spirit of the moment. His wartime and
postwar-reconstruction papers, the later ones geared to "peace-
ful coexistence" as against the cold war, may be found in *Freedom
Is the Right to Choose* (1951). He was skeptical of the Truman
Doctrine but favored the Marshall Plan.

Withdrawn from government posts, MacLeish enjoyed a long
academic career at Harvard as the Boylston professor of
rhetoric and oratory from 1949 to 1962, and after a short inter-
val served for four years (1963–67) as Simpson lecturer at
Amherst College. His almost twenty years of teaching turned
out to be one of the richest periods for his art, especially as a
playwright. He has published four more verse plays, one of
which, *J. B.* (1958), gained the Pulitzer Prize for drama in 1959
(MacLeish had already won two Pulitzer Prizes for poetry — one
in 1933 for *Conquistador* and one in 1953 for *Collected Poems
1917–1952*); several volumes of literary criticism and incidental
social commentary; and three additional volumes of poems,
Songs for Eve (1954), *The Wild Old Wicked Man, and Other
Poems* (1968), and *The Human Season: Selected Poems* (1972).

When MacLeish assembled his *Collected Poems 1917–1952*, he
conformed to usual practice in suppressing most of the early
work; but as one examines the early poems they are seen to
relate, in various and sometimes contradictory ways, to his ma-
ture verse. The first volumes, *Songs for a Summer's Day* (1915) and
Tower of Ivory (1917), display a lively interest in verse forms as
such. The former contains sonnets only; but the latter includes,
as well, a number of stanzaic exercises and one precocious
dramatic piece, "Our Lady of Troy" (which, despite a Swinburn-
ean promise in its title, is akin rhetorically to Jonson's humor
plays). The sonnets in *Tower of Ivory* show the inevitable debt to
Shakespeare; some of them, the best indeed, could only have
derived from the "soldier" sonnets of Rupert Brooke. What is

more significant, they imply a taste and probably a need for strict formal boundaries within which to manipulate tone, music, imagery, and argument. A few Keatsian couplets (in "A Library of Law"), examples of ballad measure (notably in "A Sampler"), some regular quatrains (as in "Escape"), a ballade (so entitled), paired sonnets ("Certain Poets"), a Petrarchan sonnet but with two octaves ("Baccalaureate"), and miscellaneous lyrical stanzas fill out this group. The themes are amatory and visionary, mainly in the Aesthetic tradition: there is some superficial paganism, sometimes yoked with Christian symbols, and a great deal of hedonism and a rather Yeatsian preoccupation with an enchanted realm of dream. Antiscientific or at least antipragmatic sentiments, characteristically late Victorian, come out in the dream poems "Jason" and "Realities." A time-worn motif of mutability, devouring Time, and Death the inexorable recurs abundantly. Yet, even with their intellectual representations, most of these poems seem to achieve more through music than through argument. Often the sound is more *interesting* than the sense. Imagery appears not to be handled deliberately or for the sake of symbolic possibilities, but to be mainly decorative. (At the same time a few emblematic images strike the attention, as in MacLeish's sonnet "The Altar," which uses a metaphysical conceit. Here certain carved garlands, intended as symbols of beauty in general, are discovered to have accidentally shaped the letters spelling a particular woman's name. Various baroque analogues may have influenced the poem.)

In his *Dialogues* with Mark Van Doren (1962; published 1964), MacLeish remarked that when he began writing verse he "took off from Swinburne." That, certainly, was Swinburne as musician only: Swinburne the sensualist was no model in any of MacLeish's early poetry. The decorous "Realities" is as Swinburnean as you please; in fact, it is quite good, though of low intensity — Swinburne sober. After a few years' fascination with such music, MacLeish reacted against it. It seems that his reaction was a vehement one: his later poetry has, if anything, avoided musicality and has often been downright unmusical. At any rate sense and argument reasserted themselves strongly; an intricate, even devious, rhetoric began to dominate. For a time the sonnet retained his favor, as in the title piece of the volume *The Happy Marriage, and Other Poems* (1924). That long poem (a sort of nontragical *Modern Love*) is made up partly of sonnets and partly of other regular forms, and the verbal effects produced with these are very skillful. Two sections of "The Happy Marriage" in rhyming couplets (beginning respectively "The humid air precipitates" and "Beside her in the dark the chime") have survived into *Collected Poems*, where they may remind the reader that MacLeish's next important model, after Swinburne, was Eliot. The first of these lyrics was indebted to Eliot in his "Sweeney" period, the second to his "Portrait of a Lady." Both employ symbolistic imagery in a quasi-dramatic context of emotional confrontation — as Eliot's poems had done.

Between 1917 and 1924 MacLeish's style acquired the features of its maturity — conscious symbolism; witty, almost metaphysical strategies of argument; compressed and intense implications — all of these owing much, though quite certainly not everything, to Eliot's example. MacLeish was usually able to resist the Eliot rhythms. His cadences were to have great diversity and to echo many predecessors. His voice, moreover, did not have much in common with the self-conscious orotundity of Eliot's middle period (it had something in common with the Prufrockian tones), and he seldom undertook vocal productions such as dramatic monologues. Indeed, a lasting mark of MacLeish's work has been the weakness of the persona. At times the diction is remote from speech; at other times it may be close to speech but bare of individuality, diffuse, as though spoken by a chorus. For this reason, despite his partial debt to Eliot, MacLeish belongs not only outside of the Browning-Tennyson traditions of monologue but also outside of the American schools which have stemmed from those, the diverse movements represented by E. A. Robinson and Vachel Lindsay, by Frost and the early Pound. Like stream-of-consciousness fiction, which owes a great deal to it, the dramatic monologue indulges introspection in the safety of a disguise. (Perhaps in fiction, as in the poetry of Yeats, freedom rather than safety is in request — the *complexification* rather than the *disengagement* of the writer.) MacLeish's poetry, for the most part, is not introspective, and this is why indeed no persona is wanted. According to its own purposes, its diminution of the persona is a strength: by this means it turns the reader away from the endless labyrinths of subjective illusion and irony, the "echoing vault" of the poetic self, and invites him to contemplate the phenomenal world. It does not vocalize that self: it can and often does fabricate a kind of disembodied speech, or speech whose origin need not be known. It aspires to be, and sometimes becomes, a poetry of spectacle — not always, but especially when, as in the near masterpiece "Einstein" (1926), it is wholly under the control of an intellectual concept. Then the images arrange themselves as objective counterparts of the progress of an idea — Eliot's "objective correlative" intellectualized.

MacLeish in the 1920s increasingly took pains with the formal structure of his poetry. Only through form could the swelling rhetoric be channeled. After the 1924 volume, the sonnet was neglected for a while, but it was not discarded even in *Streets in the Moon* (1926), where free verse of a highly regulated type alternates with blank verse and stanzaic patterns. Blank verse, with a few rhyming lyric passages, was used also for his symbolistic poem *The Pot of Earth* (1925) and his closet drama *Nobodaddy* (1926).

The theme and scope of *Nobodaddy*, referred to by MacLeish as a "poem," are indicated in his preface, which adds that the "emotional experiences" treated there are "not unlike" those dealt with in *The Pot of Earth*, written after it but published before. *Nobodaddy* takes its title from Blake's derisory name for the scriptural god of prohibitions. It adapts the Adam-and-Eve, Cain-and-Abel story to dramatize what MacLeish calls "the condition of self-consciousness in an indifferent universe"; it is a poetic essay, of course, not biblical commentary. In it, Adam has emerged into humanity, into consciousness of himself as a being distinct from the rest of creation. In this condition he has two choices, a fact which disquiets him and in itself presumably inclines him to the choice he makes. He can either stand in awe of nature ("the Gardener"), accepting the inferiority implicit in obedience to a system he does not understand, or else assert his will to become a god — that is, a rational being superior to nature. Urged by the Voice of his will (metaphorically the Serpent) and by Eve, who does not fear what she has never experienced, natural harshness, Adam eats the forbidden fruit and thus alienates himself by act as well as by will. The consequence is misery: his daring to break the bond of obedience brings down upon his head a flood of superstitious terrors. The Gardener, far from changing into an Avenger, seems to have vanished; but frantic with guilt Adam flees the garden, and he and Eve seek the desert. It remains for their sons, Abel and Cain, to complete the drama by, in effect, modernizing the situation. Abel, representative of Adam fallen and burdened with guilt, attempts a mystical reconciliation with the supposed Avenger. Longing to return to the garden, to ignorance and servitude, he invents a relationship with an invented god: religion is born. By blood sacrifice he strives to atone. His brother, Cain, realist and rationalist, and similar to Adam as he was when he heard the Voice of his humanity exhorting him to free himself, asserts human values and the will to power. Abel grovels before the voice of thunder and tries to pull Cain down to his knees in humility. Cain, already godlike in mind, kills him.

It is not clear why Adam is so constituted that he cannot profit from his fall, but because he cannot his son Abel cannot either. It is left for Cain to vindicate reason against superstition; that he has to do so by murder is ironic, to say the least. At any rate none of the four characters comprehends the meaning of these actions. It is for the reader to understand in terms, primarily, of acceptance and rejection. So long as man believed himself to be simply part of nature, he lived in a paradise. Death was there already, the biological cycle had begun, but man had not yet taken it personally — it was still objective. When man became self-conscious, his acceptance of nature changed into resistance, and with its normal machinery of death it seemed a threat to him. Not only was he utterly different from nature, but it was indifferent to him — though physically he remained within it.

He had imagination; nature was all process. The "Gardener" of
Nobodaddy is merely the principle of life viewed as sympathetic
harmony. When this view disappears, and reason replaces it with
the stark vision of process, the Gardener gives way to the enemy,
the unsympathetic. Physical nature converted into the an-
tagonist of man's will is a desert, a region which will not behave
as man desires. The harmony of prelapsarian Eden was that of
man's acquiescent ignorance; the disharmony of the natural
world, to fallen man, is that of its uncontrollability. His selfhood
defies nature and battles with it, but at the last must sink de-
feated. Abel's attempt to return symbolically to the unfallen state
takes the form of a conscious imitation of nature's unconscious
cruelty; he grafts human motives upon the indifferent. Abel's
sacrifice of a ram is wrong because consciousness cannot atone
with unconsciousness. Nature's own profuse bloodletting sets no
store by covenants and bargaining; apart from man's imagina-
tion such "deals" are meaningless. If human ideals estrange man
from nature, and if, nevertheless, with the justice of indiffer-
ence, nature punishes every act not in harmony with its laws,
then man is automatically unhappy.

The idea that human feelings meet nothing like themselves,
no sympathetic responses, in nature, and that nature governs
the life of the body as if the desires of the mind did not occur, is
present in *The Pot of Earth*. But the theme of this poem is the
bitterness and pity of those desires so subjected to the
Gardener's indifference. Here is the case of the toad beneath the
harrow. The poem was published three years after *The Waste
Land* of Eliot. The two works are of roughly the same length.
They have much similarity, in technique and symbolism alike. In
certain notable ways they are dissimilar. *The Waste Land* is a
first-person monologue to which are subordinated various genre
adaptations. *The Pot of Earth* is mainly a third-person narrative,
though with some first-person stream-of-consciousness effects.
Stylistically *The Waste Land* is by far the more experimental and
radical. Both poems, however, draw upon Sir James Frazer's
work *The Golden Bough* for vegetation symbolism which,
mythologically and ceremonially, represents the death and res-

urrection of a fertility god (e.g., Adonis) as a type of the sea-
sonal decay and revival of nature. Both also, in applying this
symbolism within a modern context of life, emphasize not the
victory of life over death but the reverse of this. On the other
hand, they again differ most significantly in what they apply
such symbolism to. *The Waste Land*, exploring a gnostic and
"spiritualized" sense of death and rebirth, uses a special myth
(the Grail legend) concerning an *arrest* of fertility, whose equiv-
alent in the poem is the male protagonist's state of emotional
aridity and despair. *The Pot of Earth* applies the vegetation sym-
bolism to its female protagonist's organic functions: the biologi-
cal cycle takes place in her, as if in a plant springing up,
flowering, being fertilized, bearing fruit, and dying. Or, more
exactly, the girl or woman herself can be regarded as such a "pot
of earth," or Garden of Adonis described by Frazer in the pas-
sage which MacLeish prefixed to his poem as a general epi-
graph. For, like those shallow-rooted plants forced into brief and
hectic life under the Syrian sun, only to wither and to be thrown
into the sea as symbols of the god bewailed by his sectaries, she
leads a transient existence, devoid of any lasting meaning except
the biological one. The resurrection of the fertility god means
new life for nature, not for the individual. At the conclusion of
The Pot of Earth, the woman has borne a child and has died; a
chestnut tree is in flower; but she rots in the earth. Here the
Adonis myth becomes the vehicle for a realization of the inex-
tricability of life and death. MacLeish's second epigraph to the
poem (later transferred to part I) is the "god kissing carrion"
passage from *Hamlet*; and part III is called "The Carrion Spring."
In *Hamlet* "carrion" is the prince's coarse designation for
Ophelia: evidently the woman in *The Pot of Earth* has a sacrificial
role like that to which the Ophelia personage is doomed in *The
Waste Land*. But she has been sacrificed by the indifference of
nature, not the brutality of man.

The 1925 text of *The Pot of Earth*, several pages longer than
the text printed in *Poems, 1924–1933* (1933) and thereafter,
adopts the *Waste Land* technique of making the past and pres-
ent interpenetrate, so that the modern woman's life cycle is de-

picted in timeless fusion with that of a primitive world: its inci-
dents are abruptly juxtaposed to details from the Adonis ritual.
But the three principal passages in which this effect is created
have been omitted from the later printings, leaving the poem free
of the startling "intertemporal" counterpoint typical of Eliot,
and with a contemporary texture purely. Yet, beneath this, con-
tinual allusions to the Adonis ritual remain to suggest a theme of
unending recurrence. Perhaps recapitulation, rather than re-
currence, is the universalizing motif in *The Pot of Earth* (as for
example it is in Joyce's *Finnegans Wake*): this woman is eternal
woman, and eternal woman typifies reproductive nature, whose
dream is her life. She, like the Garden of Adonis in antiquity,
blossoms as an emblem, a signature, of some omnipresent and
all-involving archetype of cyclical life and death. Her anonymity
is as profound as that of Tiresias, the *Waste Land* persona; but
whereas he is obscured by Eliot's pretentious legerdemain with
literary cross references, she has a constant, though shadowy,
identity.

There seems to be a philosophical difference between *The Pot
of Earth* and *The Waste Land* in the ways they pose their pro-
tagonists against the world. Eliot's poem is very much in a "psy-
chological" tradition; that is, starting from an Idealist's assump-
tion that the individual point of view is of paramount impor-
tance because it uniquely focuses knowledge of externals, *The
Waste Land* attains form by offering a view from a single point,
or through a single narrow peephole. It recalls Bergsonian and
stream-of-consciousness fiction. MacLeish's poem seems to start
from a Realist's assumption that there is nothing special in point
of view as such; that the law of things is common to all. It depicts
a *typical* relation of the natural to the human, indeed choosing to
examine the fate of someone quite average. Whatever the re-
semblance of MacLeish's techniques to those of subjectivists and
symbolists, his *fond* was otherwise. His poem, like Eliot's, uses
Aesthetic and symbolist procedures to assist naturalistic state-
ment, but his is closer to a philosophical naturalism which as-
sumes the total subjection of man to time and chance.

There was much of the eighteenth-century rationalist in the

MacLeish of the 1920s and in his political character later; much, also, of the scientific observer of life. He had made an almost complete break with his antiscientific and aesthetical beginnings as a poet. He now accepted the scientists' description of reality — only boggling at its falsification of experience. The external world he confronted was the one described by the astronomers, by the biologists, and above all by the mathematical physicists of his own day. Whereas Eliot and Pound and Yeats were ancients, MacLeish was a modern. One may believe that Einstein's space-time-energy continuum receives, in the work of MacLeish, its most important poetic treatment to date — a treatment not through casual allusion for contemporary color, but through exact intellectual integration with the subject matter of felt life. A thematic carry-over takes place from *The Pot of Earth* to later . poems — the conflict between personal hopes and natural law, developed first, perhaps a little less pessimistically, in *Nobodaddy*.

The volume *Streets in the Moon* scrutinizes the state of man the conscious animal in the disheartening universe of curved space and irreversible entropy. In his "Prologue" to this collection, MacLeish salutes a hypothetical "crew of Columbus" who are westward bound but, as in nightmare, toward a "surf that breaks upon Nothing"; and he comments, concerning this apparent fate of the whole human race,

> Oh, I have the sense of infinity —
> But the world, sailors, is round.
> They say there is no end to it.

The paradox of infinite aspirations confined in a world closed and therefore without "end" to aspire beyond is a leading theme of *Streets in the Moon*. The title of the book suggests the double vision: "streets" a symbol of the here and now of consciousness, the "moon" a symbol (defined partly by the counter-romantic use to which Jules Laforgue put it in his poetry) of a myth degraded by science. The volume concludes with the wry humor of "The End of the World," in which a temporal "end" to the circus of life reveals the nothingness above man's head. The poems in between, several of them conspicuously indebted to

Laforgue ("Nocturne," "Selene Afterwards," "Hearts' and
Flowers'"), to Eliot, or to Pound, and one of them most notably
("Einstein") written in a symbolistic manner recalling Mallarmé's
"L'Après-midi d'un faune" (but in a rather Miltonic strain!), deal
variously with the mystery of existence, with the problem of time
(symbolized by the sun, among other things), with death, with
love and other relations, and with human character. A few are
imagistic; others are elegiac, anecdotal, or narrative and Brown-
ingesque. One of the finest poems in this fine collection is the
three-part "Signature for Tempo," a meditation on the relativity
of time and movement:

> Think that this world against the wind of time
> Perpetually falls the way a hawk
> Falls at the wind's edge but is motionless;

on fourth-dimensional extension:

> How shall we bury all
> These time-shaped people,
> In graves that have no more
> Than three dimensions?

(though why not, one could retort, since in fact the graves have
the same number of dimensions as the people); and on death as
the point in time where all are united:

> Whom time goes over wave by wave, do I lie
> Drowned in a crumble of surf at the sea's edge? —
>
> And wonder now what ancient bones are these
> That flake on sifting flake
> Out of deep time have shelved this narrow ledge
> Where the waves break.

"The Too-Late Born," rhetorically very brilliant, is most
meaningful in the context of the time poems (its later title, "The
Silent Slain," constricts its meaning); it, too, is about the com-
munity of the dead. The death of Roland at Roncesvalles has
been made archetypal: the "silent slain" could belong to any
army, and the fact that "we" survive them is an accident of time
— an ironic one, for in due time we shall join them in the

universal graveyard of the earth. Themes of mortality are
further explored in "No Lamp Has Ever Shown Us Where to
Look," "Interrogate the Stones," and "Le Secret humain," in
terms of speculations on the "answer" that death is supposed to
have in reserve for man, an answer that may simply annihilate
the questioner. "Raree Show" asks whether the question is
within the mind, but ends with a new question, "Where?" "L'An
trentiesme de mon Eage" (its title taken from a line by François
Villon which was a favorite of Pound's, and which was used by
Eliot in an epigraph and by Pound in "Hugh Selwyn
Mauberley") is somewhat in the mood of Eliot's "Gerontion."
Through a multiplicity of memories its speaker has arrived at his
present place; he then asks, "And by what way shall I go back?"
One could answer that there is no need of going back, for
"place" is temporal as well as spatial, and what belongs to time
contains its past. The poem, having reviewed the past, has al-
ready returned to it, through art. But this reply would be satis-
factory only to a Bergsonian. In any realistic analysis the ques-
tion is unanswerable, though MacLeish was to continue asking it
in later poems.

One of the most often cited anthology pieces from *Streets in the
Moon* is the paradoxical and enigmatic "Ars Poetica." In spite of
its Horatian title, which seems to imply simply a verse essay in
legislative criticism, a poem about the art of poetry, its true
workings are otherwise. It does not frame an address to poets
generally, much less to their critics; it is no essay in criticism. Nor
yet does it introspectively comment, like Eliot's poem "La Figlia
che Piange," on the poet's relation to his own creative process.
Perhaps some readers, remembering chiefly the distichs "A
poem should be equal to: / Not true" and "A poem should not
mean / But be," have interpreted what "Ars Poetica" *says* (that a
poem should be like an object beheld in stasis, not like a message
or a paradigm) as what it is *for*. If so, they have taken it for a
critical essay and have violated its supposed counsel! The central
paradox of "Ars Poetica" is that it makes sense only when the
reader accepts its sense as a function of form. It then survives as

the aesthetic object it approves — with the proviso that the approval must be held as an utterance *in vacuo*, a silence:

> A poem should be palpable and mute
> As a globed fruit,
> . . . .
>
> A poem should be wordless
> As the flight of birds.

The real subject of "Ars Poetica" is itself, by a sort of narcissism of the written word as "pure poetry"; this poem exhibits aestheticism circling round, as it were, and returning like the equator upon the round earth. The result contrives a stasis indeed, free or nearly free of time's rotation. The moon of the second part, MacLeish's recurrent symbol of the imaginative world ideally transcending the naturalist's inner and outer landscapes, drifts as poetic subjectivity defying its antithesis, the solar clock. "Ars Poetica," somewhat Yeatsian like various other short poems in the volume, looks also Keatsian: the whole poem speaks with a voice which, like that of the Grecian urn when it equates beauty and truth, belongs to a realm of ideality and is relevant only to that. Such a realm, proper to poetry, conflicts with nature; MacLeish's long poem "Einstein" reviews the naturalistic conception that man, at least, cannot quite escape the prison of his time-bound flesh. That, too, is a Keatsian thought.

"Einstein" in theme recalls *Nobodaddy*; the resemblance proves useful in the unraveling of its complexities. Not only is the subject difficult (like most subjects) unless one already understands it, but the rhetoric lumbers in obscurity. Nevertheless the poem operates compellingly upon the emotions, and it ought to be one of the best known philosophical poems of the period. The Einstein of the title is modern intellectual man, scientist, represented microcosmically as a sort of Leopold Bloom, atomic and entire (*ein Stein*, perhaps — a stone, or at least a pebble!), who has inherited the problem and the mission of MacLeish's Cain, the mission of rationality. The Einsteinian universe is rationality triumphant, as indeed it is the triumph of the modern spirit. The poem (a narrative showing the process of "going back," by reason, to a condition which seems to repeal Adam's alienation from nature and to reunite his posterity with the primal creator — i.e., in effect deifying man) reveals the way back by re-capitulating the way forward, from any infancy to full con-sciousness. First there is Einstein, man secure in his body-sense and self-contained. Then, his awareness of sense impressions. Then, his mental abstraction of these into a coherent world —

> A world in reason which is in himself
> And has his own dimensions.

Then, his discovery of his ignorance and impotence in the world's vastness and mystery. Then, his attempt to gain mystical identification with this mystery by sensory and aesthetic con-templation, and most through music,

> When he a moment occupies
> The hollow of himself and like an air
> Pervades all other.

Then (in a passage to which Eliot, who seems to owe several points to this poem, suggests a reply in the closing lines of *Burnt Norton*), his realization that there is no longer a "word" which can translate beauty into thought and thus into himself (the word described as known to the Virgin of Chartres but as now become "three round letters" in a carving was presumably the "AVE" which hailed, in effect, the Incarnation). Then, upon his rejection of mysterious access and Abel's quest, his intellec-tual formulation of Albert Einstein's theories. And finally, the godlike subduing of nature to himself, so that the physical uni-verse is comprehended in his consciousness, which itself be-comes all.

Only one stage remains, and this is denied him. His own flesh cannot melt into his thought: he keeps "Something inviolate. A living something." These phrases return him to the state which was his at the beginning of the poem, where, at minimal definition, the "something inviolate" is the fact "that / His father was an ape." The original Adam, sprung from nature and subject to it, by it condemned, to die, persists despite this victory. Those critics are surely wrong who see "Einstein" as antiscientific; rather, the poem, like *Nobodaddy*, affirms the necessary destiny of man to subdue everything to his knowledge — everything but the stubborn, atavistic ape within, which *must* refuse to yield. The anecdotal poem "The Tea Party" says all that need be said about man's sense of his primitivism; "Einstein" says something further, that the animal residuum is man's very life. The tragic fate awaiting this life has already been revealed in *The Pot of Earth*. "Einstein" is not tragic; it is not even precisely critical. It is an intellectual celebration of an intellectual triumph, attended by a voice bidding the *triumphator* remember that he is dust.

MacLeish's tragic sense of the buried life, exposed in the impersonal symbolism of *The Pot of Earth*, is deeply sounded in *The Hamlet of A. MacLeish* (1928). An observation by MacLeish more than a decade later, in his essay "Poetry and the Public World," was made to introduce a kind of renunciation of this poem or at least of the attitudes it expresses: "The Hamlet of Shakespeare was the acceptance of a difficult age and the demonstration of the place, in that age, of poetry. The Hamlet of Laforgue, and after him of Eliot and after him of the contemporary generation, is the rejection of a difficult age and a contemptuous comment upon the hope of poetry to deal with it. . . . [N]ot until contemporary poetry writes the Hamlet of Laforgue and Eliot out of its veins, will poetry occupy, and reduce to the order of recognition, the public-private world in which we live." *The Hamlet of A. MacLeish* is in the tradition of Jules Laforgue's *Hamlet* and of Eliot's Prufrockian and wastelandish poems; and it focuses, certainly, upon the sufferings of the sensitive man, not upon the problems of the age in its "public" bearings. From the point of view of 1939, after a decade of experiment with "public" themes and at a moment of intense uneasiness about the future of civilization, MacLeish saw his *Hamlet* as too negative, as too much lacking in what the same essay called "acceptance" and "belief." Yet it was probably just as well that he aimed his criticism expressly against Laforgue and Eliot and only lumped his

Hamlet implicitly with theirs; for really there is a difference in kind between their pessimism and his own in that poem. Quite simply, their pessimism is social, whereas his is cosmic. What Laforgue and Eliot (in his early poetry) found fault with was the special uncongeniality of life for the special personae in their poetry. What MacLeish complains of in his *Hamlet* is the injustice of the universe. Surely a poem which says that life is a fraud is hardly to be criticized for not telling us how to live optimistically.

In "Einstein" there are marginal notes with the double purpose of punctuating the stages of consciousness and locating these in the mind of one individual. In *The Hamlet* such notes have a different purpose: they key the psychological action to Shakespeare's *Hamlet*, from which (being quotations, stage directions, or episode descriptions) they are taken. MacLeish's poem can be thought of as analogous to a transparent overlay which, when superimposed on the map or chart to whose details it is keyed, provides new information or modifies the old. In this case the so-called overlay is fully a map in its own right. It is divided into fourteen sections, corresponding to as many scenes of the Shakespeare play. What it maps with these is the world of consciousness belonging to its protagonist, the modern Hamlet; and this world, like that of the play, shows temporal movement or more properly historical movement, for it is a world common to mankind, whom this Hamlet represents. (As with *The Pot of Earth*, some resemblance to *Finnegans Wake* may be seen.) And if Hamlet is mankind, it would appear that the Ghost is the mysterious father-god of creation, the unknown Nobodaddy, maybe to be known in, or as, Death; Hamlet's mother is the Earth; and the Claudius figure, symbolized in the opening section as both Hyperion (the sun) *and* a satyr, is the tyrant enemy, Time. The characters in this cast do not emerge allegorically, as in a morality play, but symbolistically. That is, as addressed by Hamlet they are persons, but as described and further characterized they become actions, narratives, even landscapes; and the actions take the place of drama. The poem is not dramatic except in that sense in which a speaking voice implies a dramatic situation; nor is that implication a vivid one, Hamlet being mainly a stage-managing consciousness, like Tiresias in *The Waste Land*. The protagonist's mood and temper, conforming to the "nighted color/choler" of Shakespeare's Hamlet, do, however, determine the tone of anguish throughout the poem.

Two of the episodes or symbolic actions of MacLeish's *Hamlet* are particularly bold and memorable. Part III, corresponding to Horatio's description of the Ghost (*Hamlet*, I, ii), is presented in terms of that portion of a Grail romance (the Bleheris version, freely adapted) which contains the adventure of the Chapel Perilous and the adventure of the Grail Castle, including the disclosure of the Grail talismans. The point of this (and of part IV, answering to the appearance of the Ghost to the prince) is the inscrutability of the death mystery from whose silence there can be no appeal and into whose secret there can be no initiation — such as the initiation supposed by Jessie L. Weston, in her book *From Ritual to Romance*, to have given rise to the Grail legends. A theme is here restated from *Streets in the Moon*. Part IX, corresponding to the play within the play, the play of the mousetrap, has a subject recalling St.-John Perse's "migration" poem *Anabase*, namely the movements of peoples and tribes into new lands, the rise and fall of cultures, the cycle of civilization. And the point of this, in relation to the Shakespearean scene, is that, as the memorial of human aspirations, the whole earth is a blood-stained chronicle of the guilt of nature and time. These episodes of the poem have the profoundest import because they establish the necessity of the cosmic pessimism which is the mainspring of its tragic movement. They furthermore universalize the rage and grief of the protagonist, inviting all mankind to take part in execrating the conditions of life.

The gloom pervading *The Hamlet of A. MacLeish* is left behind in the next collection, *New Found Land: Fourteen Poems* (1930). Here the over-all tone is one of acceptance — not the unreflecting acceptance urged but resisted in the closing part of the earlier poem, but something urbanely detached. There is a return to the meditativeness of an even earlier period, in poems about memory and time; along with this there is an advance toward a new theme of affirmation, for which a tone of op-

timism comes into being. Such poems as "'Not Marble Nor the
Gilded Monuments,'" "Return," "Tourist Death," and "You,
Andrew Marvell" are retrospective in two senses: they look back
to the years and places of MacLeish's sojourn abroad, and they
recall his obsessive concern, in those circumstances, with the
erosion of life by time. "You, Andrew Marvell" has been an-
thologized too often, but it is as nearly perfect a poem as Mac-
Leish has ever written. Yet it is only one of a group (part IV of
his *Hamlet* belongs with these) in which he again used the
"cinema" technique of passing across the mind's eye a succession
of places and faces, each an objective repository of some emo-
tional association for him. The subject of "You, Andrew Mar-
vell" is the poet's past as lodged in the places named, quite as
much as it is the poet's present conceived as a moment in the
light which is soon to be covered by the darkness inexorably
rising in the east. The specific wit in his highly serious
"metaphysical" handling of this subject depends not merely on a
paradoxical view of diurnal motions (the night rises in the east)
but on his present geographical position in relation to the re-
gions reviewed in his mind. Being now presumably in the
middle of the American continent, he, at noon, imagines the
eastern world slipping into physical night just as, figuratively,
it darkens by receding into his personal past.

The new, affirmative theme, though not fully realized in this
poem or perhaps anywhere in the collection before the conclud-
ing piece, "American Letter," seems to grow out of a personal
sense of the east-west imagery. At least "American Letter"
defines the line of separation between the past, Europe and
Asia, old lands of darkness, and the future, America the "new
found land," by declaring that for the American born his life
must unfold here: the Old World may enshrine a remembered
joy, but the man of the New World is not fulfilled by it. And in
"Salute" MacLeish hails the sun, dayspring and midday, as if to
assert the preeminence of his symbol of the West. Indeed, he
tends now to neglect the moon, which becomes a symbol no
longer of that sought realm of myths and dreaming but of a
world of stasis, sterility — something praised only in the almost

hymnal "Immortal Autumn." His style tends toward greater impersonality as, following Perse, he cultivates dissociated concrete images of immense but vague significance. One very successful instance of this practice occurs in "Epistle to Be Left in the Earth," where its gnomic qualities suit the speaker's list of specific phenomena unreduced to abstract classification.

Conquistador (1932) is a long poem but not an epic, though of epic magnitude in theme, nor yet a chronicle, though based on an account of the Spanish rape of Mexico, *The True History of the Conquest of New Spain*, by Bernál Díaz del Castillo. Its interest derives neither from the portrayal of heroic character nor from adventurous narrative, but from its rendering of discrete episodes as experiences recollected by its narrator. It can hardly be termed panoramic; it is kaleidoscopic, a fantasia of emotions. Though not primarily a narrative at all but a series of tableaux with subjective coloring, it would perhaps remind one of Dante's *Divine Comedy* even if, typographically, its verse did not resemble *terza rima*. Like the *Divine Comedy* it presents a psychological, if not quite a spiritual, quest. This quest, outlined in fifteen books, has the usual temporal and spatial dimensions — temporal into the past buried within the speaker's self, spatial into the Mexican interior and the death of the Aztec culture. The hallmark of the poem, unfortunately, is an unrelieved sense of enormous confusion. In the memory of the speaker, the successive episodes are crowded with detail; and an effect of "nonlinear" construction is heightened by the frequent use of parataxis. That is, the language depends a good deal on coordinated statements, whether or not with conjunctions. That this device was intentional is evident from the special use of the colon as a divider; it is made to separate phrases of all kinds. The elements which are thus compounded stand in any order: logic seems not to be in question, since free association controls largely.

If the influence of St.-John Perse dominates the larger framework of the poem, affecting the shape of its "grand sweep," still another influence, that of the Ezra Pound of the *Cantos*, often prevails at close quarters. The arbitrary juxtaposition of "significant" details is Poundian. So, too, is one ingre-

dient of MacLeish's subject matter, the use of Book XI of the
Odyssey in the "Prologue," where Bernál Díaz is given a role
like that of the Homeric Tiresias, summoned from the dead
along with fellow ghosts to speak to the living. MacLeish drops
this mythological device after the "Prologue," in favor of Díaz's
book narrative; but the latter may be considered a realistic equiv-
alent to ghostly speech. Though more in key with the biblical
rhapsodies of Perse than with the social grumblings of Pound,
Conquistador lacks optimism. For one thing it is based on one of the
bloodiest and most barbarous exploits in history, one which de-
stroys the empire it conquers and which ends in a retreat. Fur-
thermore it is set forth by a spokesman for the dead and disil-
lusioned, himself aware, in his very book, that death hangs over
him. At the last he longs for the impossible resurrection of youth-
ful hope:

> O day that brings the earth back bring again
>
> That well-swept town those towers and that
>   island. . . .

In general this poem, far from acclaiming the origin of the New
World as the harbinger of American civilization, is negative as
well as confessional. Díaz, like MacLeish's Hamlet, is a waste-
lander, and what he longs for is a lost innocence that in fact was
never real at all: certainly it did not dwell in the Aztec priestly
slaughterhouse or in the hearts of the Spanish butchers either.
In the poem it only tantalizes like a gilded dream of El Dorado.

Whatever its defects — and its failures, for if it succeeds it
does so as a sequence of vibrant short poems, not as a big poem
— *Conquistador* brings MacLeish back definitely to American
scenes. *Frescoes for Mr. Rockefeller's City* (1933) restores the
affirmative tone. What is affirmed now is the American dream
— the wholesome one — not as an abstraction but in its embod-
iment by the American land and the pioneer past. The first of
the six poems, "Landscape as a Nude," revives an allegorical
convention (like *Finnegans Wake*, by the way) to romanticize the
land as a voluptuous woman. "Wildwest" and "Burying Ground
by the Ties" pay tribute to defeated energies of a past era, to

Crazy Horse and to the laborers dead after laying the tracks of
the Union Pacific; and at the same time these poems satirize the
millionaire railroaders, as does the opening section of the fifth
poem, "Empire Builders." The longer, second section of the
latter invokes for its contrast the unviolated wilderness explored
by Lewis and Clark on their expedition to the Northwest — the
description being treated as an "underpainting" beneath a sup-
posed series of panels beautifying the robber barons Harriman,
Vanderbilt, Morgan, and Mellon, and for anticlimactic good
measure the advertising executive Bruce Barton. The fourth
poem, "Oil Painting of the Artist as the Artist," lampoons the
anti-American expatriate snob — the T. S. Eliot type, who

> . . . thinks of himself as an exile from all this,
> As an émigré from his own time into history
>
> (History being an empty house without owners
> A practical man may get in by the privy stones . . .)

A final poem, "Background with Revolutionaries," makes a
point with regard to the controversy (current at the time Mac-
Leish was writing but now almost forgotten) surrounding the
Diego Rivera murals for Radio City in New York. Rivera had
depicted Lenin among his inspirational figures; Nelson Rock-
efeller had demurred; and the painting was expunged, to the
accompaniment of howls from the Left, amusingly reinforced
with the aesthetical plea that art is sacred beyond politics.
MacLeish's point in the concluding poem was that Lenin is ir-
relevant to the spirit of America, which lives in the communion
of land with people; a further point, which involves one's read-
ing the fifth poem, optionally, as a coda to the other four, can be
that Lenin in his irrelevance is somehow analogous to J. P. Mor-
gan.

There are not only ideological but functional problems in the
Frescoes. Ideologically it is dubious whether MacLeish quite con-
veyed the absurdity of Leninism with his selected profiles of ig-
norant, neurotic, or simply enthusiastic believers in it; a sugges-
tion emerges from "Background with Revolutionaries" that the
fault with these communists may lie in their intellectual preten-

sions, which do not suit the nonintellectual mystique urged in
the poem. And by the same token, earlier in the series, that
mystique has been manipulated in order to pillory the railroad
magnates, who were not "men of the people" and who ravaged
the land for their money making. Crazy Horse was admirable,
apparently, and the virgin wilderness was good and so were the
track gangs; but beyond this mystique of the primitive and the
peasant the *Frescoes* offered little to a people who owed their
power to the railroads and who, in distinction of achievement,
had long since outdone the spike-drivers. Obviously the *Frescoes*
laud a homegrown radicalism; they reject Leninism as sophisti-
cated (and foreign); but they ignore the complex life of a mod-
ern people. Calling themselves frescoes and claiming a pictorial
function, they fail to cover, as it were, the wall. They say almost
nothing about what Americans do, or why. Given pictorial form,
they would pose as great an irrelevance — to Mr. Rockefeller's
or anyone's city — as Diego Rivera with his intrusive Lenin.

MacLeish's next volume, *Poems, 1924–1933*, not only re-
printed the best of his work up to 1933 but arranged it in
nonchronological order. This order could form the subject of a
separate study: it seems to indicate many of the relations which
MacLeish intended to hold in balance between separate poems.
The volume begins with the *Hamlet* and ends with *Conquistador*,
the long poems most antithetical to each other as "private" and
"public" documents. Scattered through it are previously uncol-
lected pieces; at least six of these rank among the finest of his
middle period, namely "The Night Dream," "Broken Promise,"
"Before March," "Epistle to Léon-Paul Fargue," "Invocation to
the Social Muse," and "Lines for an Interment." A sardonic note
recalling a few of the poems in *Streets in the Moon* comes up
occasionally; of these six, "Invocation to the Social Muse" is the
poem most ruled by it. In "Lines for an Interment" a similar
note heard before in "Memorial Rain" is intensified into a savage
agony. Elsewhere the tone is dispassionate, conveyed through
imagery and syntax of a crystal precision reminiscent, almost, of
Dryden's noble renderings of Horace and worthy of Landor or

Housman at their most painstaking. Of this character are "Before March" and a slighter poem, "Voyage":

> Heap we these coppered hulls
> With headed poppies
> And garlic longed-for by the eager dead . . .

Such effects are concentrated in the poems having great intimacy of theme and voice.

The short volume *Public Speech: Poems* (1936) is strong in social implication, like MacLeish's plays in the same decade; but for part of its length it is different in manner from the usual "public" poetry. It ends with a series of ten poems in various lyric forms, assembled under the general title "The Woman on the Stair"; this, more than anything else in the volume, harks back to an earlier period. One thinks especially of "The Happy Marriage," which also is a series of this type: "The Woman on the Stair," too, is made up of meditative descriptions which chart an emotional relationship. Why should this sequence have been inserted in a book whose very title points to MacLeish's new preoccupation with what poetry can deliver to the public concerning themselves? The answer is that the adjective *public* is not synonymous with *national* or with *political* or with *cultural* in a social scientist's sense; it connotes all that is common, all that touches everyman. Those of MacLeish's poems that treat of the individual in society, or of society in history, do seem public in a more "communal" sense than is possible to a lyric commemoration of love; but this subject, too, can be so treated that its private values become general meanings. Moreover, the first poem in the volume, "Pole Star," celebrates social love, the observance of charity for all, as a guiding principle in an age of misdirections; almost the whole collection is about human bonds of feeling. What *public* meant to MacLeish at this juncture seems to have been dual: in one aspect it came close to our recent slack sense of *relevant*; in another it rather implied *impersonal* in something like Eliot's sense, that is, marked by avoidance of self-absorption. In "The Woman on the Stair," personal subject matter becomes archetypal.

"The Woman on the Stair" is really about the psychology of love. The Eros who rules here is the god of maturity; it would be instructive to set beside this another group of lyrics, also a sequence and also a chronicle of love's progress, but focusing on youthful love — Joyce's *Chamber Music*. There the intensities of feeling wear romantic disguises which in turn undergo transformations into fabrics of symbol. Here, viewed alike from the masculine and the feminine sides, are the great intensities — need, selfishness, shame, jealousy, fickleness, boredom — and time's deadly gift, detachment, all of them functions of a pragmatism that often governs human relations in the mask of the romantic spirit. This sobering vision culminates in the remarkable closing poem, "The Release," a meditation on past time as stasis. What "The Woman on the Stair" projects as a "cinema" sequence, a passional affair involving two people only, becomes in projection a far-reaching commentary on behavior and motivation.

Not only "Pole Star," concerning love, but several other poems at the beginning of *Public Speech* meditate contemporary bearings for traditional wisdom. "Speech to Those Who Say Comrade" defines true as against specious brotherhood. "Speech to the Detractors" rebukes debunkers and petty journalists and acclaims the love of excellence, arguing that a people unwilling to honor its outstanding men is a self-degrading people. "Speech to a Crowd" exhorts men to be self-reliant, not to wait on leadership, not to *be* a crowd. These poems, along with a few in the middle of the volume, may be too inspirational to appeal to readers who are moved by the psychological shrewdness of "The Woman on the Stair." One poem, "The German Girls! The German Girls!" (its title to be understood as a sardonic toast?), takes the form of a quasi-choric exchange and is therefore dramatic in structure though not in form. It damns the militaristic spirit by cataloguing the coarse, brutal, and perverted types that abound among the Nazis. Propaganda though this is, the poem remains fresh because it is dramatic and also because it escapes "pulpit diction."

Two separately published poems on social themes, *Land of the*

Free — U.S.A. (1938) and *America Was Promises* (1939), both with topical bearing, relate to diverse areas of concern. The first is hard to judge as poetry because, as published, it was tied to a series of eighty-eight contemporary photographs in order that (according to a note by MacLeish) it might illustrate *them*. The photographs were already collected before the poem was written. The letterpress still makes a poem, but is at some disadvantage in proximity to the pictures. The two arts combine to tell a horrifying before-and-after story of the pioneer settlers in a rich land who, after many generations, have sunk into poverty and squalor through disease, overcrowding, economic exploitation, soil deterioration, industrialization, and all the rest. The horror is conveyed mainly by the impact of the photographs as a set, which embraces many contrasts; but the most distressing, i.e., pathetic, are far beyond the power of the poem to annotate. The pictures are violent, shocking; the poem is "cool," relying on irony. Certainly the contrasts are intrinsic to the two modes: photography is presentational, ruminative poetry representational. The style is itself cool, in form a kind of collective monologue; but the pronoun *we* serves also to make the voice impersonal, as if the speaker were radiobroadcasting the report of a disaster. MacLeish's use of a "broadcast announcer" voice was frequent in the 1930s. Whether radio was responsible directly (other poets having experimented with the same device — Auden, for example, and Eliot in "Triumphal March"), the fact that MacLeish had written radio plays, in which such a voice was normally essential, suggests that the medium exerted some influence. One problem with having this voice accompany a photographic series is that, *ex hypothesi*, it belongs to a subject confronting human objects seen by the camera, yet it purports to speak in the character of those objects, and this without so much as adopting their dialect.

America Was Promises is indisputably the most eloquent of the "public" poems. It contrives an absolute alliance between theme and voice; actually the theme helps to flesh the voice so that it surmounts its usual anonymity and acquires the solidity of a persona. Who the persona is, is unclear, but what he is, is obvious, a prophet but contemporary, a liberator but traditionalist, a revolutionary but sage. The working question asked is "America was promises to whom?" — one answered in several ways, by Jefferson, by John Adams (philosopher of usury for Pound's *Cantos*), by Thomas Paine, and finally in the oracular formula *"The promises are theirs who take them."* The rest of the poem beseeches the vast community of America to believe that unless they "take the promises" others will; but there is something inconclusive about this, for a rhetoric capable of sounding a call to arms seems to have been expended on a plea for faith. References to nations made captive by the Falange, the Germans, or the Japanese might imply something like a war message (the year being 1939); on the other hand, the historical material is of the sort that, unlike MacLeish, a Marxist would have exploited seditiously. In its intellectual ambiguity *America Was Promises* had much in common with the philosophy of the national administration at that period. So seen, of course, the poem is milder than the rhetoric of its conclusion: it is simply urging people to remain loyal to New Deal doctrines at home and American policy abroad. Really it is much better as a poem than as a message: for once, MacLeish's adaptation of St.-John Perse's geographic evocations seems precisely right.

The long lapse before the appearance of *Actfive and Other Poems* (1948) would itself suffice to set this volume apart. But the double circumstance of the war and MacLeish's public service, along with the new personal vitality he seems to have experienced at this time, may account for its energies. In spirit this book is fully postwar, and it contains the perceptions of a man who had worked within government and who now had a far more exact idea of the gulf between political dreams and reality. It is the book of his second renaissance. A number of the poems, quite apart from the title piece, are of immense interest technically. They range from "Excavation of Troy," an amusing metaphysical exercise in the slow manipulation of imagery and simile (in the mind of a drowsing girl her lover of many nights gone is like Troy buried under many intervening "layers"), to "What Must," a quick medley of narrative, dialogue, and meditation (telling virtually in a cataract of rhymes the events of a brief love idyl). Several of the poems are ideological: thus "Brave New World," a ballad to Jefferson in his grave (in the tradition of Yeats's "To a Shade") taunts postwar America for its indifference to the plight of nations still unliberated.

The title piece, "Actfive," was the most significant poem by MacLeish since the publication of his *Hamlet*. It does what a major work by a developing poet has to do: it clarifies the meaning of his previous major works in relation to one another, and it subjects to new form the world which his art is trying now to deal with. This poem relates to *The Pot of Earth*, to "Einstein," and to *The Hamlet of A. MacLeish*; and though quite intelligible independently of those, it gains depth and complexity by the relation. The general title, with the ranting manner of part I ("The Stage All Blood . . ."), brings the *Hamlet* to mind; "Actfive" continues, in a manner of speaking, the actions of that nightmarish poem, advancing them beyond the circle of a single protagonist's mind and showing that they involve all men.

Part I proclaims the death of God, of Kingship, and of Man deified — the last murdered by tyrants; and it appeals for one who can become in their stead "the hero in the play," a hero to restore not only peace but Eternity, the principle of very reason. Implicitly both *The Pot of Earth* and, at some distance, *Nobodaddy* are drawn upon here, the one for the indifference of the Absolute, the other for, as well, the human alienation from it. In turn both are implicitly criticized: they have too palely depicted the stark loathsomeness of the death which proud man has inherited. Part II, "The Masque of Mummers," parades before the reader an absurd train of expressionistic figures, nonheroes yet "each the Hero of the Age"; it is an age whose inhabitants, stripped of privacy and individuality, cling together as in a public amphitheater and witness a charade of social lies — those of the Science Hero, of the Boyo of Industry, of the Revolutionary Hero with the Book, of the Great Man, of the Victim Hero or "pimp of death," of the Visitor or dreamer of millennium, of the State or utopia, of the I or egotist-introspectionist, of the lonely Crowd. Part III, "The Shape of Flesh and Bone," identifies the sought hero at last; it is flesh and bone, unidealized, existential man, instinctive, physical, able to define the meaning of his universe to himself — man the transitory but in spirit indomitable. Archetypes present themselves: "The blinded gunner at the ford," an image borrowed presumably from Hemingway's *For Whom the Bell Tolls*; a profile of Franklin D. Roosevelt, "The responsible man . . ./[who] dies in his chair . . ./ The war won, the victory assured"; and other images, of an invalid and a hostage. These exemplify the unposturing, unselfish performance of duty,

> Some duty to be beautiful and brave
> Owed neither to the world nor to the grave
> .   .   .   .
> But only to the flesh the bone.

The closing lines reaffirm the unutterable loneliness of man in his universe of death, but, like "Einstein," leave him with his inviolate creaturehood. It is ironic that "Actfive" should so circuitously return to the point insisted upon in "Einstein"; for it steers by the opposite pole, assuming that man's lordly reason, far from having subdued nature to its understanding, has been dethroned utterly. Equally, the animal self here, which can still "endure and love," is all that preserves man from destruction; whereas in "Einstein" it is the only thing that debars him from godhead.

Collected Poems 1917–1952 incorporates a section of "New Poems" which might have made a book by themselves. They protract the *Actfive* renaissance (indeed it has lasted MacLeish into old age). Some half-dozen of them are modern "emblem" poems, being dominated by single images (often elaborated) with connotative value. Blake's "Ah! Sun-flower" is analogous; in MacLeish's "Thunderhead" the physics of lightning symbolizes an aspect of conjugal behavior; in "Starved Lovers" chrysanthemums symbolize sensuality; in "The Linden Branch" a green bough is metaphorically a musical instrument playing silent music. The newness of this effect consists in the way whole poems are now built round it, as Emily Dickinson's or (using symbol rather than metaphor) Yeats's often are. Yeats, who was to become a major inspiration for MacLeish, must have influenced the style of the end poem of "New Poems," the meditation on metaphor "Hypocrite Auteur," which essentially offers a justification for the effect.

Songs for Eve (1954) really consists of two collections joined together: first the twenty-eight tight, riddling poems (corresponding to the days of the month?) called "Songs for Eve"; then "Twenty-One Poems" of miscellaneous kinds. Despite the general title of the initial set, some of its pieces are for Eve but others are for Adam, the Serpent, the Green Tree, Eve's children, and so on. Perhaps in some sense all indeed are "for" Eve, she being central in the mythic context. Like Yeats's Crazy Jane, Eve is carnal and vicariously creative — in short, Blakean. Through her, Adam is enabled to wake from animality into consciousness; with her, he falls upward "from earth to God," his soul growing as the awareness within his body, his children succeeding him as rebels and creators destined to rear, in place of the Green Tree of consciousness, the Dry Tree (the Cross) of godlike knowledge. The theme is that of *Nobodaddy* enriched with that of "Einstein." The twenty-eighth poem ends the sequence by lauding "man / That immortal order can"; and in like manner the last of the "Twenty-One Poems," entitled "Reasons for Music" and dedicated to Wallace Stevens, defines the poet's task as the imposition of form upon the fluid world (a theme of Stevens's own; MacLeish would ordinarily refer to the *discovery* of natural, intrinsic order, except probably in the aesthetic or the moral sphere). The fine keynote poem "The Infinite Reason" paraphrases "Songs for Eve" in effect by speaking of the human mission to read meaning in external reality:

> Our human part is to redeem the god
> Drowned in this time of space, this space
> That time encloses.

Clearly the leading theme of *Songs for Eve*, the whole book, is man's ordering function; the collection is closer to "Einstein" and the other space-time poems of *Streets in the Moon* than are the works in between. Here much is made of the origin of the human soul within space-time, particularly in "Reply to Mr. Wordsworth," where the proposition that the soul "cometh from afar" is refuted by an appeal to Einsteinian physics and — paradoxically — to the felt life of the emotions. The poems "Infiltration of the Universe," "The Wood Dove at Sandy Spring," "The Wave," "Captivity of the Fly," and "The Genius" are emblematic, and they happen also to compose a miniature bestiary. The volume pays tribute impartially to matters of intellect and of feeling; these compressed parables divide between them.

The Wild Old Wicked Man (1968) explores the whole scale of MacLeish's concerns, still optimistically. Old age and youth, time, domesticity, contemporary manners, love, death — these predominate. Introspection is not overworked, but two of the most arresting poems in the volume are "Autobiography," on childhood vision, and "Tyrant of Syracuse," on the subliminal self. In a memorable group of elegies, MacLeish bids farewell to Sandburg, Cummings, Hemingway, and Edwin Muir. The Hemingway poem, only eleven lines long, is one of numerous tributes paid by MacLeish to that one-time friend; it adapts Yeats's concept of "the dreaming back" for a skillful and moving analysis of the unity of the man Hemingway in his life and death. The Muir poem quotes "The Linden Branch," applying to a *green memory* the graceful conceit of the green bough as a musical staff with leaves for notes. Yeats furnished the title of the volume; and the title poem, placed at the end, closes on the theme of

> . . . the old man's triumph, to pursue
> impossibility — and take it, too,

which is a signature for MacLeish's poetry, restating the theme of Adam victorious, fallen upwards into a stasis of art and eternity.

As playwright, MacLeish began with closet drama, with *Nobodaddy* (not to forget the rhetorically lively dramatic poem

"Our Lady of Troy" behind that). Though excellent as a trial of philosophical drama, such a work could not have taught him much; thus the strength of his first stage play, *Panic* (1935), is very impressive. For the dialogue, as he explains in a prefatory note, he chose a five-accent line in free (or sprung) rhythm; other passages, those of a choric nature allotted to various supplementary voices, he wrote in three-accent lines. The experiment was contemporary with Eliot's *Murder in the Cathedral*; and while MacLeish's verse shows less flexibility than Eliot's there, it is at least as stageworthy. The play is an admirable and curious hybrid. In sum, it is an Aristotelian tragedy with a special catastrophe, the withdrawal of the supporting characters' loyalty (the protagonist, a great man, suddenly ceases to be accepted as that); and this plot is superimposed on a proletarian drama conveyed by expressionistic techniques (anonymous voices of the poor and unemployed in a time of financial crisis). It is the unemployed who make the protagonist's fellow bankers lose confidence in him; and not what he does because of pride, but his vulnerability to the hatred of the mob because of who he is, precipitates the "panic" causing his downfall. The play remains solidly in the classic tradition; for the protagonist, the superbanker McGafferty (the play was first called "J. P. McGafferty"), possesses nobility of spirit and authentic powers of leadership: he really could avert his country's economic collapse if his colleagues would rally round him and pool their resources instead of defaulting. Their refusal to do so might support a "proletarian" interpretation, but in fact the whole botch happens because the proletariat prophesy that it will, when they invade his office and one of their number (a blind "Tiresias") pronounces his doom. "Proletarian" is converted into "psychological." The weakness in *Panic* consists in the unintegrated role of the feminine lead, McGafferty's mistress Ione, who exercises only a reflector function of emphasizing his arrogance. Her role is crucial theatrically, but in structure the play suffers from it.

In his foreword to *The Fall of the City* (1937), MacLeish discussed the advantages of radio as a medium for verse drama. Looking back a third of a century, one must now regret bitterly the lost opportunities for this genre, which was killed when, in America, radio was killed by television. MacLeish's claims for radio verse were not exaggerated, but the moment was wrong and the remaining time too short. His own early contributions, notably this play and its successor *Air Raid* (1938), have, alas, chiefly a memorial importance. *The Fall of the City*, in which the radio announcer's unique function as described by MacLeish is essential, appears to follow expressionistic models. The Announcer, the Dead Woman, the Messenger, the Orator, as voices bring the most presentational style into the most presentational medium. The poetry has absolute immediacy: since it must express action, it hews to what happens, never deviating into mere lyricism. The techniques are of the simplest: the play employs the unity of (supposed) place, with everything taking place under the Announcer's eyes. *Air Raid* is at once more realistic in terms of radio drama, and more conventional — although less realistic in one sense, for it uses the "newsreel" technique of picking up scenes at which the Announcer is not present. And in this play the poetry ranges away from the main action, as the characters' feelings digress from their imminent danger, so that it has a more various texture. Both plays use a poetry of vivid images and plain colloquialism. In *The Fall of the City* the unit is a line of varying length in sprung rhythm; in *Air Raid* it is a line of five or, less commonly, fewer accents.

When, in the postwar television age, MacLeish returned to radio verse drama tentatively, it was with recognition of its anachronistic status. He called *The Trojan Horse* (1952) a play for broadcasting or for reading without scenery (i.e., like Dylan Thomas's *Under Milk Wood*). It is a one-act piece with one moment of high drama, when Helen realizes that the wooden horse contains those who will destroy her happiness. Otherwise the speeches seem unduly level — a problem in the play for voices, which often thus depends on elocutionary artifice for sharp characterizations. The verse line is of three accents, except in formal speeches, where blank verse occurs. In place of an announcer, there is a brief prologue in which a "modern" voice calls upon an "ancient" voice (Homer) to explain the action;

within the play there are a blind man (also Homer) and a girl, whose dialogue serves for choric commentary. This structure foreshadows *J. B.* The effect is of a kind of Chinese-boxes perspective. *This Music Crept by Me upon the Waters* (1953) has been staged as well as broadcast. It is conversational, with no fewer than ten characters filling the one act; they speak a three-accent verse a little like Eliot's in *The Cocktail Party*, but with less straddling from line to line and much tighter rhythm. The people are contemporary, the setting Caribbean, a Paradise island like Prospero's; the theme is the impossibility of a return to innocence and Eden, except for saints or primitives. Others, the romantics, sink into dreams but soon are recalled to reality; still others, the merely idle, are overwhelmed with boredom and drink. The play chides the rich and irresponsible who demand Eden without earning it.

J. B.: A Play in Verse (1958) and *Herakles* (1967) are respectively based on the book of Job and on the Greek hero myth; between them they represent man suffering and acting. J. B. is a King Lear who, divested of all illusions about a benevolent universe, is taught to endure and love, like the survivors in *Actfive*. Herakles is an Einstein mastering nature, a Cain seeking godhead, confronted finally by the limits of human power and made to see his mere humanity. *J. B.* is constructed as a play within a play, with a remote director-prompter as deity offstage. The God and Satan of the scriptural drama are here impersonated by actor-clowns, Zuss the circus balloon-vendor and Nickles the popcorn-seller, who first stage a play in the deserted circus tent and then become involved in it as chorus for J. B.'s tribulation. J. B. triumphs both over Zuss's humiliation of him and Nickles's temptation to hatred. Learning the truth about his god, he forgives him his injustice. With a love stronger than the unreasoning tyranny of heaven, he justifies that love by beginning to live again when his torment is finished.

Against this eloquent, superbly theatrical play, *Herakles* seems brittle; yet, fantasy though it is, it is founded on a sacred and profound myth. A modern scientist, Professor Hoadley, has received international recognition for his discoveries. Symbolically he is Herakles, his work for human knowledge and power analogous to the hero's labors. His wife corresponds to Herakles' wife Megara. The analogy extends to the Hoadleys' son, effeminate and hostile, alienated by his father's profession; he represents the sons slaughtered by Herakles in his overweening frenzy after returning from the underworld. If, like Euripides' play (from which MacLeish drew hints), this action begins as a triumph in Act I, it continues as a fantasy of pathos. In Act II Mrs. Hoadley and Megara occupy the stage together, as their two worlds of history and myth interpenetrate and the myth is shown as eternal meaning: Herakles' homecoming and his reunion with the mother of his dead children, at once the repetition and archetype of Professor Hoadley's (the two parts are presumably doubled in production), become symbolic of the mere ruin of life to which the Promethean hero is condemned. He obeys the necessity of fighting evil and harnessing power for man's welfare, but he is destroyed by hatred and the unnatural burden of godhead.

Herakles and *J. B.* show Janus faces of the human struggle to neutralize the blind sentence of death passed upon mankind. Their two scales of poetry, exemplifying MacLeish's maturest talents, correspond to extremes of lyricism and tragic realism in speech.

The prose drama *Scratch* (1971), amplifying Stephen Vincent Benét's 1936 story "The Devil and Daniel Webster," creates a parable with ethical overtones of "Actfive" as well as MacLeish's Blakean exaltation of liberty over law. The story, transformed by MacLeish, achieves a certain mythic dimension, not really because it deals with inveterate problems of American life (though it can indeed symbolize these as MacLeish's "Foreword" contends), but because its hero, Daniel Webster, thinks and acts as if, obedient to a categorical imperative, he embodied the meaning of civilization: he is a type of Prometheus. This strong drama involves a more complex system of implication than *J. B.* Its actual events reduce to a simple linear form. They begin with the leveling of charges against Webster by two accusers, a moral New Englander (Webster's friend Peterson) and the Devil himself (Scratch). They continue with Scratch's attempt to "fore-close" the soul of Jabez Stone, who has bartered it for seven years' good luck. They end with Jabez's legal defense by Webster before a ghostly judge and jury consisting of thirteen dead and damned enemies of American freedom. In the story by Benét, Webster is pure lawyer: he argues successfully on behalf of Jabez that the terrible forfeit must be ruled null and void because the Devil, as a foreign potentate, cannot exercise dominion over a freeborn American. In MacLeish's version a protagonist more like the historical Webster must argue both Jabez's case and *his own* — the latter amounting in fact to the whole substance of the drama. The charges against Webster in *Scratch* concern his al-leged expedient "sellout" of liberty to preserve the American Union, through his adoption of the Compromise of 1850. In accepting the Fugitive Slave Law, he seems to have betrayed his fundamental axiom "Liberty and Union, now and forever, one and inseparable." When the jurymen bring in a verdict favorable to Jabez, they do so because touched by Webster's *argumentum ad hominem*, his appeal to their own sense of the "huge injustice" of man's life and death. In particular this appeal holds that every man, even such as the feckless Jabez, has the liberty to alleviate his poverty, his suffering, without being accountable to the strictness of the law. Webster's argument itself is a sufficient reply to his own accusers: it demonstrates his devotion to liberty but does not undermine his resolution as a statesman. Accord-ingly the jury's verdict, like that of any audience, finds not only for Jabez but for Webster as in effect a codefendant; and in purely dramatic, theatrical terms the "case" against Webster ends simultaneously with the suit against Jabez Stone. In the forum of history, as Webster sadly acknowledges, the charges against him for accepting the Fugitive Slave Law remain un-quashed. MacLeish, too, seems to believe that the historical Webster erred; but in *Scratch*, paradoxically, he arrays against his protagonist only two accusers, the Father of Lies and a New England Abolitionist.

Scratch is a lively and moving drama. Yet it had only a brief New York run in 1971. Perhaps, in the years between *J. B.* and

Scratch, the strong, representative or mythic hero went out of fashion. Perhaps the improvident blasphemer Jabez Stone, intent on getting something for nothing, would better have fitted the occasion and the age if glorified as an antihero. Perhaps *Scratch* is both too intellectual and too highly civilized for the American theater of the 1970s.

MacLeish from the beginning has held to a course of lonely exploration. His standards are classical and aristocratic. Once his friend Mark Van Doren, presented with an award for "services to poetry," responded with slow and deliberate emphasis that, as for himself, he had tried to serve only the *best* poetry. The remark could have been made by Archibald MacLeish with equally merited pride (the pride which knows the humility exacted by such service) and with equal truth. Part of his devotion has been accorded to craftsmanship. One can praise poets for this, not too much, certainly, but with too much exclusiveness. Often when one has praised it, in Frost or Stevens or Eliot, say, or in Rimbaud, it does not seem sufficient. This century still paddles in the backwash of Aestheticism; but there have been ages, before the subjectivist era, when poetry and the other arts pertained to the things of man — Cicero's *artes quae ad humanitatem pertinent* — and not just to one man's special quirk of vision, to express which he devises exquisite forms. Part of MacLeish's devotion has gone to the human state. Such concern is not poetry, but one is entitled to ask whether, without it, good poetry, let alone the best, can come into being. It must be set down that MacLeish, like the great poets — Yeats, for example — has striven to give form to what pertains not just to himself but to his fellowmen.

Richard Eberhart

Anyone surveying the developments in American poetry during the last four decades and noting the emergence of a new and powerfully equipped generation of poets in the period between the middle 1930s and the close of World War II must be attracted immediately by the figure of Richard Eberhart. Born in 1904 at Austin, Minnesota, he is the oldest of three senior poets (the other two are Stanley Kunitz and the late Theodore Roethke) who broke ground for that generation, which also includes Robert Lowell, John Berryman, and Karl Shapiro. But recognition has come to him, as it has to Kunitz and Roethke, slowly and belatedly. Together with them Eberhart explores the possibilities of a personal lyricism enclosing a broad spectrum of human experience and boldly testing the forms and language for articulating what imagination gives and intuition seizes. Dispensing for the most part with the device of the persona or fictional speaker so profitably employed by Eliot, Pound, and Stevens, and lacking any inclination to commit themselves to systematic frameworks of ideas or to build private mythologies to support the imaginative interpretation of experience, these three poets and the others of their generation openly engage the material of their work in fresh, dramatic, and often original ways.

55

While certain general affinities may be traced among these poets when they are viewed in the perspective of the literary historian, it is not the intention here to look for them. Indeed the individual achievement of a writer such as Eberhart can be seriously distorted if examined through the odd lenses of similarities and relationships, for he has found a prominent place in the generation of which I have been speaking only by traveling an independent route and appearing from a different direction than his contemporaries. In background and youthful experience, in many of the artistic and intellectual influences that contrived to shape his thought and poetry, Eberhart needs to be sharply distinguished from most other American poets of his approximate age. Not easily classifiable, he continues over the years to stand out as a highly individual, sometimes even slightly eccentric poet who is unswervingly dedicated to the life of the imagination and the craft of poetry.

Eberhart studied for a year at the University of Minnesota, then attended Dartmouth, where he received his B.A. in 1926. When he was only eighteen his mother contracted cancer of the lung and suffered a "nine-month birth of death through utmost pain" which he "witnessed intimately" and which became a turning point in his life. Subsequently he wrote that this terrible ordeal was the probable cause of his selection of a poet's career, and in fact his mother's illness and premature death appear several times in poems as well as in one of the verse plays.

Before resuming his studies in England, Eberhart journeyed to the Orient as a steamer hand. In 1929 he was awarded a B.A., in 1933 an M.A. from St. John's College, Cambridge. While at Cambridge he was exposed to the teaching of I. A. Richards and F. R. Leavis; two young poets, Kathleen Raine and William Empson, were students there at the same time. Eberhart read thoroughly the then excitingly new and radical poetry of Gerard Manley Hopkins (whose work did not become available until after World War I), T. S. Eliot, D. H. Lawrence, and other pioneer modernists, but he must have devoted himself equally to the writings of Shakespeare, Donne, Wordsworth, Coleridge, and Shelley. The influence of some of these poets shows, naturally enough, in his earliest verse.

From this milieu, rather than an American one, Eberhart launched himself as a poet. His first book, *A Bravery of Earth* (1930), was published in a year which the author spent tutoring the son of King Prajadhipok of Siam — an exotic beginning for a lifetime of service as a teacher of literature and of poetic accomplishment of a high order. From 1933 until 1941 he taught at St. Mark's School, Southboro, Massachusetts, where he met Robert Lowell, then a pupil. During the war Eberhart acted as a naval gunnery officer and instructor, a role which prompted several of his fiercest and most dramatic poems, and afterwards returned to teaching, with a six-year interlude in the business world. Since 1956 he has been a professor of English and poet in residence at Dartmouth College, has spent a term as consultant in poetry at the Library of Congress; his *Collected Poems 1930–1960* was honored with the Bollingen Prize and *Selected Poems 1930–1965* was awarded the Pulitzer Prize.

Eberhart's poems set themselves in a curiously singular relationship to established canons of modern poetic practice, which they seldom heed. These poems treat philosophic themes abstractly; their method is frequently deductive rather than inductive, as Philip Booth has persuasively argued; they rely much of the time on inspiration, in the poet's own words, "burst into life spontaneously," during a period in which critical opinion emphasizes careful craftsmanship, the poem as a discovered but also a *made* object; as a final impertinence they are apt to level undisguised moral judgments while still fighting shy of dogma and firmly insisting on the ultimate mysteriousness of existence, the impenetrable heart of reality. In his handling of words Eberhart may be playful and witty, as in this excerpt from a speech in "Triptych," a play for voices:

> Shallow? Then air is shallow,
> Through which we see to heaven.
> Shallow? Then water is shallow,
> Of which we are composed.

> Shallow? Then morning's atmosphere,
> Lakes, rivers, rills and streams
> Are shallow. What is your jealous depth
> But layers and layers of shallows?

Or to take one of many possible examples, this from "The Recapitulation," he can be austere and reflective:

> Not through the rational mind,
> But by elation coming to me
> Sometimes, I am sure
> Death is but a door.

Or he can express, with the impatience of anger and disgust, his judgment of the inhumane folly of men in conflict, as in "At the End of War":

> For they cannot think straight, or remember
>   what they said,
> Cannot keep their word,
> Or realize how soon they will be dead,
> Nor distinguish between verities
> Who lust over presences,
> Nor be faithful
> Who are wrathful,
> Nor escape animal passion
> With cross-bow, slit-trench, Napalm bomb,
>   atom bomb.

Or at the opposite end of his emotional range he can become purely lyrical:

> Cover me over, clover;
> Cover me over, grass.
> The mellow day is over
> And there is night to pass.

These passages give a mere sampling of the variety of moods to be found in Eberhart's writing and the language he uses to evoke them. It ought also to be remarked in passing that sometimes emotional pressure or the love of wit exceeds the poet's control and discrimination with consequent faults in diction, tone, and rhythm; but that seems a small price to pay for many

successes and for a recognizably original voice. Eberhart's notion
of poetic creation, of the act of composition, and of the opera-
tions of the poet's mind, all of them so intimately connected with
what he conceives to be his essential artistic task, makes him
vulnerable to these dangers as well as leading him to an abun-
dance of fine poems. In the following pages we shall examine
briefly this poetic theory and some of the work which is its con-
crete manifestation.

To start with, Eberhart thinks of the poem as being, at its
highest level, inspirational in origin, an idea which, if not criti-
cally popular in our century, has managed to survive as a legacy
of the Romantics and has received confirmation in varying de-
grees by modern poets as different as Rainer Maria Rilke, D. H.
Lawrence, Herbert Read, and Robert Graves. Of course it is
doubtful that any of these poets would say *each* of his poems
arrived in its entirety, bursting upon the mind in a moment of
trancelike vision or imaginative possession, nor would Eberhart
himself make such a claim; yet all of them could point to some of
their best work as originating in luminous instances of this sort.
In a response to comments in a recent symposium on one of his
own poems Eberhart refers to and quotes Plato's *Ion*. He desig-
nates several of his pieces "as coming under this [Platonic]
theory of creation": namely "'Now Is the Air Made of Chiming
Balls,'" "'If I Could Only Live at the Pitch That Is Near
Madness,'" "1934," "'Go to the Shine That's on a Tree,'" and
"Only in the Dream." Several others, including "The Ground-
hog," "Maze," "For a Lamb," and "'In a Hard Intellectual
Light,'" are also cited but are "less purely" the result, in the
words of Plato's dialogue, of "falling under the power of music
and meter," of being "inspired and possessed." Eberhart does
not, however, stop with these disclosures; he goes on to remark
how he "grew up in the convictions of ambiguity, ambivalence,
and irony as central to poetry and cannot rationally accept
Plato's last words 'when [the poet] has not attained to this state,
he is powerless and is unable to utter his oracles.'" Thus poems

which are *given in their totality* are few and far between, the
product of rare occasions of unalloyed inspiration.

Nonetheless the infrequency of poems dictated with no neces-
sity for alteration does not preclude another kind of inspiration
at work in the rest of Eberhart's poetry. This second type of
inspiration likewise derives from moments of special percep-
tiveness and extraordinary sensitivity, in short, moments of reve-
lation; but the difference from the first, or higher, inspirational
experience lies in the fact that now the dictation is less complete
and must be augmented by the poet's conscious efforts. In this
case the poem does not come, as it were, gratuitously, and he
tries to grasp in an order of language as much as he can of a
fleeting intuition before it vanishes. Eberhart's "Notes on
Poetry" offers further explanations: "A poet does what he can
do. Poetry is dynamic, Protean. In the rigors of composition it
seems to me that the poet's mind is a filament, informed with the
irrational vitality of energy as it was discovered in our time in
quantum mechanics. The quanta may shoot off any way. (You
breathe in maybe God.) If you dislike the word inspiration, say
then that the poet in a creative state of mind is in a state differ-
ent from that of his ordinary or logical state. This leads on not to
automatic writing, but to some mysterious power latent within
him which illuminates his being so that his perceptions are more
than ordinarily available for use, and that in such moments he
has the ability to establish feelings, ideas and perceptions which
are communicable in potential degree and with some pleasure."

Whatever may be felt about the applicability of the analogy
with modern physics this passage holds up as one of the best of
several statements Eberhart has written insisting upon the poet's
unusual condition of attentiveness and receptivity immediately
preceding a seizure of creative activity. The validity of his ac-
count rests on its experiential nature, for it is quite without
theoretical pretensions and simply essays a description at first
hand of what happens to Eberhart when he writes a poem. Yet
the passage does more than tell us generally how many of his
poems come about; we will find on reading through the body of
Eberhart's work that the observations here have an additional

relevance both to its formal aspects and to its themes. A sense of
the processes of his art is indispensable for a full understanding
and appreciation of what it attempts.

In view of these procedures in poetic composition, sketched
here rather hastily, it should not be surprising to the reader that
the primary qualities he notices in Eberhart probably will be
spontaneity and the immediate presence of, involvement with, a
particular experience. Even *A Bravery of Earth*, which is a book-
length autobiographical poem, achieves such effects, though as a
whole it is not very satisfactory. Like many initial endeavors with
a long poem this one is packed with everything that has seemed
important in the writer's life thus far. The book divides into two
parts, the first of which, opening with a lovely lyric section,
forms a kind of allegory of the self from innocence to experi-
ence, from the natural life and the free enjoyment of the senses
through the acquaintance with love to the discovery of reason
and the shocking knowledge of death. Too often the poet loses
himself and control over his material in the currents of his
strong but conflicting emotions. Yet the movement of the poem,
in spite of its awkwardness and confusion (interspersed with
fine, compelling passages), and as Peter Thorslev has said, its
obvious indebtedness to Wordsworth, carries the reader along at
a rapid pace and impresses on him a sensation of the vital flow of
living experience, even if that experience is not always ade-
quately directed and defined. Of course this sort of sensation
belongs to literature generally, but in Eberhart's case, as no
doubt in others, it makes special claims on our consideration and
endows his poetry with uncommon energy and drama.

Of his long poem Eberhart has retained only three rather
brief portions for inclusion in his *Collected Poems*, and the best of
these is a lyric prologue which I quote in part as evidence of
already estimable gifts:

> This fevers me, this sun on green,
> On grass glowing, this young spring.
> The secret hallowing is come,
> Regenerate sudden incarnation,
> Mystery made visible

> In growth, yet subtly veiled in all,
> Ununderstandable in grass,
> In flowers, and in the human heart,
> This lyric mortal loveliness,
> This earth breathing, and the sun.

In the second half of the poem Eberhart continues his autobiographical narrative but now shifts from the lyrical account of his affective inner life to a detailed picture of the external world, of person and place as he meets them on his global voyage, working aboard a steamer. This transition from inner to outer focus at last brings about the completion of a pattern in the poet's existence:

> Into the first awareness trembling,
> Girded with mortality;
> Into the second awareness plunging,
> Impaled upon mentality;
> Into the third awareness coming
> To understand in men's action
> Mankind's desire and destiny,
> Youth lies buried and man stands up
> In a bravery of earth.

Looking back on these lines from the poem's conclusion with the advantage of time one is apt to think that while they round off nicely the author's formal intentions here, the three types of awareness he distinguishes are not, as it seems, easily succeeded in later poems by a point of view unhindered by their troubling presence. In fact "mortality," "mentality," and "men's actions" may be said to become Eberhart's chief themes throughout his career. For our purposes we might better read the end of *A Bravery of Earth* as an announcement of things to come, of thematic resources yet to be tapped. With the publication of *Reading the Spirit* (1937) these resources are opened and the long phase of this poet's genuine accomplishment, extending to his newest collection, *Fields of Grace* (1972), begins. With few exceptions he confines himself after his first book to the short or medium-length poem, kinds more suited to the alternatively meditative and intuitive character of his imagination. Poems of these proportions can more readily approximate to the flashes of perception which usually initiate them. As we know, for Eberhart the poet's primary obligation is to voice the truth disclosed by a specific experience with all the force of the revelation itself, and so it is a note of immediacy or urgency that his poetry most often, if not always, strikes.

Reading the Spirit still contains traces of its author's deep attachment to Wordsworth, coupled with some evidence of Hopkins's influence, in "Four Lakes' Days," and indeed Eberhart has a love for nature, for land- and seascape, that associates him with these two English poets, though he rapidly develops his own manner of treating it. Most apparent in this second book, however, is not a feeling for nature but a terrible intensity of vision, a radical, piercing insight into psychic and spiritual processes reminiscent of Blake, which was hardly to be predicted on the basis of *A Bravery of Earth*. Themes we noted in that poem are now embodied in the dramatic presentation of experiences at once peculiarly individual and clearly universal.

"Maze," for example, starts out as a pastoral poem in which we expect to find a fundamental harmony of man with nature elaborated:

> I have a tree in my arm,
> There are two hounds in my feet,
> The earth can do me no harm
> And the lake of my eyes is sweet.

The unity proclaimed in this stanza is, nonetheless, of short duration; not only has a fire destroyed the tree and a lack of blood starved the hounds but questions of "will" and "a human mind that has bounds" interrupt what was obviously a mode of existence from which intellectual calculation was quite absent. In the third stanza disruption is completed by a more pointed questioning which is answered in oracular fashion in the fourth:

> It is man did it, man,
> Who imagined imagination,
> And he did what man can,
> He uncreated creation.

This leads to a concluding stanza which is an ironic version of
the poem's beginning:

> There is no tree in my arm,
> I have no hounds in my feet,
> The earth can soothe me and harm,
> And the lake of my eyes is a cheat.

Undoubtedly the reader will have several ways of interpreting
various details in this poem, but puzzling as some things may
seem we can be fairly certain of what has been taking place. In
archetypal or symbolic terms the poem recounts a fall from in-
nocence, wholeness, and a sort of grace into a state of experi-
ence, characterized by the intrusion of self-consciousness, in-
quisitiveness, and intellectual activity. The maze of the title is
what reality becomes after the breakup of the original unity:
there the individual, driven by will, relentlessly seeks knowledge.

This theme of "mentality," to use Eberhart's word from *A
Bravery of Earth*, appears regularly in his poetry, often in connec-
tion with different experiences of knowing. One early poem,
"Request for Offering," pursues the theme in a strictly allegori-
cal manner through the figures of a "baleful lion" and "the
virgin pap / Of the white world." If seen as showing ferocious
intellect poised to attack the beautiful mystery of the cosmos the
poem makes sense; it also suggests a violation or rape, so that the
intended assault takes on a more specific moral cast. But the
poem's direction is halted abruptly in the fourth stanza, where
the lion's attack meets a surprising resistance:

> Amaze your eyes now, hard
> Is the marble pap of the world
> And the baleful lion regard
> With the claws of the paw curled.

The next, and final, stanza merely repeats the first one, which
utters the "request" for the sacrifice or "offering," the implica-
tion being that it will probably be made again and again but that
the impenetrability of the world will remain secure.

Another poem, "'If I Could Only Live at the Pitch That Is

Near Madness,'" from Eberhart's third book, *Song and Idea*
(1942), examines the same fall from innocence and the unified
life into knowledge that we saw in "Maze," but here the emphasis
on perception — the childish vision as the clearest and most
discerning one — is pronounced. The first two stanzas belong to
a tradition in modern poetry, reaching from Blake through
Rimbaud to E. E. Cummings and Dylan Thomas, which equates
the child's intensity of vision with a hallucinated perception lib-
erated from routine habits of mind that impose a conventional
method of looking at the world without ever seeing it:

> If I could only live at the pitch that is near
>   madness
> When everything is as it was in my childhood
> Violent, vivid, and of infinite possibility:
> That the sun and the moon broke over my head.
>
> Then I cast time out of the trees and fields,
> Then I stood immaculate in the Ego;
> Then I eyed the world with all delight,
> Reality was the perfection of my sight.

In this instance of enlightenment the visible universe discloses
its hidden energies, time is overcome, and selfhood is enjoyed in
all of its pristine innocence and completeness. We know from
the poem's beginning that this vision does not survive as a con-
stant mode of seeing and experiencing reality; only at extraor-
dinary moments, when the individual approaches the sheer un-
reason and heightened consciousness of madness, will that kind
of perceiving be reawakened. Stanza three makes plain the fact
that "the race of mankind" cannot countenance a world where
"fields and trees" have "a way of being themselves," and so the
child is required to supply "a moral answer" for his vision, to
learn the adult's distinction between good and evil, to share the
adult's burden of guilt, with disastrous results:

> I gave the moral answer and I died
> And into a realm of complexity came
> Where nothing is possible but necessity
> And the truth wailing there like a red babe.

The poem ends, then, in a confirmation of human misery and torment, in a divided, fateful state very like the confused one with which "Maze" finishes. The "moral answer" brings evil into the child's universe, shattering his unified, positive view. The point should be stressed that the fall from simple harmony with creation and the loss of the vision which is so essential a part of it appears quite unavoidable. As it does for T. S. Eliot, Edwin Muir, Kathleen Raine, and a number of other modern poets, the lapse from grace and wholeness in the child has for Eberhart metaphysical and religious implications prior to any merely psychological effects, though these are not always set forth in specifically Christian terms. Yet the English poet and critic Michael Roberts in his introduction to *Reading the Spirit* remarked that Eberhart's poetry "represents the Western, Christian, Aristotelian view of life against the Oriental and platonic view; its music is alert and energetic rather than mellifluous and drowsy; and the delight at which it aims is the delight of intense mental and physical activity, and not of passivity and disembodied ecstasy." This description is quite accurate; only in some of his later poems, of which more presently, does Eberhart contradict it.

Man's fallen condition, his inner disunity, as we have seen it represented in these poems certainly furnishes the poet with a basis for his ambivalent role with regard to his intuitions and for the tension which so often obtains between them. In an autobiographical sketch for *Twentieth Century Authors*, Eberhart calls himself a "dualist" and a "relativist" rather than a "dogmatist." The poet needs to adopt a "sitting on the fence attitude" which "allows him to escape whole decades of intellectual error, while it provides radical use of the deepest subjective states of mind toward vision felt as absolute when experienced." What he trusts is the intuition or perception which comes from the poetic imagination and the sudden unique truth it extends. Such intuitions occasionally conflict with one another, but that is because they emerge from the opposing forces operating in man's divided state. In "Notes on Poetry" Eberhart says: "Divisive man can know unity only at death (or so he can speculate), and he cannot know what kind of unity that is. He lives in continuous struggle with his imperfection and the imperfection of life. If one were only conscious of harmony, there would be no need to write." The relativism of Eberhart therefore consists in a submission to the dictates of each imaginative experience as it takes hold of him without concern for its close agreement with other experiences or with any preexisting structure of ideas: in Wallace Stevens's words, "The poem is the cry of its occasion." Consequently, while poems might seem to challenge each other in attitude, such apparent inconsistencies should not obscure the poet's larger purpose, which is his endeavor through "vision felt as absolute when experienced" to attain to what deep if partial truths, what glimpses and approximations of a transcendent and, from a limited human position, unfathomable unity, he can.

"The Skier and the Mountain," included in *Undercliff* (1953), is a poem about the difficulties of reaching any firm and final plane of reality, of opening up a clear route of access to the supernatural; it is only one of many poems in which Eberhart proceeds toward the extremes of his "mentality" theme, moving into regions of divinity on the "elusive" and tricky waves of the imagination. Though the visionary events of the poem occur in the midst of a day's skiing, the first line prepares us for them by introducing spiritual realities before physical ones:

> The gods are too airy: feathery as the snow
> When its consistency is just the imagination's,
> I recognize, but also in an airy, gauzy way
> That it will capture me, I will never capture it.
> The imagination is too elusive, too like me.
> The gods are the airiness of my spirit.
> I have dreamed upon them tiptop dreams,
> Yet they elude me, like the next step on the ski.
> I pole along, push upward, I see the summit,
> Yet the snow on which I glide is treachery.
> The gods are too airy. It is their elusive nature
> I in my intellectual pride have wished to know.

We begin with "the gods," and snow, summit, and skis may strike the reader as obvious metaphorical devices used to sup-

port Eberhart's speculations on the life and activity of the imagi-
nation rather than substantial things in their own right. Up to a
point that interpretation is correct, but only so far as the first
stanza is concerned; the second stanza incarnates the actual ex-
perience of vision, which took place sometime in the past during
a skiing expedition. Thus Eberhart has reversed the temporal
order in the poem, perhaps to underline its reflective character:
stanza one, composed in the present tense (with hints of the
past: "I have thought I knew what I was doing"), contains medi-
tations prompted by the experience recounted in stanza two,
which is written in the past tense. To get at the center of the
poet's thought here we must also confront this experience:

> I saw an old country god of the mountain,
> Far up, leaning out of the summit mist,
> Born beyond time, and wise beyond our wisdom.
> He was beside an old, gnarled trunk of a tree
> Blasted by the winds. Stones outcropped the
>   snow,
> There where the summit was bare, or would
>   be bare.
> I thought him a dream-like creature, a god
>   beyond evil,
> And thought to speak of the portent of my
>   time,
> To broach some ultimate question. No bird
> Flew in this flying mist. As I raised my voice
> To shape the matters of the intellect
> And integrate the spirit, the old, wise god,
> Natural to the place, positive and free,
> Vanished as he had been supernatural dream.
> I was astonished by his absence, deprived
> Of the astonishment of his presence, standing
> In a reverie of the deepest mist, cloud and
>   snow,
> Solitary on the mountain slope: the vision gone,
> Even as the vision came. This was then the
>   gods' meaning,
> That they leave us in our true humanity,
> Elusive, shadowy gods of our detachment,
> Who lead us to the summits, and keep their
>   secrets.

The first half of the poem is devoted to affirming the impossibility of coming into close contact with "the gods," who are not only independent beings but are also identified with the ethereal nature of the poet's own spirit. Eberhart recognizes how his "intellectual pride" wishes rationally to conquer and explain these puzzling deities, but the single means of approach is through the imagination, itself an elusive instrument. In fact the "soaring" of the imagination leads to the poet's realization that he is "the captured actor, the taken one" of the gods, and he knows finally that he is "their imagination, lost to self and to will." At the stanza's end pride has melted to "humility."

Stanza two, as we have seen, concentrates on the vision and pursuit of a god. The incident, haunting in the detail Eberhart has given it, provides matter for the more abstract thinking done in the previous stanza and demonstrates the ultimate failure to establish direct relations between man and the divine. Will and reason may be thwarted, but the last lines tell us something important all the same. The gods will not lift us from our "true humanity," Eberhart says there, and this notion serves to enforce his interpretation of the human estate as a fallen, disharmonious one. Yet the gods do compel us "to the summits," stirring our latent fascination for a higher plane of reality while remaining forever mysterious. Whether we assume them to be projections of the poet's imagination or find them to be forms of the supernatural, these gods, by their enigmatic attractions, urge us toward "our detachment," by which I take Eberhart to mean the release and free exercise of the spirit in its quest for enduring truth.

But Eberhart never intends that a quest of this sort shall lose itself in regions where earthly, human nature is alien or forsaken: "the saving grace of a poem may light the reader likewise out of some darkness," he writes in "Notes on Poetry," "and art is essentially social." In "'The Goal of Intellectual Man'" from *Song and Idea*, one of his poems about the artist's responsibilities, he defines the object of the quest. The "intellectual man," by which term he certainly designates the poet in the broadest sense, seeks "To bring down out of uncreated light / Illumination to our night," that is, he can aim at a visionary knowledge through the imagination, a knowledge which reflects divinity. The "uncreated light" of the first stanza and the "fire" of the second are both used here and elsewhere as traditionally representative symbols for God or Ultimate Being (see also, for example, the poems "The Incomparable Light" and "A Meditation"). Quite clearly, however, the poet does not wish to possess this divine fire for himself, nor does he desire the annihilation of his own human identity in an absolute. Unlike Prometheus, he does not defy the deity. His "goal" is not, either, a deathly "imageless place,"

> But it is human love, love
> Concrete, specific, in a natural move
> Gathering goodness, it is free
> In the blood as in the mind's harmony,
>
> It is love discoverable here
> Difficult, dangerous, pure, clear,
> The truth of the positive hour
> Composing all of human power.

Love, as Eberhart employs the word here, includes compassion, understanding, a respect for the inviolability of the individual person, an awareness of the abundant beauty of the natural world and all its creatures, the relationship between man and woman, but this true center of feeling and value must encounter inevitably in his work as in his life the strongest opposition. The chief forces of that opposition manifest themselves in those poems which fall under the two other thematic headings mentioned earlier: "mortality" and "men's actions."

Death readily captures prominence as the most obvious opponent to Eberhart's values, and, not surprisingly, we shall see that it blends into the theme of human behavior. Mortality constantly occupies the poet's mind from *A Bravery of Earth* on. Some of this concern stems from the profoundly disturbing experience of his mother's untimely death and her long, agonizing battle against it. While the signs of that terrible initiation never disappear entirely from the poetry, the shocking confrontation with death

puts Eberhart in the way of a variety of imaginative considera-
tions of mortality, of the sundering of spirit from body, the
separation of the dead from the living. Occasionally he uses a
dead animal as an object to draw his mind into meditation on the
fate of all creatures. In "For a Lamb" the analogies with man are
not stated, but they hardly need suggesting. At the beginning
the poet comes upon the carcass of "a putrid lamb, / Propped
with daisies"; the juxtaposition of the mutilated physical body
and the indifferent serenity of nature fixes the paradoxical
mood of the poem. With the start of the second stanza Eberhart
asks a pointed question, the answers to which, if we can call them
that, are provokingly ambiguous and end the piece:

> Where's the lamb? whose tender plaint
> Said all for the mute breezes.
> Say he's in the wind somewhere,
> Say, there's a lamb in the daisies.

The question is really that perennial one we ask when faced
with the still, emptied body we once knew so full of life: where
has that life, that vital being, gone? Eberhart gives us no certain
or comforting reply. First he is boldly crude and spiritual at the
same time, for in locating the lamb in the wind he is referring
both to the offensive stench of the disemboweled carcass which
hovers in the air and to the traditional identification of the life
principle or spirit with the element of air or the wind. Yet in the
final line he withdraws from these subtleties to the only sure
answer: the lamb is *there*, he is *that* dead heap lying in the grass
and flowers; beyond such facts we cannot go. We should not,
however, accept this poem as proof of a settled conviction on the
poet's part; we have to remember his avowed artistic method of
expressing a subjective intuition as it occurs. Poems "become
what one was at the moment of composition."

"The Groundhog," included in the same volume, *Reading the
Spirit*, with the elegiac "For a Lamb," also focuses on a dead
carcass, but here there is an intense visualization, an elaboration
of physical detail and of the poet's response to it, that are miss-
ing from the other, much briefer poem. These qualities put it in

a line of descent from Baudelaire's terrifying poem "Une Charogne." In the present piece Eberhart finds the groundhog's body lying "amid the golden fields" of June; his accidental discovery resembles that of "For a Lamb." From then on, however, the poem gathers its own very potent dramatic strengths. Drama springs from the tension generated between observing poet and observed object over a considerable period of time, a period marking the gradual disintegration and, at last, the total disappearance of the groundhog's carcass. Watching this process of decay with an extraordinary but very human fascination, the poet leaves us only faintly aware of the transitions in time from one visit to the field to the next; we seem almost to be witnessing the entire decomposition, so intently is the imagination brought to bear upon the actual details of change and their implications. Though the facts of violent death are presented bluntly in "For a Lamb," they are set forth in an objective, ironical manner which is in distinct contrast to the mode of presentation in "The Groundhog." The poet's reaction to the corpse now is instantaneous; he appears startled not merely by what he has unexpectedly found but also by a piercing realization of its significance for himself as a creature: "Dead lay he; my senses shook, / And mind outshot our naked frailty."

Aroused by what he sees, the poet obsessively decides to investigate further the relentless progress of destruction:

> There lowly in the vigorous summer
> His form began its senseless change,
> And made my senses waver dim
> Seeing nature ferocious in him.
> Inspecting close his maggots' might
> And seething cauldron of his being,
> Half with loathing, half with a strange love,
> I poked him with an angry stick.
> The fever arose, became a flame
> And Vigour circumscribed the skies,
> Immense energy in the sun,
> And through my frame a sunless trembling.
> My stick had done nor good nor harm.

The aggressive gesture with the stick stirs the maggots to a fury of activity; but the poet is suddenly exposed to an awakening still more frightening, for the seething energy about the corpse releases in him an almost hallucinatory sensation of nature's all-consuming power which brings in its wake a fearful comprehension of the precariousness of his own personal existence. In spite of his terror Eberhart's fascination is hypnotic and complete; he stays rooted to the spot, "watching the object, as before." At length the efforts to calm himself, to master the curious "passion of the blood" aroused in him by the awful vision of decomposition, fail, and he kneels, "praying for joy in the sight of decay." The dark and fiery god of nature, the pantheistic "Vigour," has won his submission.

In the space of the next two lines several months pass; the season turns to autumn and the poet "strict of eye" revisits the groundhog, "the sap gone out" of it and only "the bony sodden hulk" remaining. His attitude has likewise altered, his passionate response become a slightly aloof thoughtfulness:

> But the year had lost its meaning,
> And in intellectual chains
> I lost both love and loathing,
> Mured up in the wall of wisdom.

Eberhart implies in this passage that the first jolting vision of disintegration has robbed the year and its seasons of their sense — that is, the rhythm and pattern of time in his perception of them dissolve into chaos — and has deprived him of his feelings: his whole being is now subordinate to the shattering knowledge of death and reabsorption by nature's thriving energies. "Wisdom," as Eberhart applies the word in this poem, consists in knowing death and guilt; it signifies the knowledge discussed earlier as integral to the descent from innocence to experience. On this occasion the same kind of knowledge is equally crippling because it traps the poet in his intellect, a life-denying bondage.

Two more returns to the scene of the groundhog's death, one in the following summer, the other three years later, occur be-

fore the poem's climactic finish. The first of these summer days,
"massive and burning, full of life," recalls the previous June, the
time of the poet's discovery, but the atmosphere of the day con-
trasts noticeably with the barren appearance of the animal's re-
mains when Eberhart has again "chanced upon the spot" (the
word *chanced* suggests that while his original encounter with the
dead groundhog imposed upon him a heavy burden of knowl-
edge not readily disposed of, he may still have forgotten the
object which was its cause until he found it once more during a
walk):

> There was only a little hair left,
> And bones bleaching in the sunlight
> Beautiful as architecture;
> I watched them like a geometer,
> And cut a walking stick from a birch.

The bones retain hardly a semblance of the flesh and blood they
once structured; Eberhart scrutinizes them dispassionately as he
would something formally pleasing but nevertheless coldly ab-
stract. Around him nature hums and blazes with renewed vital-
ity and with an abundance whose price is death and anonymity.

Perhaps it is this dreadful combination, the loss of life and the
loss of any indication that a particular life was ever lived, which
hastens Eberhart to a resurgence of emotion at the end. After
three years "there is no sign of the groundhog," though the poet
stays standing in the midst of a "whirling summer," nature's
eternal return. He cannot avoid feeling the life drying up in him
as it has done in that animal carcass; the terrible human message
of his experience breaks in waves upon his consciousness: how
long is memory, how can civilization or individual achievement
finally endure?

> I stood there in the whirling summer,
> My hand capped a withered heart,
> And thought of China and of Greece,
> Of Alexander in his tent;
> Of Montaigne in his tower,
> Of Saint Theresa in her wild lament.

To the emotional outburst of these last lines Eberhart has no counterbalance of reasoned explanation, nor can he satisfy himself as Yeats does in "Lapis Lazuli" and elsewhere with a pose of desperate Nietzschean gaiety at the spectacle of civilizations collapsing and being replaced: such theoretical apparatus is alien to his poetry. Death holds a central, unquestioned position in his imagination, and its relationship to the endless cycle of nature remains visible throughout his work. Even in a rather recent poem, "Sea Burial from the Cruiser *Reve*" included in *The Quarry*, dispersal into and assimilation by two of the traditional four elements seems quite appropriate for someone whose life was characterized by the other pair:

> She is now water and air,
> Who was earth and fire.
>
> *Reve* we throttled down
> Between Blake's Point and Western Isle,
>
> Then, oh, then, at the last hour,
> The first hour of her new inheritance,
>
> We strewed her ashes over the waters,
> We gave her the bright sinking
>
> Of unimaginable aftermaths,
> We followed her dispersed spirit
>
> As children with a careless flick of wrist
> Cast on the surface of the sea
>
> New-cut flowers. Deeper down,
> In the heavy blue of the water,
>
> Slowly the white mass of her reduced bones
> Waved, as a flag, from the enclosing depths.
>
> She is now water and air,
> Who was earth and fire.

Eberhart's artistic interest in this relationship of death and nature does not always show itself with the dramatic power of "The Groundhog" but can be lyrical and elegiac, as the lines above prove. So far each of the poems we have looked at keeps the treatment of death to the material and historical levels and refuses to venture beyond them. On such a basis death appears absolute, but that is merely a partial view, easily contradicted by our previous examination of poems directed toward experience of a visionary or mystical order.

Death never really loses its essential strangeness of appeal for Eberhart, and in a number of poems he does attempt imaginatively to trespass its shadowy, indefinite boundaries. In "Grave Piece" and "'Imagining How It Would Be to Be Dead'" he tries, as Dylan Thomas does in certain of his early poems, to envisage his own dissolution. The concluding lines of both pieces leave the poet poised on the threshold of a spiritual reality, but before he arrives at that stage it is necessary for him to participate through a moment of vivid imaginative possession in the process of decay imposed by death. The earlier of the two poems, "Grave Piece," from *Song and Idea*, is somewhat encumbered by the influence of Hopkins, Blake, and Empson, though the authenticity of perception cannot be denied:

> There in the vasy tomb of bone-green icicles,
> And gelid grasses of cold bruise to touch;
> Of looking roots, night agate eyed . . .

This excruciating process ends with a liberating and transcendent vision in which the poet sees growing "A crystal Tear / Whose centre is spiritual love." The second poem, collected in *Burr Oaks* (1947), has that unabashed directness of speech that is so compelling a feature of Eberhart's work. In this poem the imagined death consists of an expansion and transformation of self dominated by one element, air, and from the outset it is presented as a desirable rather than a difficult or terrifying series of events. The weight of time, consciousness of which comes as a consequence of the fall from innocence and the disappearance of the child's vision, is thrown off as the body itself disperses into the air and the omnipresent nature of that element is enjoyed:

> I lost my head, and could not hold
> Either my hands together or my heart

> But was so sentient a being
> I seemed to break time apart
> And thus became all things air can touch
> Or could touch could it touch all things,
> And this was an embrace most dear,
> Final, complete, a flying without wings.

The concluding lines clarify the release into a further dimension of spiritual reality, but the poem halts at the frontiers, so to speak, of what is felt yet stays unseen and intangible. Eberhart must rest content to point the direction in which his experience has taken him, for language too has its limits and is attached to the world of things:

> From being bound to one poor skull,
> And that surrounded by one earth,
> And the earth in one universe forced,
> And that chained to some larger gear,
> I was the air, I was the air,
> And then I pressed on eye and cheek
> The sightless hinges of eternity
> That make the whole world creak.

The poem "A Meditation," published in *Song and Idea*, does, however, project itself daringly beyond the borders of mortal existence; in form it is the monologue of a dead man who addresses a living person through his skull, probably discovered by the latter in some ancient ruin or graveyard, though such details are irrelevant to the piece. While it is not stated, we understand that the individual who holds the skull wishes it could yield up its secrets to him. But true to what we have already remarked about Eberhart's attitudes the emphasis of the monologue falls on life, on what should be found there before it vanishes, rather than on any secrets which the dead can disclose:

> I cannot get back, cannot reach or yearn back,
> Nor summon love enough, nor the intellectual care —
> Being dead, you talk as if I had spirit at all —
> To come back to you and tell you who I am.

He places the responsibility for prophesying on his listener, who is still among the living, who is yet "full of imagination" and can create images beyond himself: oracular and speculative activities "can only be talked of by men," for those ideas belong exclusively to earthly existence. The speaker lightly chides the living man for his intellectual labors and their remoteness from the truth, then offers him a *memento mori* in the repeated line: "Life blows like the wind away."

As the poem proceeds and the speaker stresses the perennial "wish" of man "to know / What it is all about, meaning and moral dimension," we are brought nearer to a glimpse of supernatural reality. This revelation is composed mostly of warnings about the utter difference between the human estate and the pure life of the spirit existing in a region completely foreign to earthly experience. A total transformation apparently separates the two realms of being, and the mortal flesh shrinks from this frightening change, as the voice of the dead speaker declares:

> You would withdraw in horror at my secret,
> You would not want to know, your long-lashed eyes
>   aglare,
> Of the cold absolute blankness and fate of death,
> Of the depths of being beyond all words to say,
> Of your profound or of the world's destiny,
> Of the mind of God, rising like a mighty fire
> Pure and calm beyond all mortal instances
> Magnificent, eternal, Everlasting, sweet and mild.

In this passage, with its visionary perception, we find once again the confirmation of Eberhart's fundamental religiousness. His convictions are often tested and shaken by tragic or brutal circumstances, by agonies of doubt and questioning; nevertheless they hold firm against these storms of experience, touchstones of belief to which the poet continues to return. The lasting riddle of death and of man's situation afterwards is no further unveiled than we have seen; the stanza below enunciates the obligation to live out the human span in human terms. The difficult but "simple truth" is

> That you are to be man, that is, to be human,
> You are imperfect, will never know perfection,
> You must strive, but the goal will recede forever,

> That you must do what the great poets and sages say,
> Obeying scripture even in the rotten times . . .

Of course death will close out each life and let it "blow like the wind away." In the final stanza the speaker explains the value of his listener's "solemn meditation" on mortality as an enterprise that should lead him back to "seek among [his] fellow creatures whatever is good in life." As before, Eberhart directs the results of spiritual vision to the conditions of existence in *this* world.

The utilization of visionary or mystical experience to illuminate life here and now, and, more particularly, the emphatic sounding of moral imperatives in the concluding portions of "A Meditation" bring that poem near in spirit to the third category of Eberhart's work: "men's actions." I have indicated how he frequently and unashamedly adopts the role of moralist and critic, a role usually disowned in theory by modern poets but one very evident in their practice. Eberhart's best known works as a moralist are, rightfully, his war poems, surely among the finest and most outspoken pieces of that variety in American literature, but his achievement in other areas should not be neglected: his judgments of contemporary society also merit our consideration.

If some authors of excellent poems about World War II — Randall Jarrell and John Ciardi are exemplary in this respect — write from actual combat experience and from the point of view of the soldier or airman totally immersed in war or in the military life, Eberhart chooses the transcendent, objective role of the prophet or seer-poet who envisages the conflict in terms of moral absolutes and of all humanity. War looked at from this position is a cosmic event drawing into play the larger forces of good and evil in the universe and exhibiting to men — should they notice it — their basic imperfection, their underlying savage desire for complete destruction. The adoption of a vatic mask might seem to the skeptical reader an easy way to handle the problematic matter of warfare in poetry, but I think this interpretation would be wrong. No voice is more difficult to raise and to sustain authentically in a poem than the prophetic one, which requires great skill and imagination for its realization. Thus Eberhart's technique must function smoothly and effortlessly, as it were, within the period of inspirational seizure that is germane to his method of poetic production; if it does not the poem may develop rough or awkward spots, however pure the inspiration. Similarly an excess of emotion, of outrage at man's evil, or of abstract thinking can severely damage a poem of this sort — and does so in several instances.

We may take here the justly famous and moving poem "The Fury of Aerial Bombardment" in *Burr Oaks* to exhibit Eberhart's prophetic manner at its best. The poet starts off the first stanza exaltedly, on a cosmic plane boldly challenging God for His apparent refusal to intervene in the affairs of men and to put an end to the viciousness and slaughter of war:

> You would think the fury of aerial bombardment
> Would rouse God to relent; the infinite spaces
> Are still silent. He looks on shock-pried faces.
> History, even, does not know what is meant.
>
> You would feel that after so many centuries
> God would give man to repent; yet he can kill
> As Cain could, but with multitudinous will,
> No farther advanced than in his ancient furies.

The use of the "you" in these two stanzas is a brilliant stroke because it establishes contact between poet and reader at the same time that it serves as part of an opening passage of vigorous rhetorical appeal.

Having called upon "history" in general and the figure of Cain, the first murderer, to support the portrayal of man's age-old desire to kill rather than love his brother (the implied contrast between the single murder committed by Cain and the wholesale killing accomplished by the latest inventions of war is, of course, intentionally disturbing), Eberhart begins to wonder if God is after all simply "indifferent"; this third stanza closes with the somber thought that "the eternal truth" perhaps consists only of "man's fighting soul / Wherein the Beast ravens in its own avidity." Such a question really means to ask if God exists at all: should the answer be negative, the inner malice of mankind emerges as the ultimate, eternal reality. But if the poet poses this question he does not pretend to give a reply of any general sort; instead the last stanza of the poem moves suddenly into the realm of the particular, borrowing from Eberhart's personal acquaintance:

> Of Van Wettering I speak, and Averill,
> Names on a list, whose faces I do not recall
> But they are gone to early death, who late in school
> Distinguished the belt feed lever from the belt
> holding pawl.

Even the relatively specific character of these lines is not permitted to do more than modify a bit the aloofness and exaltation of the poet's speech, and then only to drive home his point in another way. The oddly formal construction of this one-sentence stanza strengthens the feeling of distance maintained in spite of the introduction of personal details and names. Various meanings may be attributed to the stanza: possibly most important is the shock which occurs in shifting from the universal, philosophical level of the three preceding stanzas to the frank, objective enumeration of facts — the deaths of certain named individuals. The ravening "Beast" abruptly takes on real and deadly proportions: its victims are listed.

The religious or metaphysical implications of the poem are not, as I have said, brought to any conclusive formulation, nor should we expect them to be when we remember Eberhart's avowed dedication to the truth of each poetic vision as he receives it. With that commitment in mind we should also observe that other poems than the present one ("New Hampshire, February" and "Reality! Reality! What Is It?" are two of them) assert with great forthrightness the moments of deepest doubt, of religious belief assaulted by seemingly chance fatefulness. Over against the poems of metaphysical anguish, which originate in the crushing pressure of events on the poet's reason and conscience, one has to set the larger bulk of poetry that surpasses suffering, injustice, and doubt to approach the zone of what

Eberhart calls "Psyche." In one of several lectures he has deliv-
ered on Will and Psyche in poetry he defines the latter: "Psyche
poetry pertains to the soul, to peace, quiet, tranquillity, serenity,
harmony, stillness and silence. It provides psychic states of pas-
sive pleasure." We will recall how Michael Roberts indicated that
the young Eberhart avoided this style, but in recent years he has
produced with some frequency poems representative to one de-
gree or another of the category. These poems coincide with
their author's intellectual and artistic maturity, with an attitude
of calm reflectiveness, and with the contemplation through a
number of suggestive terms and images (*light, love, unity, the
unfound beyond, height*, or, taken altogether, *God*) of a transcend-
ent reality, a divine source.

By way of contrast, Eberhart's war poems belong to the class
of "Will" poetry, as do his other pieces which express a moral
view of human behavior. "Will poetry exists because of the
power in the cell beyond its energy to maintain itself. Will results
in action, through wish, zeal, volition, passion, determination,
choice, and command. Will makes something happen in poetry."
Not all Will poems, occupied with men's actions, employ the
vatic manner of "The Fury of Aerial Bombardment." Eberhart
takes the part both of intimate witness and of commentator in
"Fragment of New York, 1929" from *Undercliff*, which has as its
chief metaphor for the cold, vicious character of modern society
the slaughtering and butchering of animals. The poet begins
with an early morning awakening and depicts himself as the city
dweller, whose movements are habitual and mechanical, whose
awareness of his own identity is often shaky, who fears the direc-
tion in which his thought will lead him. As he goes out into the
predawn urban streets under "the one untormented integer,"
the "surprise moon, four-thirty moon," he feels as if he were
going "into Hell again."

In subsequent stanzas Eberhart's graphic rendering of the
routines of the slaughterhouse creates a highly charged symbolic
vision of contemporary life, of those buried desires and an-
tagonisms that seek their fulfillment in the act of killing. We can
elicit for ourselves a variety of topical analogies with the ac-

tualities of twentieth-century history — with concentration
camps, city gangs, or the sick fantasies of the mass media. The
poet gives us a shockingly effective image of our sex and death
obsessions in the figure of the beasts' executioner at his daily
task:

> The killer's face! He is baffled now,
> Seems. Moment. He poises
> The tip of the knife at the throat.
> So little is life. He cannot make
> The one swift entry and up-jab.
> Curious copulation, death-impregnation.

As if indeed this nightmare experience were a journey into hell,
Eberhart ends his poem with indications of emergence and re-
birth:

> Death I saw,
> And wormed through it. And make fragment
> Of the end of a time, when seethed
> So thick the life, it knew not,
> In savage complexity, modernity,
> The harsh omnipotence of evil.

Obvious reference is made here to the time specified in the
poem's title: the year of the stock market crash, the beginning of
the Depression, the finish of a frenzied postwar era. But the
substance of the poem has no more special relevance to that
period than it does to the present day; rather it fashions a gen-
eral picture of inhumanity and spiritual vacuity.

  If we want to see Eberhart's definite handling of the quality of
life in American society at a certain level, then we must turn to
the play *The Visionary Farms*, which is, in addition, his most am-
bitious and successful effort as a verse dramatist. Denis Dono-
ghue, who has discussed the play shrewdly and at length, speaks
of it as "expressionist" in style, "a *drame à thèse* . . . with a
difference"; the difference lies in the fact that while Eberhart
pictures the triumph and failure of a huge business empire and
the three men who are its executives he does not attack his
material in the spirit of naturalism or social realism but blends
elements of fantasy and extravagant comedy with, as he has said

himself, "a study of evil Will in a man" and the insidious tempta-
tions of money and success, the American dream ("Money is
stronger than life, Adam, much stronger," the president of the
company tells his vice-president, a man whom he is about to ruin
and whose wife is dying). The conventions of realism are further
avoided by the poet's use — common to almost all of his plays —
of a group of characters, including the Consulting Author, who
gather on the stage as in a living room to joke, talk, pun, and
finally to watch the play *The Visionary Farms*; but the Consulting
Author puts the group under a spell so that they become more
than an audience: they are metamorphosed into the actors of
the drama they came to see:

> Each thus becomes a part of Everyman.
> What is, is what might happen to him.
> And each can share in the scenes of fabulous life
> As if imagination were reality,
> For reality is strange as imagination.

Considered from another angle, the portion of "reality" in the
play is not negligible, for the plot is clearly grounded in the
experience of Eberhart's father, a businessman who, his son
wrote, "was betrayed by the notorious Cy Thompson, who em-
bezzled over a million dollars" from George A. Hormel and
Company, of which Eberhart senior was vice-president. Here he
has been developed into the character of Adam Fahnstock, sec-
retary and vice-president of the Parker Corporation, a soap
manufacturer. During the course of the play his wife, Vine, is
discovered to have an incurable cancer. The main figure is not
Fahnstock, though, but "Hurricane" Ransome, the company
treasurer, a man of extraordinary business daring whose wild
ideas and enormous expenditures (marvelously and wittily cari-
catured by Eberhart), have brought the firm very high sales and
have made him, Fahnstock, and the president, Roger Parker,
rich men.

Yet things are not all they seem. The play opens with Ran-
some giving a Sunday School sermon to the children of the small
midwestern town in which the company's employees and execu-
tives live. He shows them a silver dollar — "See how clean it is,

hard and pure" — as "a symbol of the American dream," and
then by thrusting the coin into hydrochloric acid, where it turns
"black, fuming," demonstrates how "If you do evil, your soul will
turn black / Immediately, like this hideous dollar." A silver dol-
lar makes an odd symbol for the soul and prepares us for what
follows. As the play continues we learn that Ransome is, ironi-
cally enough, very like that blackened dollar himself. Though a
man prodigiously gifted, he has become inwardly warped; over
a number of years he has embezzled increasingly large sums of
money from the company and by clever maneuvering of the
accounts has kept his thievery hidden. "Success," Ransome re-
marks at one point, "is a trick," and the trickery exacts a destruc-
tive price of the spirit and of human dignity. What started as a
relatively harmless borrowing of five dollars from the company
has expanded into a monumental swindle. The Visionary
Farms, an extraordinary venture in chicken farming, is invented
by Ransome simply as another means of keeping money circulat-
ing, the books balanced, and his robbery concealed; thus the
American dream of fantastic financial success appears to be a
crippling delusion. As Ransome confesses to himself, echoing
King Lear by the way:

> It is the evil getting me from the inside.
> The slightest, innocent-seeming insinuation
> When it all began, back in 1914,
> Has grown in my hand to my most monstrous sin.
> I am bound upon a wheel of fire.
> There is no end to the agony I am in.

Ransome's crime is uncovered by the president's son, and the
calculating executive is imprisoned; with hilarious irony
Eberhart has him at the play's finish ruling the prison and its
warden with the same energetic business daring and hocus-
pocus as he lavished on the Parker Company and his surrealist
chicken farms. Ransome typifies an indefatigable American de-
sire for success, fortune, manipulative powers; and while
Eberhart shows us this embezzler reaching a tragic moment of
self-recognition we still find that his knowledge does not in any
fashion curb his basic impulses or cause him to change.

Differing noticeably from Ransome, the figure of Adam Fahnstock stands out as representative of innocence, goodwill, endurance, victimization, love, and loss. Not only is his wife dying but he is forced at last to relinquish his stock in the company to Parker, a move by which the latter betrays Fahnstock's friendship and ruins him financially. Success for Mr. Parker, or the next thing to it, the salvaging of his honor, is also a trick. Fahnstock remains the embodiment of genuine values in the play; in a scene in his apple orchard he is compelled to explain to his children the impending death of their mother and the collapse of his fortunes. Against the fateful circumstances that have overtaken them and the death which will intrude upon one of them prematurely Adam proposes the single worthy countermeasure:

> While there is love there can be no death
> For we carry love with us to our own end.
> Love we carry in our memories.

In an earlier poem, "Orchard," from *Song and Idea* Eberhart composed a somewhat different version of the disclosure of his mother's mortal illness. There the mother is herself present; she and her husband are cognizant of what must come, but the children can merely guess it from the extremely troubled atmosphere surrounding them. The two brothers are "placed in the first light / Of brutal recognition," though their sister registers the disturbance without comprehending its source. The concluding stanza elevates the forces in conflict within this family group to a stage at which they exemplify, as they do in *The Visionary Farms*, the inescapable vicissitudes of life and the human will to meet them. These lines from the poem help us to perceive the role of Fahnstock and his family, as well as his sturdy opposition to cheating, greed, and misfortune, in the play:

> And in the evening, among the warm fruit trees
> All of life and all of death were there,
> Of pain unto death, of struggle to endure,
> And the strong right of human love was there.

Eberhart's experiments in the theater, all of them rather recent (with the exception of the brief "Triptych" they date from 1950 when he began to work in earnest on verse drama), have had some interesting effects on his poetry too. These are most evident in his collection *The Quarry*, where, besides poems of philosophical speculation, elegies, and visionary lyrics, one finds an assortment of pieces unusual in Eberhart's writing: letters in verse (to W. H. Auden and the late William Carlos Williams), dramatic monologues utilizing fictional speakers ("A New England Bachelor," "A Maine Roustabout," "The Lament of a New England Mother") or character sketches ("Ruby Daggett"), and dialogues which are indeed miniature dramas ("Father and Son," "Father and Daughter"). The high quality of these poems indicates yet another direction in which Eberhart's free and generous imagination may operate.

In spite of such influences deriving from his experiments with verse drama, however, the predominant trait of Eberhart's later poetry is of another kind. I am referring to the reflective or Psyche poems, in which the author contemplates sympathetically and dispassionately the nature of life, the function of his art, the full spectrum of experience discussed here under separate and partial thematic headings of perception, death, and human behavior. Not all of this poetry fits into the category of Psyche of course, but much of it does, to use Eberhart's own words, because it "works partially through a religious attitude." Progression away from the world of desire and act toward the lasting realities of spirit, toward contemplation entered upon for its own sake or for the sake of vision alone, without any wish to turn the experience to practical account, is characteristic of the purer types of Psyche poem. "Life as Visionary Spirit," a piece from his *Collected Poems*, exhibits this mood of the imagination but also contains certain inherent qualifications of the mood, for Eberhart never produces the absolutely pure Psyche poem:

> Nothing like the freedom of vision,
>   To look from a hill to the sea,
> Meditating one's bile and bible: free
>   From action, to be.

> The best moment is when
>   Stillness holds the air motionless,
> So that time can bless
>   History, blood is a caress.
>
> Neither in landwork nor in seawork
>   Believe. Belief must be pure.
> Let the soul softly idle,
>   Beyond past, beyond future.
>
> Let it be said, "A great effulgence
>   Grows upon the sandspit rose.
> A rare salt harrows the air.
>   Your eyes show divine shows."

Though retaining some traces of place, of the physical cosmos, at the start, this poem departs in the third stanza for the world of spirit or psyche, for the regions outside time, for a reality beyond what is immediate to the senses, and advocates a passivity of the soul as the way of attaining such a superior state of being. The realm of appearances, though substantial in itself, becomes illusory if it is believed in as *all* that exists, yet Eberhart neither ignores nor tries to do away with it. The human and the particular, if we look, are stubbornly there, merging and exchanging themselves with the spiritual: while touched with unearthly radiance, the rose in the final stanza keeps its natural identity; the air, element of the spirit, is cut by the salt of the sea; and the manifestations of the divine are seen mirrored in a pair of human eyes. These persistent attachments to earth, even in Psyche poems, put us in mind once again of Eberhart's feeling for location, for man's position in the middle kingdom of the natural world. He writes very accurately of his attitude in the last two stanzas of "Autumnal":

> We have been living the full year,
>   It is still full, it is here
>   In the late recline of sun,
>   A grand red one.
>
> What is going on beyond
>   I have not found, am bound

To the love of the unfound
Beyond, but here.

The first of these stanzas purposefully recalls the poetry of
Wallace Stevens, not only in diction and tone but in attitude; the
view expressed closely resembles Stevens's statements about the
earthly paradise, about life lived to its completion within the
precincts of the material universe and transfigured by the pow-
ers of the imagination. I think there can be no doubt that
Eberhart also wishes to evoke feelings of fulfillment with regard
to life in this world: earlier stanzas of the poem dwell on nature's
richness, on the details of creation, praising both their multiplic-
ity and their beauty. These feelings he communicates are ones
which he obviously shares with Stevens. But the closing stanza of
"Autumnal" marks an unequivocal return by Eberhart to his
own voice and to the balance between earthly and visionary
commitment which, as frequently noted in this essay, he never
fails to hold. Eberhart, with the onset of his later years ("the late
recline of the sun"), joins Stevens in approving the profusion of
gifts extended by creation even as he travels toward death; how-
ever, where Stevens limits reality to the physical world and the
work of imagination within it, Eberhart reaffirms his acquaint-
ance with a transcendent and divine reality which he may be
incapable of penetrating altogether but which is not less real to
him for that.

Eberhart continues in a number of these more recent poems
to test, by thought and meditation or in the sudden disclosure by
an observed scene or event of a previously unrecognized
significance, the extent and validity of that acquaintance. Some
of the best pieces are, like "Life as Visionary Spirit" and "Au-
tumnal," representatives of the Psyche poem, though again they
are perhaps less than pure examples of their type because they
too hold firmly to images of the natural world. In "Light from
Above" Eberhart stands alone on an October afternoon in the
"vigor and majesty of the air," which is "empurpled" by rays of
sunlight showing through wind-blown clouds onto the land-
scape he surveys. This light, first described as "the imperial

power / Greater than man's works," becomes as the poem pro-
ceeds the visible manifestation of a transcendental "unity" for
the poet, who has already confessed himself to be delighted by
"unsymbolic gestures of eternity." (I gather "unsymbolic" means
here something natural as opposed to something designed or
imagined by man.) At its conclusion this poem — and we could
profitably read it along with "The Illusion of Eternity," from
Selected Poems 1930–1965, which has similarities of season, set-
ting in nature, and timelessness — rises toward an affirmation in
which the natural and supernatural blend before the poet's eye
in the actual scene witnessed:

> here, the great sky,
>
> Full of profound adventure beyond man's losses,
> Tosses the locks of a strong, abrasive radiance
>
> From the beginning, and through the time of man,
> And into the future beyond our love and wit,
>
> And in the vigor and majesty of the air
> I, empurpled, think on unity
>
> Glimpsed in pure visual belief
> When the sky expresses beyond our powers
>
> The fiat of a great assurance.

Given his methods of composition and his understanding of
what, in his own practice, the poem is, we can hardly expect him
to claim for his work the coherent structure of a total aesthetic
universe, and of course he does not do so. Yet much in his work
compensates for its absence. Reading and rereading his poems
one comes to recognize — and to appreciate more completely
each time — the marvelous and fruitful vantage point he has
secured for himself as an artist; this vantage point is actually a
condition of the lyric poet's inner life or consciousness and its
primary quality remains throughout his career an independent
availability to experience which permits him to embrace with
equal ardor and sympathy the events of existence in the world
and the revelations of the spirit. This position, with all its risks
and uncertainties, cannot have been an easy one to maintain

over the years, but Eberhart has been amply rewarded in the poetry that has resulted from it. The end of "The Incomparable Light," the poem with which he concludes his *Collected Poems 1930–1960*, should keep us reminded of Eberhart's constant dedication:

> The light beyond compare is my meaning,
> It is the secret source of my beginning,
> Issuance of uniqueness, signal upon suffering,
> It is the wordless bond of all endings,
> It is the subtle flash that tells our song,
> Inescapable brotherhood of the living,
> Our mystery of time, the only hopeful light.

RALPH J. MILLS, JR.

Theodore Roethke

It is sometimes said of modern poetry that its day is over, that the revolution which swept through all the arts from about 1910 until a decade after World War I died out in the political anxiety and commitment of the 1930s, and that while the great poets who created the modern idiom — Yeats, Eliot, and Pound, for example — pursued their own ways to artistic maturity, writers growing up after them could no longer find the stimulating atmosphere of participation in what Randall Jarrell so aptly called "an individual but irregularly cooperative experimentalism." To a certain extent that view is correct: there has been no concerted poetic movement of real consequence here or in England since the work of Auden, Spender, Day Lewis, and MacNeice in the thirties. Yet even if the excited collective activity inspired by radical and widespread creative ferment gradually dissipated in those years, there was no lack of purpose and talent among the American poets who began to publish notable work near the outset of World War II or the others who appeared soon afterwards.

In his essay "The End of the Line," from which I quoted above, Randall Jarrell acted as a brilliant self-appointed spokesman for his contemporaries, for Robert Lowell, John Frederick Nims, Karl Shapiro, Richard Eberhart, Richard Wilbur, and

Theodore Roethke, as well as for himself, when he defined the situation of the younger poet in 1942. "Today, for the poet," he said, "there is an embarrassment of choices: young poets can choose — do choose — to write anything from surrealism to imitations of Robert Bridges; the only thing they have no choice about is making their own choice. The Muse, forsaking her sterner laws, says to everyone: 'Do what you will.'"

The American poets of that generation did exactly what they willed and have produced, without the impetus of any common enterprise other than devotion to their art, a remarkable body of poetry. Ironically enough, they are poets on whom the label of academicism has been fastened occasionally; yet outside of the fact that many of them like Roethke have taught for a living that word, with its pejorative overtones, would seem to have little application. We have academic verse when a poet, instead of learning from the poetic tradition by remaining alive and open to its possibilities in relation to his own gifts and aspirations, submits himself to it automatically or, to change the metaphor, polishes the surface of old conventions. The weakness of the academic writer lies in an acceptance of literature before personal experience and imagination as the source of his art. But the poets I have named, and some not mentioned, showed originality, concern for language, and an abiding honesty toward the facts of their experience. If comparisons with the pioneer writers of twentieth-century modernism do not offer these successors the historical advantage, there is still no doubt in my mind that two or three of the latter can already hold their own surprisingly well in such formidable company.

Of all these later poets Theodore Roethke appears the most considerable, in terms of imaginative daring, stylistic achievement, richness of diction, variety and fullness of music, and unity of vision. From his first book, published in 1941, to his posthumous volume of 1964 he consistently proved himself a poet discontented with the restrictions of a settled manner of composition. This is not to say, of course, that Roethke lacked steadiness or certitude, that he was frivolous or insubstantial; quite the reverse. His poetry grew in distinct stages, each one with its own peculiar qualities and aims, each one expanding and developing from its predecessor, each providing its own special means of furthering the poet's central themes and subjecting them to different modes of apprehension. We should not be surprised then in reading through Roethke's books to discover a wide range of moods and styles: tightly controlled formal lyrics, dramatic monologues and something like an interior monologue, nonsense verse, love lyrics, and meditative poems composed in a very free fashion. His experience reaches from the most extraordinary intuition of the life of nature to lightning flashes of mystical illumination.

To fit Roethke definitely within a given tradition or to link him finally with other poets, past or present, who share certain of his predilections is tempting but too easy. He expressed an affection for John Clare and borrowed the title for his third book from Wordsworth's *The Prelude*, yet he was not drawn to the natural world in quite the same way as either of them, though he maintained affinities with both. Again one might like to proclaim him an investigator of the irrational, a poet obsessed with the pure flow of inner experience, with the preconscious and the unconscious: a poet similar to the young Dylan Thomas or Paul Eluard. Or perhaps he should be classed with the visionary poets he so admired: Blake, Whitman, and Yeats. No doubt every one of these attempts at classification would tell us a partial truth about Roethke, but none would give us the whole of it. He was, in fact, equally at home with any of these other poets, though we will be defeated in the endeavor to read his poetry honestly if we settle for a particular category in which to lodge him and so avoid further thought. Roethke needs first to be seen through his own work.

Behind the profusion of experience we have noted in Roethke's writing one comes upon a preoccupation with the poet's own self as the primary matter of artistic exploration and knowledge, an interest which endows the poems with a sense of personal urgency, even necessity. What do we mean by this self? I think the self, as we shall want to use the word here, can best be called the main principle of the poet's individual life — or for that matter, of any human life — a principle of identity and of being which is generally spiritual in character but also reaches into the realm of the physical. It partakes of what Martin Buber includes in his definition of the "primary word *I-Thou*," which is the speech of a person's entire being in relationship with the other creatures and things of the world, for Roethke viewed the self as continually seeking a harmonious dialogue with all that is. The bulk of Roethke's poetry derives its imaginative strength from the author's restless quest for that communion in which self and creation are joined. Though they take the self as theme we cannot look in these poems for the sort of personal element we associate with the later work of Robert Lowell. Yet they are in their way just as intimate, maybe even more intimate, since some penetrate the protective screen of conscious thought. Lowell focuses often on other personalities, the family, the world of historical time, while Roethke's concentration either is inward, almost untouched by public happenings or by history, or turns outward to the existence of things in nature. But in order to understand his fundamental attachment to this theme of the self we must now look closely at its development within a growing body of poetry.

By any standards *Open House* (1941) is a remarkable first collection of poetry. Roethke's sensitive use of language and his craftsmanship stand out on every page; and if one returns to this book after reading his other work it becomes plain that the author's main interests were already present here. The title poem is a frank announcement of his intention to use himself in some way as the material of his art, but we are not told how. The poem is sharp in its personal disclosure and might justifiably serve as a motto for all of Roethke's subsequent verse:

> My secrets cry aloud.
> I have no need for tongue.
> My heart keeps open house,
> My doors are widely swung.

> An epic of the eyes
> My love, with no disguise.
>
> My truths are all foreknown,
> This anguish self-revealed.
> I'm naked to the bone,
> With nakedness my shield.
> Myself is what I wear:
> I keep the spirit spare.

These sparse, carefully rhymed stanzas characterize Roethke's earlier poetic technique, and their kind is visible everywhere in *Open House*. A certain economy and simplicity of diction, as well as insistent, forceful rhythms, more freely employed as he matured, are in fact lasting trademarks of his style, even though he abandoned some of them almost entirely on occasion in favor of experiments with considerably looser forms. Such departures are especially evident in the long sequence of interior monologues from *The Lost Son* and *Praise to the End* and in the "Meditations of an Old Woman" from *Words for the Wind*, to say nothing of poems later than that. But the experiments are always interspersed, even in his last work, with returns to the simple lyric. Here, as an illustration, is a stanza from "Once More, the Round," with which Roethke concludes his final book:

> Now I adore my life
> With the Bird, the abiding Leaf,
> With the Fish, the questing Snail,
> And the Eye altering All;
> And I dance with William Blake
> For love, for Love's sake.

The two subjects on which Roethke's imagination most often fastens in *Open House* are the correspondence between the poet's inner life and the life of nature, and the strengths or weaknesses of the individual psyche. Frequently he tries to demonstrate hidden relationships in the processes of both, as in "The Light Comes Brighter," a poem which begins with a very direct account of winter's end and the arrival of spring to a particular landscape:

> The light comes brighter from the east; the caw
> Of restive crows is sharper on the ear.
> A walker at the river's edge may hear
> A cannon crack announce an early thaw.
>
> The sun cuts deep into the heavy drift,
> Though still the guarded snow is winter-sealed,
> At bridgeheads buckled ice begins to shift,
> The river overflows the level field.

The observation and description are quite accurate and undoubtedly derive from the poet's childhood experience of the Michigan countryside. But as in the poetry of Léonie Adams, which Roethke always admired, nature yields a secret analogy with human existence, though it does not appear until the closing lines:

> And soon a branch, part of a hidden scene,
> The leafy mind, that long was tightly furled,
> Will turn its private substance into green,
> And young shoots spread upon our inner world.

Mind and nature are bound in these lines by certain laws and enjoy a common awakening. Still we are left to tease out most of the implications for ourselves because the poet merely hints at the possibilities of this comparison in the present poem. In many of the other poems in this volume Roethke offers further seasonal descriptions but never makes the implied correspondences with human life any more definite than what we have already seen in the lines quoted.

Elsewhere in the book he takes the durability of the mind by itself as artistic material; and in a few poems which show an indebtedness to W. H. Auden he portrays the opposition to this mental stability through the figures of those victimized by unconscious forces, inherited sicknesses that threaten to destroy psychic balance:

> Exhausted fathers thinned the blood,
> You curse the legacy of pain;
> Darling of an infected brood,
> You feel disaster climb the vein.

These last poems, though they are of little aesthetic interest so far as the bulk of Roethke's writing is concerned, possess some value in foreshadowing the motives behind the tremendous imaginative leap he took in the seven years between *Open House* and *The Lost Son*. For the hostile powers of the unconscious had at last to be dealt with, and are dealt with in the astonishing sequence of interior monologues which record the poet's odyssey through subterranean regions of the psyche, a spiritual journey that remains one of the boldest experiments in modern American poetry. Taken altogether the poems in *Open House* are indicative of Roethke's major themes, but they hardly prepare the reader for the change to an intensely subjective vision in the next book or for the readjustment of his perceptions demanded by this shift. With *The Lost Son* (1948) he emerges as a poet of undeniable originality and stature, whose writing bears its own stylistic signature.

The section of poems with which *The Lost Son* opens may catch by complete surprise the reader who has seen nothing but Roethke's previous work. While emphasis on nature is still maintained attention has now moved away from the earlier images of natural and seasonal activity in the larger sense to a reduced, microscopic scrutiny of plant life that seems almost scientific in its precision but is obviously prompted by the poet's intuition, passion, and sympathy. What in preceding poems would most likely have been a careful description of the outer appearance of a plant or flower becomes an attempt to seize imaginatively the essential life of the flower, as in the haunting "Orchids," where it overlaps ours:

> They lean over the path,
> Adder-mouthed,
> Swaying close to the face,
> Coming out, soft and deceptive,
> Limp and damp, delicate as a young bird's tongue;
> Their fluttery fledgling lips
> Move slowly,
> Drawing in the warm air.

The basis for this sudden alteration in distance and perspective must have been the poet's decision to utilize his close experience in childhood with plants and flowers as substantial matter for his art. However it came about the choice was fortunate because it marked out the route his poetic imagination was to take and, one likes to think, even urged him on his way by revealing the similarities existing between his human life and that of the inhabitants of the plant kingdom which had played so important a part in his youth. Through this new personal vision of the vegetable and mineral, insect and animal, knowledge of which he owed to his boyhood, Roethke found before him the difficult problems of spiritual evolution and the search for psychic identity.

The poet was born in Saginaw, Michigan, in 1908, received his education at the University of Michigan and Harvard, and subsequently taught at Lafayette College, Pennsylvania State University, Bennington College, and for some time at the University of Washington in Seattle, where he was professor of English and poet in residence at the time of his death on August 1, 1963. As a boy he grew up in and around the greenhouses that were the center of the Roethke family's floral establishment, one of the largest and most famous of its time. The business was both retail and wholesale; it was operated by Roethke's father and his Uncle Charlie, aided by a staff of trained florists and also by a working crew of eccentric figures which included the three marvelous old ladies, Frau Bauman, Frau Schmidt, and Frau Schwartze, about whom the poet wrote a wonderful and moving elegy that captures the beauty and pleasure of these women at their task. I quote here only a few lines from the first stanza:

> Gone the three ancient ladies
> Who creaked on the greenhouse ladders,
> Reaching up white strings   ·
> To wind, to wind
> The sweet-pea tendrils, the smilax,
> Nasturtiums, the climbing
> Roses, to straighten
> Carnations, red
> Chrysanthemums; the stiff
> Stems, jointed like corn,

> They tied and tucked, —
> These nurses of nobody else.

   As a boy Roethke played and worked around these green-
houses. Many of his experiences he transformed elegantly,
and often humorously, into poems: we need only look at "Big
Wind," "Old Florist," "Child on Top of a Greenhouse," and the
poem above to be conscious of that. But from the same intimate
knowledge of his father's greenhouses he began those poetic
ventures into the scarcely visible — except to the eye of a deter-
mined and fascinated observer — motions of plant life that we
noticed in "Orchids." In another poem, appropriately entitled
"The Minimal," Roethke renders himself in the act of watching:

> I study the lives on a leaf: the little
> Sleepers, numb nudgers in cold dimensions,
> Beetles in caves, newts, stone-deaf fishes,
> Lice tethered to long limp subterranean weeds,
> Squirmers in bogs,
> And bacterial creepers
> Wriggling through wounds
> Like elvers in ponds,
> Their wan mouths kissing the warm sutures,
> Cleaning and caressing,
> Creeping and healing.

   In the poet's attentive gaze this tiny world increases its size and
comes curiously near in its procedures to the one we would like
to believe is exclusively man's. Something in the human psyche
responds to these minute activities, discovers a mysterious, even
terrifying, attraction to levels of existence to which reason or
intelligence would quickly assign an inferior value. But an indis-
pensable part of the imaginative breakthrough Roethke achieves
in his second book is just this exposure of himself to subrational
elements. Thus the disturbing quality in these poems results
from the dramatic re-creation of affinities with the lower orders
of life, parallels we have banished from thought. And how star-
tling it is for the scientific, technological mind of contemporary
man to countenance such images of his origins, of archaic
sources of life he shares with lesser forms than himself. If

Roethke's endeavors start with a return to his own past experience, the poems surpass the barriers of privacy to delineate hidden patterns in creation; and they accomplish this with a freshness of language and imaginative energy unmatched by any other poet since Dylan Thomas. A poem like "Cuttings, *later*" brings poet — and thus reader — and the newly born plants into a correspondence so delicate and yet profound that there can be only one true conclusion: a kind of psychic rebirth for the poet through his sympathetic contemplation of propagating plants:

> This urge, wrestle, resurrection of dry sticks,
> Cut stems struggling to put down feet,
> What saint strained so much,
> Rose on such lopped limbs to a new life?
>
> I can hear, underground, that sucking and sobbing,
> In my veins, in my bones I feel it, —
> The small waters seeping upward,
> The tight grains parting at last.
> When sprouts break out,
> Slippery as fish,
> I quail, lean to beginnings, sheath-wet.

Roethke's inclination in these poems to reveal a deep and permanent tie between the "minimal" world of flowers, plants, and small creatures he so benevolently scrutinizes and the inner world of man prepares for the sequence of experimental monologues, the first of which appear in the last section of *The Lost Son* and which are continued in *Praise to the End* (1951). The sequence poems are, so far as I know, unique in modern literature. Undoubtedly they owe their inspiration to the poet's pursuit of the correspondences just mentioned and to the fact that his previous work keeps insisting on such an immersion in the prerational and unconscious areas of experience in the hope of bringing unity to the self and gaining a new harmony with creation.

The poems are grouped around an associational scheme, as Roethke once suggested, and seem closer perhaps to certain experimental tendencies in the modern novel, such as stream of consciousness, than they do to the efforts of most contemporary poets. "Each poem" — there are fourteen in all — "is complete in itself," Roethke says in his "Open Letter" from *Mid-Century American Poets*, "yet each in a sense is a stage in a kind of struggle out of the slime; part of a slow spiritual progress; an effort to be born, and later, to become something more." The poems treat portions of a spiritual journey undertaken by a child-protagonist, a journey the narrative of which does not develop in a direct, logical manner because it is viewed internally through the fluid movements and reactions of the protagonist's mind. This protagonist, through whom we comprehend whatever happens in the poems, plays a double role: he is both a mask for the poet and a universal type, any man, for Roethke is at pains to avoid the limitations of a totally personal significance in the experience created by this poetic sequence. The journey, while it is basically psychic and spiritual, also has similarities with quest myths: the hero's descent into the underworld of the self; a series of ordeals he must pass or an enemy to be vanquished; his victorious return to familiar reality, which is now changed by his efforts. This sort of parallel will make it clear at once that while Roethke's primary intention is the "struggle for spiritual identity" (his phrase) in the individual protagonist, that struggle symbolizes a more general body of human experience. This last dimension is, however, implied rather than heavily outlined through a detailed system of allusion.

In several of the poems we have seen from *The Lost Son*, as well as in a number of others that cannot be discussed here, Roethke presses back toward the very beginnings of existence in his concentration on the life process of plants. This practice by itself is sufficient to separate his interests from his contemporaries' and to display his genuine innovation. Roethke wishes in these poems to uncover through his imagination the laws of growth in a flower and relate them to the development of the human self, though it is done metaphorically rather than scientifically. But short lyric poems are ultimately unsatisfactory as vehicles for such ambitions because they are not flexible enough and do not readily permit the singular approach to experience the poet now envisages. What he is aiming at is a poetic "history of the psyche" (his phrase) which opens with the earliest stages of life and traces the evolution of the spirit in its ordeal of inner and outer conflicts, its desire for "unity of being," to borrow a term from Dante by way of Yeats, that final condition of grace which is a harmony of the self with all things. In Roethke's later work the love of man and woman is involved in this idea of unity and so is an awareness of the Divine. Yet the protagonist's route in the poems is anything but easy, for regressive instincts, desires to remain on the lowest plane of existence or to become a lump of inanimate matter, war upon the natural impulse to growth. The spirit tries to release the self from these destructive attractions and to rise toward the full embrace of life. Nature is the context in which the individual assumes at last his rightful identity, finds love, and engages the spirit in further encounters. Roethke depicted some of the terrors and humiliations attending this venture into buried regions in a poem entitled "The Return":

> A cold key let me in
> That self-infected lair;
> And I lay down with my life,
> With the rags and rotting clothes,
> With a stump of scraggy fang
> Bared for a hunter's boot.

The self-imposed, and no doubt personally necessary, journey on which the poet sets forth with the first poem of the sequence (as rearranged by Roethke in the order he wishes in *Words for the Wind*), "Where Knock Is Open Wide," immediately alters ordinary spatial and temporal dimensions. Spatial because the poems view a secret landscape of the inner self that resembles the external world only in fragmentary details supplied by memory or momentary perceptions, and these are heightened, distorted, or transfigured, as in a dream, by the various struggles of the spirit in its search for freedom and unity. Temporal because the poet, or the projection of himself which is the protagonist, needs to go back to his childhood experience so that he can relive this evolutionary process in writing about it. Thus we

witness the activity of the poems from the standpoint of the
poet-protagonist himself.

It has already been suggested that these poems carry echoes of
archetypal patterns from other modes of experience, particu-
larly mythical and religious. Because the protagonist travels into
the regions of memory, the preconscious and the unconscious,
he shows distinct similarity to the heroes of myth whom Jung
saw as representative of the quest for psychic wholeness. Like
those fabulous heroes or the lesser ones of fairy tales Roethke's
lone protagonist must endure the trials and dangers of a mission
into the darkness of personal history. The prize to be won is
rebirth and illumination, what is called in one of the poems "a
condition of joy."

The title of "Where Knock Is Open Wide" is taken from
Christopher Smart's poem of praise and celebration, "Song to
David," LXXVII, but Roethke's piece, which presents the sensa-
tions and thoughts of earliest childhood, seems to use the line
from Smart to imply birth and entry into the world. From this
aspect Roethke's poem somewhat resembles Dylan Thomas's
"Before I knocked," which describes experiences of a child (in
this case, Jesus) in the womb. Indeed, Thomas is probably the
only one of Roethke's immediate contemporaries who also inves-
tigates successfully the fluid exchange of past and present within
the self. Roethke establishes his atmosphere with childish per-
ceptions:

> A kitten can
> Bite with his feet;
> Papa and Mamma
> Have more teeth.

He goes on in a few lines to what appears to be an image of birth:

> Once upon a tree
> I came across a time . . .

The tree is a species of the common symbol of the Tree of Life,
and the next line recalls the protagonist's introduction to time. A
stanza further on we learn the nature of the journey and some-
thing of its method:

What's the time, papa-seed?
Everything has been twice.
My father is a fish.

This brief passage draws the protagonist back toward the in-
stant of his conception and fixes our attention on the movement
into his personal past, which is a reversal of the temporal order.
The middle line makes plain the fact that the poet is not simply
rendering the original stages of development in a fictional indi-
vidual but reliving them in himself to interpret their meaning.
We seem to hear the voices of the protagonist and the poet
blending in this line. The identification of the father with a fish
has again a double reference: first, in alluding to a fishing trip of
the father and son, bits of which are given later; second, in
hinting at the evolutionary scheme emphasized previously. This
process of evolution we witness in the protagonist is universal
and leads away, as Roethke writes in his "Open Letter," from
"the mire," where "man is no more than a shape writhing from
the old rock." In the third section of the poem he sounds the
same theme by employing the word "fish" once again, but now as
a verb instead of a substantive. This change marks a step for-
ward from domination by an image of ancestry among the lower
forms of life to an active desire on the protagonist's part for
self-completion:

A worm has a mouth.
Who keeps me last?
Fish me out.
Please.

Since our point of observation is located within the
protagonist's mind, though not at the level of reason or calcula-
tion, certain external facts such as his changing age are not
always easily determined. We gather, however, that the poems
extend over a period from early childhood into late adolescence.
Roethke's associative technique allows him to shift back and
forth freely in the history of his protagonist, and so he can bring
his artistic weight to bear on the themes which matter to him
without particular regard for the consistency of linear time. The

present poem ranges from the first years of life with their scraps
of nonsense verse and nursery songs, through a brief section
touching on the small boy's religious emotions, then his fishing
trip, and ending with the initial signs of anxiety and guilt which
accompany the feeling of desolation caused by the father's
death. The narrative progression of the poems, if we may thus
speak of it, depends upon Roethke's concern for the advances
and setbacks of the evolving spirit.

The loss of his father empties the protagonist's world of its
paternal image of God as well:

> Kisses come back,
> I said to Papa;
> He was all whitey bones
> And skin like paper.
>
> God's somewhere else,
> I said to Mamma.
> The evening came
> A long long time.

The last two lines predict a period of deprivation and loneliness
to come. And in the next poem, "I Need, I Need," with its title so
sharply indicative of the child's terrible hunger for affection and
stability, he alternates between a search for the mother:

> A deep dish. Lumps in it.
> I can't taste my mother;

solitude and melancholy:

> Went down cellar,
> Talked to a faucet;
> The drippy water
> Had nothing to say;

and a final resort to the diversion of children's habits, rhymes,
and games:

> A one is a two is
> I know what you is:
> You're not very nice, —
> So touch my toes twice.

But, clearly enough, these diversions exhibit the inner divisions and turmoil of the protagonist, too. In later sections of the poem a gradual easing of tensions occurs, succeeded by intimations of human possibility and of an abiding kinship with physical creation: "Hear me, soft ears and roundy stones! / It's a dear life I can touch." The poem finally closes by emphasizing two of the traditional four elements thought to compose the universe, water and fire:

> I said to the gate,
> Who else knows
> What water does?
> Dew ate the fire.

Here the gate symbolizes all that prevents the protagonist from rebirth into the world, from the potential of his existence. Like beings, objects, and places in fairy tale and folklore, creatures and things in Roethke's poetic cosmos are invested with magical properties, can hinder or help the spirit in its growth. Thus the protagonist seeks the true way by asking questions in this subterranean and animistic kingdom from which he must obtain new life or sink back into the "dark pond" — as Roethke calls the deep unconscious — where oblivion awaits him. The water mentioned in the passage above should not, however, be identified with that sinister place; rather it signifies a continuation of the journey into daylight, the constant will of the self to accomplish, in Robert Frost's words, this "serial ordeal."

Dew consumes one fire in this same stanza only to disclose another kind in the next. The first should probably be understood as the fever of discord in the protagonist, while the second, which appears momentarily in the poem's final lines — "I know another fire. / Has roots." — surely is meant to remind us of fire's ancient use as a symbol of spirit. So we realize that the entire movement of the first two poems in the sequence constitutes an ascent from origins, from the introduction to death, the experience of fear and isolation, to the recognition of freedom and possibility beyond present conditions, though such prospects are never mistaken for a guarantee of security. Life, as it is seen in Roethke's poetry, can best be defined as always becoming.

"Bring the Day!" fulfills the promise of spiritual progress implied before. It is a celebration of self and nature together in a newly won relation, and as such it marks the conversion of the haunted landscape of unknown terrors and hidden demons projected by the self into the radiant external world of insects and birds, grass and flowers. The poem begins with an exuberant burst of song which sounds as if Roethke might have had both John Lyly and Edward Lear in mind when he wrote it:

> Bees and lilies there were,
> Bees and lilies there were,
> Either to other, —
> Which would you rather?
> Bees and lilies were there.

This mood of celebration, of self-possession and joy, prevails throughout the poem. Nature guides the protagonist further along the path he must travel and hints in symbols which recall those of "I Need, I Need" at the pattern of his journey from confinement to fluidity: "The grass says what the wind says: / Begin with the rock; / End with water."

The third and concluding section shows the emergent self in the image of a tiny bird waking to existence, feeling a little its own possibilities, and facing a life that has cast off its ties with the past and only looks forward. The gentle lyricism of the stanza again points up Roethke's uncanny sensitiveness to the subtlest details of nature and their covert human meanings:

> O small bird wakening,
> Light as a hand among blossoms,
> Hardly any old angels are around any more.
> The air's quiet under the small leaves.
> The dust, the long dust, stays.
> The spiders sail into summer.
> It's time to begin!
> To begin!

Following this poem three others, "Give Way, Ye Gates," "Sensibility! O La!" and "O Lull Me, Lull Me," lead up to "The

Lost Son," which is the key poem of the sequence and, as
Roethke said himself, the one with the most obvious narrative
construction. The poems preceding "The Lost Son" continue to
test various lines of inner tension we have already noted in the
protagonist. Sexual agony, lack of identity, and solitude are cast
as barriers against the vital energy of the spirit in its evolution
but with no lasting success. The closing portion of "O Lull Me,
Lull Me" measures the spirit's achievement and attests once
more to the protagonist's intuition of harmony with creation:

> I'm more than when I was born;
> I could say hello to things;
> I could talk to a snail;
> I see what sings!
> What sings!

Light, movements of air, flowing water, and the music of song
supply Roethke with some favorite metaphors for these sudden
revelations of increase and communion. And they are peculiarly
appropriate and effective metaphors because their source is the
great world of nature, which stands, as we have seen, as the
foundation and setting for the poet's investigation of human
reality. In Roethke's writing man is always viewed in the
framework of nature, or at least is never far distant from it.
Whether the immediate subject is the individual self, love be-
tween man and woman, or some kind of visionary experience, it
partakes of that natural world in evident or indirect relation-
ships, in the physical details of imagery. Finally, in some of his
more recent poems such as "The Far Field," "Meditation at
Oyster River," and "The Rose" Roethke sees the realm of the
spiritual beginning in nature; yet he never denies the validity of
the natural in favor of the transcendental. He tends rather to
hold them in his vision simultaneously, for to his imagination
they blend and interchange endlessly.

"The Lost Son," as Hilton Kramer wrote in his fine essay on
Roethke, summarizes the main theme and the developments
which appear loosely in the sequence as a whole. The first of the
poems from this group we examined took the early phases of life
as their point of departure, but here the reference to a cemetery

in the opening line and the attraction to death which it signifies states at once the conflict with the evolving self whose pull is toward fulfillment and maturity. The remainder of this initial section, which is entitled "The Flight," treats the confused and often tormented condition of the child-protagonist as he tries to learn the direction he must take to escape those forces working solely for his anguish or destruction. In keeping with Roethke's preoccupation with the irrational and subliminal side of his protagonist's experience the poem assumes the strange aura of dream and fairy tale we have come to expect of the entire sequence. The protagonist undertakes his journey without certainty of his bearings or his goal. All he can do, it seems, is ask questions and go where chance or the guidance of the spirit may lead him. The environment through which he travels (again we should stress the subjective character of his perceptions) displays hostility, though he has obvious feelings of sympathy for the smallest creatures, whose size and innocence resemble his own:

> At Woodlawn I heard the dead cry:
> I was lulled by the slamming of iron,
> A slow drip over stones,
> Toads brooding in wells.
> All the leaves stuck out their tongues;
> I shook the softening chalk of my bones,
> Saying,
> Snail, snail, glister me forward,
> Bird, soft-sigh me home.

As in previous poems from the sequence Roethke juxtaposes fragments of children's songs, nursery rhymes, and riddles with apparently factual descriptions; thus he keeps a balance between external and subjective reality. But even the fairly straightforward passages distill a symbolic meaning in terms of the quest on which the protagonist is bound:

> Hunting along the river,
> Down among the rubbish, the bug-riddled foliage,
> By the muddy pond-edge, by the bog-holes,
> By the shrunken lake, hunting, in the heat of summer.

The river with its steady flow, suggesting progress, intensifies by contrast the image of frustrated and unrewarded searching by the protagonist near those places, holes and slippery mud patches, that spell out the dangers of regression and defeat to his odyssey.

In "The Pit," the second part of the poem which is only one stanza long, the seductiveness of a descent into the earth, a relinquishing of self to the dark body of the mother, becomes an active threat to the protagonist. But an inner warning, perhaps by the spirit, prevents him from succumbing to what I think we must call a strong death wish or a refusal of any further hardships in the search for human completion:

> Where do the roots go?
>   Look down under the leaves.
> Who put the moss there?
>   These stones have been here too long.
> Who stunned the dirt into noise?
>   Ask the mole, he knows.
> I feel the slime of a wet nest.
>   Beware Mother Mildew.
> Nibble again, fish nerves.

The section following treats sexual agonies and alienation. Roethke builds up to a terrifying climax the tension between the protagonist and his surroundings. The short, terse lines which he handles so deftly are essential to the poet's creation of this climactic atmosphere:

> The weeds whined,
> The snakes cried,
> The cows and briars
> Said to me: Die.

But the full weight of the poem up to this point, which is brought to bear on the word "Die," is released in the next stanzas, and we suddenly realize that the protagonist has survived the worst of his trials. He finds himself at the calm center of a storm and recognizes that he is poised on the threshold of a new spiritual phase, of transformation and rebirth: "Do the bones cast out their fire? / Is the seed leaving the old bed? These buds are live as birds." Still more lines of conflict succeed these indications of change, but they terminate at last in a gentle apprehension of natural things, which is, in its turn, broken by an unexpected, violent flash of interior illumination and a period of turbulence ending in the restoration of the protagonist to the familiar climate of daily life.

The two concluding portions of the poem bring the protagonist home to his father's greenhouse and to an interval of waiting. The boy's sensitive awareness of the existence of the roses he tends and watches there ("The roses kept breathing in the dark. / They had many mouths to breathe with.") should also be understood to connote the self-recognition earned through his troublesome journey. Like these flowers he enjoys a precarious and fragile state of being; his scrutiny of their gradual response to the coming light of day duplicates a perception of his own slow ascent from the abyss of inner tensions:

> A fine haze moved off the leaves;
> Frost melted on far panes;
> The rose, the chrysanthemum turned toward the light.
> Even the hushed forms, the bent yellowy weeds
> Moved in a slow up-sway.

The stately, graceful quality of this stanza, contrasting sharply with the clipped style of previous parts, leads us without disruption into the meditative attitude of the final section, in which the winter landscape, bare yet enduring, mirrors in its stark forms and objects the present condition of the protagonist. From this symbolic notation with its imagery of the "bones of weeds" and of "light" moving "slowly over the frozen field, / Over the dry seed-crowns, / The beautiful surviving bones / Swinging in the wind" there comes a shift to the mind of the protagonist deeply immersed in what has been happening to him. His mind also moves, but "not alone, / Through the clear air, in the silence." The poem closes with two stanzas reflecting the spiritual questions raised by the boy's experience as recounted in the first three sections of the poem and, presumably, in the other poems of the sequence placed before "The Lost Son":

> Was it light?
> Was it light within?

Was it light within light?
Stillness becoming alive,
Yet still?

A lively understandable spirit
Once entertained you.
It will come again.
Be still.
Wait.

We can hardly fail to notice here a recollection of T. S. Eliot's *Four Quartets*, a series of poems which parallel Roethke's in some respects. Both works are explorations of the self, its past history and its developments, though Eliot has no intention of representing those prerational areas of the mind into which Roethke so daringly plunges. Both works seek realization in a spiritual order, but Roethke declines to step into religious orthodoxy and relies upon his own intuition, while Eliot integrates his mystical perceptions with the traditions and beliefs of Catholic Christianity. Yet Roethke's reference to the senior poet is too obvious to be merely an unconscious allusion. I think we should see it as a deliberate echo of *Four Quartets* but also as a statement of difference. The illumination which occurs in "The Lost Son" may be a divine visitation or a gift of grace; however, it lacks any explicit theological structure of the kind embodied in so many of the details in Eliot's poems. For Roethke this moment of light appears to be given as a matter of course and is accepted as completely natural. Certainly it is merited to a degree by the ordeal through which the protagonist has passed, but it surely is not achieved in the sense in which Eliot achieves those mystical experiences at the heart of *Four Quartets*, that is, by prayer, selflessness, and meditation. Roethke's is the more Protestant approach, one that bases itself firmly on personal knowledge and evidence, on the lone individual's apprehension of the transcendent. And such a description applies to mystical poems like "In a Dark Time," collected in *The Far Field* (1964).

The purpose of this visitation at the close of "The Lost Son" is clear all the same, for it displays the progress of the spirit over the longest and most difficult stage of evolution. In the seven

remaining poems of the sequence Roethke continues to record
the advances and lapses of his protagonist, though we are by
now conscious of the latter's increasing maturity. But he has not
yet escaped the pains of sexuality and of alienation: they have be-
come the problems of a person who has left childhood behind
and arrived at a more comprehensive vision of himself and of
the world around him. The poet even tells us the protagonist's
age in the third part of "Praise to the End!":

> The sun came out;
> The lake turned green;
> Romped upon the goldy grass,
> Aged thirteen.

In spite of persistent obstacles passages of lyrical exaltation
occur with greater frequency than they do in the poems preced-
ing "The Lost Son." Such superior moments, with their pleasure
in the beauty and variety of nature, look forward to some of
Roethke's last poetry. Stanzas like the following from "I Cry,
Love! Love!" (which takes its title from William Blake's "Visions
of the Daughters of Albion") prepare the way for the vision of
life we find in "The Far Field" or "Meditations of an Old
Woman":

> I hear the owls, the soft callers, coming down from
>   the hemlocks.
> The bats weave in and out of the willows,
> Wing-crooked and sure,
> Downward and upward,
> Dipping and veering close to the motionless water.
>
> A fish jumps, shaking out flakes of moonlight.
> A single wave starts lightly and easily shoreward,
> Wrinkling between reeds in shallower water.
> Lifting a few twigs and floating leaves,
> Then washing up over small stones.
>
> The shine on the face of the lake
> Tilts, backward and forward.
> The water recedes slowly,
> Gently rocking.

After the unusual and striking techniques which he intro-
duces for his special purposes in the sequence poems, Roethke
turns back again to a more formal manner in the early 1950s. In
some of this work, most notably in "Four for Sir John Davies"
and later in "The Dying Man," he makes use of cadences some-
what reminiscent of those in the poetry of Yeats, but these are
intentional effects on Roethke's part and not, as some critics
would have us believe, signs of weakness and of an unassimilated
influence. Roethke ably defended himself against such charges
in his essay "How to Write Like Somebody Else," pointing out
that the poet needs to work forward consciously from his pred-
ecessors, that "the language itself is a compound . . ." And
finally, he adds, "the very fact" that the poet "has the support of
a tradition, or an older writer, will enable him to be more him-
self — or more than himself."

What Roethke says on this subject is profoundly true and is
peculiarly applicable to himself. With his sequence finished he
could no longer exercise the devices employed there: that vein
was thoroughly mined and could only be kept open at the risk of
repetition, boredom, and stultification. But he had learned a
good deal from the sequence, and the themes which engaged his
imagination were far from exhausted; in fact, one might venture
to say that the exploration of the past, of personal history,
served to make the present very available to him. The evolution
of the self was not done, and the love poems begun during this
period show that this evolution was entering a new, more expan-
sive phase which related the self to the other, or the beloved.
Technically speaking, Roethke tested the possibilities of a formal
style, but with a daring, a liberty and passion that go beyond the
urgencies of amorous feeling. His experiments in the sequence
poems freed him to attempt an altered diction and looser syntax,
more exclamatory, interrogative, and aphoristic lines:

> I'd say it to my horse: we live beyond
> Our outer skin. Who's whistling up my sleeve?
> I see a heron prancing in his pond;
> I know a dance the elephants believe.

> The living all assemble! What's the cue?
> Do what the clumsy partner wants to do!

To get a better impression of the distance Roethke has traveled thus far in his poetic style, let us set next to those lines above from "Four for Sir John Davies" a stanza from "The Heron" in *Open House*. Though the rhythms of both passages are fundamentally iambic, the latter will call to mind the more restricted, tense character of the poet's first work:

> The heron stands in water where the swamp
> Has deepened to the blackness of a pool,
> Or balances with one leg on a hump
> Of marsh grass heaped above a musk-rat hole.

The piece which best prepares us for the considerable group of love poems gathered into their own section of *Words for the Wind* is "Four for Sir John Davies," an ambitious poetic cycle that appeared among the last pages of Roethke's Pulitzer Prize volume of selected poems, *The Waking* (1954). As the title implies a little covertly, the basic metaphor of the poem is dancing. Roethke draws openly on two other poets to enlarge the dimensions of his poems: they are the sixteenth-century English poet to whom these four pieces are dedicated and William Butler Yeats. From Davies's *Orchestra* (1594), a long philosophical poem on the harmonious relations of the various spheres of being in the universe, Roethke gains support for the cosmic scheme he includes in the first poem, "The Dance." But since *Orchestra* is constructed about a supposed dispute between Penelope and her suitor Antinous, who tries to persuade her to dance, the sexual theme has also already been evoked, though as yet only indirectly. And it is to Yeats that Roethke looks for precedence in the treatment of sexual love through the figure of the dance, as well as for certain rhythms and qualities of tone and diction.

"The Dance" begins with the poet recalling the universal system to be found in Davies's poem, then questioning whether man any longer conceives of the world in terms of the dance within his own mind. Whatever the answer to that question may be, he affirms his own participation in such a cosmic dance and even humorously identifies himself with the shambling but pleasurable gait of bears:

> The great wheel turns its axle when it can;
> I need a place to sing, and dancing-room,
> And I have made a promise to my ears
> I'll sing and whistle romping with the bears.

But Roethke intends something more than mild self-mockery here, for the bears in their dance throw into relief the sheer physical aspect of existence — in the poet as well as in themselves: "O watch his body sway! — / This animal remembering to be gay." The poem carries this note into the third stanza with emphasis now placed on the poet's own isolated dancing. In spite of the elation accompanying this joyous, willed activity there is an incompleteness in what he does that can only be corrected by the appearance of the beloved. This beginning poem of the four closes with a stanza expressing Roethke's debt to Yeats:

> I take this cadence from a man named Yeats;
> I take it, and I give it back again:
> For other tunes and other wanton beats
> Have tossed my heart and fiddled through my brain.
> Yes, I was dancing-mad, and how
> That came to be the bears and Yeats would know.

The next poem, "The Partner," brings together the poet and his beloved in the dance. It becomes clear immediately that their relationship is more than sensual, more even than love between two persons, for overtly sexual gestures generate metaphysical overtones until we sense that Roethke attains a kind of visionary intuition of human possibility through his dancing lovers:

> Things loll and loiter. Who condones the lost?
> This joy outleaps the dog. Who cares? Who cares?
> I gave her kisses back, and woke a ghost.
> O what lewd music crept into our ears!
> The body and the soul know how to play
> In that dark world where gods have lost their way.

The "dark world" of which the poet speaks is undoubtedly the
maze of love and bodily attraction. It may further imply the
realm of the human, fully realized in the sexual and spiritual
bond of the pair, as opposed to a supernatural plane of being
altogether removed from life. We enter that world more com-
pletely in "The Wraith," where lover and beloved apparently
exchange identities through their union. Though this poem
aims specifically in its imagery and reference at the intense mo-
ment of completion in the sexual act, it extends past that in
Roethke's speculations on the meaning of the act. Certainly we
do not exaggerate in saying that he wishes to reveal the spiritual
transcendence emerging from carnal love in the poem:

> There was a body, and it cast a spell,
> God pity those but wanton to the knees,
> The flesh can make the spirit visible . . .

The wraith, "a shape alone, / Impaled on light, and whirling
slowly down," who is the poet's image of his beloved, is briefly
associated with Dante's Beatrice in the first stanza of "The Vigil."
In those lines Roethke asserts the purity of the lover's vision of
the beloved. Created from his "longing" it may be contradicted
but not destroyed by the reality of the loved one as a person. But
the allusion to Dante and Beatrice goes further because it sup-
ports the transcendental experience recorded in the poem's last
stanza, an experience which never denies the physical nature of
the love relationship and yet presents it as the cause of a break-
through in the spiritual order:

> The world is for the living. Who are they?
> We dared the dark to reach the white and warm.
> She was the wind when wind was in my way;
> Alive at noon, I perished in her form.
> Who rise from flesh to spirit know the fall:
> The word outleaps the world, and light is all.

Such a visionary climax is predicted by the similar but less
comprehensive bursts of illumination in "The Lost Son" and
other poems of that sequence. Even more important is the fact

that moments of this kind recur throughout the love poems and again, of course, in the unmistakably visionary and meditative work that follows. It is necessary to understand first of all that Roethke's love poems are not just evocations of the beloved or descriptions of his aroused emotions with regard to her; these play their part in what he writes, but it is only one part. As I hinted earlier, this group of poems brings to a certain measure of fulfillment the evolution of the self begun with the childhood and adolescence poems. So Roethke tends to locate the loved woman at the center of the physical universe: through her he communes with that world and its elements, and has his vision transformed. Once more we think of the reference to Dante, of Beatrice's guidance which brings that poet to a revelation of the Divine. Surely the beloved in Roethke's poems, though she can change swiftly from a wraithlike to an earthy creature, functions in a manner closely resembling her predecessor.

A poem that is one of the most fully achieved as well as one of the most representative of the considerations discussed here is "Words for the Wind," which gives its title to Roethke's collected verse. Other of the love poems do take up various strands of the themes of death, spirit versus flesh, ultimate belief, and so forth, but they gain much more prominence in "The Dying Man," an elegy to Yeats, and "Meditations of an Old Woman." In an anthology, *Poet's Choice*, edited by Paul Engle and Joseph Langland, Roethke says that "Words for the Wind" was written as an epithalamion to his bride during their honeymoon visit at W. H. Auden's villa in Ischia, but these are merely the external circumstances of composition. The poem itself is literally a song of joy, a mood in the poet which arises from delight in his companion but overflows into the world outside. Perhaps it would be even more accurate to say that his love for this woman awakens and refines in him a knowledge of a participation in the life of creation, in the being of all things. His beloved merges with flowers, the wind, a stone, the moon, and so she appears to be present in almost every living thing, in objects or the elements. As the last line of the opening stanza intimates, he has the sensitive reverence for them we think of in a St. Francis of Assisi, who would make a particularly appropriate patron saint for Roethke's poetry:

> Love, love, a lily's my care,
> She's sweeter than a tree.
> Loving, I use the air
> Most lovingly: I breathe;
> Mad in the wind I wear
> Myself as I should be,
> All's even with the odd,
> My brother the vine is glad.

Not only does this love result in a harmony with the cosmos but it accomplishes an internal balance too. The self that was, so to speak, divided against itself in many previous poems arrives at unity through another person, a woman who is frankly physical and sexual but is furthermore a creature of spiritual and mythological proportions. In the intensified perception of the poem we see her continual metamorphosis, her changing roles, but at the same time she remains a constant image within the poet himself, the archetypal female principle dwelling in man which Jung called the *Anima*:

> The shallow stream runs slack;
> The wind creaks slowly by;
> Out of a nestling's beak
> Comes a tremulous cry
> I cannot answer back;
> A shape from deep in the eye —
> That woman I saw in a stone —
> Keeps pace when I walk alone.

In spite of this disclosure of a psychic image Roethke concentrates most of his imaginative powers on the external world and the forms of nature. The second section of the poem is devoted almost totally to natural imagery through which the course of love and the person of the beloved are traced. Here we find creation transfigured by the lovers who move within it and color it with their complex of emotions, "the burden of this joy":

The sun declares the earth;
The stones leap in the stream;
On a wide plain, beyond
The far stretch of a dream,
A field breaks like the sea;
The wind's white with her name,
And I walk with the wind.

Love in the figure of this woman "wakes the ends of life,"
Roethke tells us, and I do not believe it is misleading to say that
she and the poems about her suggested to the poet some of the
approaches and devices of his later writing. "The Dying Man"
and "Meditations of an Old Woman," the two poetic cycles which
conclude *Words for the Wind*, are meditative and both employ the
persona or mask to obtain a more objective dramatization of
viewpoint.

At the start of "The Dying Man" the imagined voice of Yeats
alternates and blends with Roethke's through the five lyrics
composing it, and the style is itself a combination of the poetic
speech of the two men. This adaptation of the Yeatsian manner
and mood is not merely casual but quite intentional. In his late
poems Yeats was, of course, paradoxical, outrageous, and ex-
tremely powerful, with a seemingly boundless reserve of energy
to dispose to these ends. He brought together spiritual and sen-
sual modes of experience in unexpected, even sensational, ways
and under the harsh light of his irony. Roethke wished at times
to use his poetry as Yeats did, to probe the extremes of percep-
tion and knowledge which the self may attain. "The Dying Man"
is just such an imaginative effort; and the fact that it is both an
elegy for Yeats and a utilization of some of his language and
techniques should not prevent us from seeing how Roethke is
really examining himself and his own situation.

The opening poem, "His Words," records the message of "a
dying man / . . . to his gathered kin." This man is presumably
Yeats, and what he says seems an amalgam of the thought of
Blake and Yeats. Here the last stanza proves most influential in
stirring the mind of the poem's narrator (Roethke himself) to
his own observations:

"A man sees, as he dies,
Death's possibilities;
My heart sways with the world.
I am that final thing,
A man learning to sing."

The second poem begins with the revaluation of his life and
work which these last words and the death following them force
upon the poet-narrator. In addition, he feels the potentialities of
existence revived: "I thought myself reborn." The subsequent
stanzas range back over past experience, the poet's love and its
opposite, the darkest moments of the spirit when he "dared to
question all." A knocking "at the gate" announces most probably
the presence of death, but the poet puts that off in the conclud-
ing line.

Three other poems, "The Wall," "The Exulting," and "They
Sing, They Sing," make up the rest of the cycle. All of them
reach beyond the bounds of a reasoned arrangement of ideas
and perceptions in favor of a terse but ecstatic and visionary
utterance. Themes are intermingled, but they include the poet's
psychic burdens:

A ghost comes out of the unconscious mind
To grope my sill: It moans to be reborn!
The figure at my back is not my friend;
The hand upon my shoulder turns to horn.

and the fusion of natural and transcendental knowledge:

Though it reject dry borders of the seen,
What sensual eye can keep an image pure,
Leaning across a sill to greet the dawn?

These passages, taken from "The Wall," both use the image of
the sill as the apparent threshold separating the conscious self
from the unconscious and from external reality. The wall turns
up in the third stanza as the limit of what can be known, and
thus the poet can recognize his dilemma as that of "a spirit
raging at the visible."

"The Exulting" begins with a statement of the childlike inno-

cence and freedom which once satisfied the poet but which now
have aroused further yearnings:

> I love the world; I want more than the world,
> Or after-image of the inner eye.

Yet the most explicit account of the object of his desires, if it can
be so described, is withheld until the final stanzas of the last
poem. There nature asserts itself as a means of revelation for
Roethke, and he has a vision of reality corresponding to the
words of the dying man in the initial section of the poem —
"Eternity is Now" — a vision that calls to mind Blake's famous
passage from "The Marriage of Heaven and Hell": "If the doors
of perception were cleansed every thing would appear to man as
it is, infinite." The world gives the poet intuitions of the eternal
and the infinite through its temporal, finite creatures and things
—if he has learned how to see or has been granted this frighten-
ing clairvoyance:

> I've the lark's word for it, who sings alone:
> What's seen recedes; Forever's what we know! —
> Eternity defined, and strewn with straw,
> The fury of the slug beneath the stone.
> The vision moves, and yet remains the same.
> In heaven's praise, I dread the thing I am.

The poem's ending lines, of great strength and beauty, set
forth the loneliness and uncertainty but also the singular deter-
mination of the poet in his confrontation of the unknowable or
the void where the Divine may be sought. Roethke furnishes no
answers and, as he does elsewhere, keeps within the strict
confines of his personal perceivings:

> Nor can imagination do it all
> In this last place of light: he dares to live
> Who stops being a bird, yet beats his wings
> Against the immense immeasurable emptiness of things.

"Meditations of an Old Woman," a longer and superior group
of poems, consists of several dramatic monologues spoken by an
aging lady, modeled on the poet's mother, who muses on her

past, on the meanings of an individual's existence, as she faces
the prospect of death. Over and above those poems included in
the collected edition and in the volume of light verse (which also
reprints the so-called greenhouse poems) *I Am! Says the Lamb*
(1961) there are a considerable number of later poems; Roethke
planned a book for them, *The Far Field*, completing it shortly
before his death. These late poems in part take the manner and
technique of the "Meditations" as their starting place. Some of
them become even looser in form; some are fragmentary, explo-
sive, and epigrammatic; some turn to a taut lyricism. Many are
shaped by that mixture of description and reflection so promi-
nent in the "Meditations." Through these poems runs a con-
tinued fascination with ultimate questions of mortality, God, the
final significance of human life. Of course these are questions
about the self too, and they constantly bring Roethke's evolu-
tionary theme to its highest level, that is, to occasions of vision-
ary knowledge. But first we should look at "Meditations of an
Old Woman," both as the foundation of later work and as the
last part of *Words for the Wind*.

The "First Meditation," which inaugurates the series of five
poems, offers the reader opening stanzas that create a harsh
mood of old age, winter, frailty, and severely restricted expecta-
tions. We can capture something of the ominous quality of this
section from the initial lines:

> On love's worst ugly day,
> The weeds hiss at the edge of the field,
> The small winds make their chilly indictments.

Thus the title and the beginning provide us with the personal
situation from which the speaker's memories and thoughts are
set in motion. As Roethke so frequently does, he expresses the
condition of a person's life through happenings or objects in
nature. The old woman's recognition of death is conveyed viv-
idly by external events: "stones loosen on the obscure
hillside, / And a tree tilts from its roots, / Toppling down an em-
bankment." And here we must remember that it is *her mind*
which entertains these images of sliding stones and falling trees.

In spite of the temporal erosion that has worn away the speaker as though she were a thing exposed to wind and dust and rain there is an essential life of the spirit preserved in her described by Roethke as "light as a seed." Small that life may be, but it has a toughness and resiliency which enables it to burst forth with a vigorous assertion of its own being. The effort of the spirit to be renewed is characteristically reflected in careful details of the actions of nonhuman creatures, a fish, for example:

> So the spirit tries for another life,
> Another way and place in which to continue;
> Or a salmon, tired, moving up a shallow stream,
> Nudges into a back-eddy, a sandy inlet,
> Bumping against sticks and bottom-stones, then swinging
> Around, back into the tiny maincurrent, the rush of
>   brownish-white water,
> Still swimming forward —
> So, I suppose, the spirit journeys.

This passage could be seen as a paradigm of the five poems, for the old woman's meditation, which spans the period of time in the poetic cycle, is analogous to the rest enjoyed by the salmon before he renews his journey against the stream. For precisely this brief duration we are allowed to enter the speaker's mind and witness her thoughts.

Within her consciousness, as might be expected, there are alternating currents of imagery and ideas. Her attention may shift rather abruptly from past to present, from the actual to the speculative, from knowledge to dream, as we would naturally imagine it to do readily in a person of advanced age who has a lifetime to think upon and its termination to face. Yet whatever these fluctuations of consciousness might be and however random they might seem at first glance, all of them contribute to a pattern of repeated affirmations of life which reach a peak of lyrical strength at the end of "What Can I Tell My Bones?"

In contrast to this pattern the poems also contain the elements of despair, evil, and nothingness: all that thwarts the steady forward movement of the spirit. One could, in a more comprehensive study of Roethke's poetry, draw up two lists, of his positive and negative imagery, and not simply for the poems under discussion but for his work in general. We have already noticed some of the recurring metaphors and symbols in passing. Most of them will be familiar to the reader who has watched the texts with care. On the positive side we find spring and summer; the sun and moon; small creatures of the bird, insect, and fish variety; wind and flowing water; flowers, plants, and grass. On the negative side would appear winter; aridity; still and muddy waters; holes, pits, or caves; dust; desolate landscapes. The old lady in her reflections also must countenance the memory of negative experience, if only to defeat it. In the following lines we can see how she conceives the life-denying by bringing it together in her mind with the life-giving and the sacramental:

> I have gone into the waste lonely places
> Behind the eye; the lost acres at the edge of
>   smoky cities.
> What's beyond never crumbles like an embankment,
> Explodes like a rose, or thrusts wings over the
>   Caribbean.
> There are no pursuing forms, faces on walls:
> Only the motes of dust in the immaculate hallways,
> The darkness of falling hair, the warnings from
>   lint and spiders,
> The vines graying to a fine powder.
> There is no riven tree, or lamb dropped by an eagle.

Like D. H. Lawrence, with whom the critic Kenneth Burke once very interestingly compared him, Roethke locates a substantial moral vocabulary in the natural order. Perhaps these uses are not intentional in every case of such imagery, but certainly his images very often serve a purpose of the kind I have named.

The moments of ecstasy in these poems, as elsewhere in Roethke's previous work, tend to occur through the life of nature or within its boundaries. "I'm Here," the second of the "Meditations," is largely devoted to memories of the old woman's girlhood years: from them arise scenes of an innocence, an awakening of flesh and spirit in concord with the surrounding world:

> I was queen of the vale —
> For a short while,
> Living all my heart's summer alone,
> Ward of my spirit,
> Running through high grasses,
> My thighs brushing against flower-crowns;
> Leaning, out of all breath,
> Bracing my back against a sapling,
> Making it quiver with my body . . .

And again:

> The body, delighting in thresholds,
> Rocks in and out of itself.
> A bird, small as a leaf,
> Sings in the first
> Sunlight.

The closing poem compels the speaker once more to encounter the forbidding prospect of a slow crumbling away to death; yet it is at last her love for all things, especially the commonplace or simple things of which our everyday world is made, that urges her back from somber meditation to the flow of existence. The tired, aging lady with whom the cycle of poems began emerges from shelter as if life had just been given her by an "agency outside . . . Unprayed-for, / And final." But Roethke is not explicit about this agency as yet. Later poems such as "In a Dark Time" recount the poet's experience of God in trancelike visions. The emphasis in the "Meditations" falls upon earthly possibility, the self's embrace of the entire horizon of existence open to it:

> The sun! The sun! And all we can become!
> And the time ripe for running to the moon!
> In the long fields, I leave my father's eye;
> And shake the secrets from my deepest bones;
> My spirit rises with the rising wind;
> I'm thick with leaves and tender as a dove,
> I take the liberties a short life permits —

I seek my own meekness;
I recover my tenderness by long looking.
By midnight I love everything alive.
Who took the darkness from the air?
I'm wet with another life.
Yea, I have gone and stayed.

Though cut tragically short by his premature death, Roethke's career is brought to a magnificent conclusion in the poems of *The Far Field* (1964). Here we find an extension of his amazing, always increasing versatility in formal arrangement and experiment, his ability to explore several avenues of poetic endeavor simultaneously without sacrificing the value of one to the interests of another. In these poems various thematic preoccupations — the identity of the self, its relation to the beloved, to nature, and to God — also achieve rewarding fulfillment.

The book is organized in four sections. The first and last, "North American Sequence" and "Sequence, Sometimes Metaphysical," though contrasting in manner, are concerned with a search for the Divine and with spiritual illumination while still expressing a recurrent sense of oneness with nature. In between there is a sizable group of love poems and a section of miscellaneous pieces aptly called "Mixed Sequence." The love poems, written for his wife Beatrice, even include, with humor and understanding, the moments of their discord; but these are far outnumbered by celebrations of the ecstasy and joy of their relationship. At the close of the section we discover the incredibly moving and prophetic "Wish for a Young Wife":

My lizard, my lively writher,
May your limbs never wither,
May the eyes in your face
Survive the green ice
Of envy's mean gaze;
May you live out your life
Without hate, without grief,
And your hair ever blaze,
In the sun, in the sun,
When I am undone,
When I am no one.

Of this kind of short lyric Roethke is a master, as we have seen in his work from the beginning. Over the years he tested its possibilities as thought and experience deepened, and in "Sequence, Sometimes Metaphysical" he brings this taut, economical formalism to a peak of accomplishment in the treatment of difficult material. The twelve-poem sequence starts with "In a Dark Time," which is a statement of harrowing mystical union, and continues with poems reflecting on this encounter, as well as with other instances and types of spiritual revelation. While these experiences are in one sense extremely personal, Roethke uses repeated images and metaphors, frequently drawn from the natural world, to objectify his inner life. Many of the poems appeared singly in journals and made impressive reading by themselves; but taken altogether they compose a cycle of visionary lyrics which must surely count among the finest in our literature. Let me quote, as one example, the first stanza of "The Tree, the Bird":

> Uprose, uprose, the stony fields uprose,
> And every snail dipped toward me its pure horn.
> The sweet light met me as I walked toward
> A small voice calling from a drifting cloud.
> I was a finger pointing at the moon,
> At ease with joy, a self-enchanted man.
> Yet when I sighed, I stood outside my life,
> A leaf unaltered by the midnight scene,
> Part of a tree still dark, still, deathly still,
> Riding the air, a willow with its kind,
> Bearing its life and more, a double sound,
> Kin to the wind, and the bleak whistling rain.

And as yet a further indication of Roethke's power and clairvoyance in these poems, here is a brief passage from "Infirmity":

> Things without hands take hands: there
>   is no choice,
> Eternity's not easily come by.
> When opposites come suddenly in place,
> I teach my eyes to hear, my ears to see

How body from spirit slowly does unwind
Until we are pure spirit at the end.

The poems of "North American Sequence" stand in marked
formal contrast to such lyrics and pursue the direction of the
reflective monologue developed in "Meditations of an Old
Woman." Now, however, Roethke dispenses with the dramatic
mask to speak in his own person and record the movements of
his spiritual consciousness in his quest for final unity. Roethke
noted in his essay "Some Remarks on Rhythm" the need for the
catalogue poem, for the careful and prolonged descriptive pas-
sage; and in these pieces with their lengthy, irregular lines, de-
liberately placed in the tradition of Whitman and Lawrence, he
has answered his own requirements. Disclosing the progressions
and setbacks of his inward states — that fundamental psychic
structure or movement integral to his writing — the desire to
escape from the self and its attachments, the sequence also
renders in loving detail the life of nature, the world of creatures,
trees and plants, rivers and stones, in profound correspondence
with the poet's inner being. It is difficult to quote from this
sequence without taking long sections, so I must make do here
with a few lines from "Meditation at Oyster River" as illustra-
tion:

The self persists like a dying star,
In sleep, afraid. Death's face rises afresh,
Among the shy beasts, the deer at the salt-lick,
The doe with its sloped shoulders loping across the
    highway,
The young snake, poised in green leaves, waiting for its fly,
The hummingbird, whirring from quince-blossom to
    morning-glory —
With these I would be.

Roethke once remarked to me, a year before his death, that
this might well be his last book, a judgment I found both de-
pressing and hard to believe. It was painfully accurate though,
and these late poems, preoccupied with death and the ultimate
phases of spiritual quest, complete his life's work as if by intuition.
Few contemporary poets can match the daring, the richness, and

the freedom — which is really to say, in summary, the beauty — of the body of his poetry. Certainly the intensity and clarity of Roethke's vision, in addition to his tremendous lyrical force and technical facility, place him, as John Crowe Ransom has said, in the company of the finest modern American poets. His art shows this poet's will to extend himself, to try his skill and imagination at every turn, and his growth was organic and true. The metamorphoses or transformations through which he and his poems passed are caught by the old lady's words near the conclusion of "What Can I Tell My Bones?" What they reveal of that speaker, her aspirations and strength, they also disclose about Roethke and the magnitude of his poetic achievement:

> The wind rocks with my wish; the rain shields me;
> I live in light's extreme; I stretch in all directions;
> Sometimes I think I'm several.

Randall Jarrell

Although Randall Jarrell wrote a very witty novel and a good deal of lively criticism as well, his most enduring interest as a writer lies in his poems. Between the appearance of an early group in the New Directions anthology *Five Young American Poets* in 1940 and his death at fifty-one in 1965, he prepared seven books of verse. Their usually melancholy titles suggest the desolation with which he constantly contended and which seems to have won out in the breakdown he finally suffered.

To review very briefly the curve of this psychological struggle as it manifests itself in the succeeding volumes: The first book, *Blood for a Stranger* (1942), reveals amid its many echoes of Auden and others certain underlying motifs of loss and confused focus. The next volumes, *Little Friend, Little Friend* (1945) and *Losses* (1948), take their main strength from a number of elegiac war poems. In these poems Jarrell was often able, because of their concreteness and directness, to objectify the motifs that had knotted up so much of his previous work. Also, he learned a good deal about immediacy from such poets of World War I as Siegfried Sassoon and Wilfred Owen. A period of broadening perspectives followed, marked by the appearance in

1951 of *The Seven-League Crutches*, in 1954 of the novel *Pictures from an Institution*, and in 1955 of *Selected Poems*. This last-named volume, containing only two new pieces, was the result of careful reconsideration and, often, revision of past work.

It was not until 1960, actually, that Jarrell published his first book of new poems since *The Seven-League Crutches*. But in the decade and a half after the war he had had a varied experience. He had been literary editor of the *Nation*, poetry consultant at the Library of Congress, visiting lecturer in American colleges and abroad, and, with occasional interruptions, a professor in the Woman's College of the University of North Carolina. He had established himself as one of a small, elite group of poets, protégés originally of Allen Tate and John Crowe Ransom. But Jarrell's outward successes did not anesthetize him against his painful need to gain inward clarification, which finally led him to write the autobiographical poems of *The Woman at the Washington Zoo* (1960) and *The Lost World* (1965).

In a sense, Jarrell tried to make a European of himself, to change over from a bright young American southerner to a sort of German-Austrian-Jewish refugee of the spirit. His interest in Rilke, in the German *Märchen*, and in the neglected European heritage of Americans seems in part an effort to repossess for himself a nourishment denied him in his childhood. Yet this effort, by a process analogous with that described in Keats's "Nightingale" ode, eventually "tolled him back to his sole self."

The word *fey*, meaning both *intensely excited or gay* and *doomed*, is perhaps too grim for Jarrell's poetic personality. Yet it is useful when we think of that side of him which is at once high-spiritedly brilliant and superciliously overinsistent, engaging yet irritating, and which assorts so ill with his capacity for gentleness and for an almost sentimental love of the quieter and more pedestrian virtues — and with the absorption of his imagination by bleakness and horror. The impact on others of this complex of qualities comes through strikingly in the collection of affectionate essays and reminiscences, *Randall Jarrell, 1914–1965*, that appeared in 1967 as a memorial volume. An unusually valuable piece in this excellent collection is "A Group of Two," written by his widow. It is a lovingly drawn portrait of a baffling man: his varied enthusiasms, his childlike ebullience and depressions, his sparkling if somewhat shrill spirit. Mrs. Jarrell is straightforward but protective. She never spells out the nature of his psychic disturbance or the exact circumstances of his death while walking on a highway. She does nevertheless suggest that he carried about with him throughout his life the burden of childhood insecurity, both psychological and financial. His parents were divorced, and for a while he lived happily with his paternal grandparents and great-grandmother, working-class people, in Hollywood, California, before his reluctant return to his mother in Nashville, Tennessee. The gifted, volatile child never "grew up" entirely. The intensity, the traumatic moments, and the accumulated guilt and resentment behind these experiences were never resolved.

He recurs to the Hollywood period a number of times in his poetry, most notably in the title sequence of *The Lost World*. The confusion and displacement of that period are crucial, though many of their implications are suppressed. "Mama" and "Pop" in Jarrell's poems are the *grandparents*, while his mother is "Anna." The sense of universal sadness, betrayed vulnerability, and emptiness at the center of the self in Jarrell's work is rooted in these childhood events and relationships, and doubtless helps account for his strong attraction to European literature of tragic consciousness.

In his poems there is at times a false current of sentimental condescension toward his subjects, especially when they are female. But more often another current carries us toward a realization of the ineradicable innocence and pity of the common life in all its alienating reality. This current did not really show itself, as a directive element in Jarrell's art, until the war poems of his second volume. In the first, *Blood for a Stranger*, some of his major themes were visible but neither voice nor tone was yet quite his own. One hears a sort of Auden-static everywhere, with other voices cutting in every so often. In the most

accomplished poem of the book, "The Skaters," the voice seems
a duet of Hart Crane and Edwin Muir:

> I stood among my sheep
> As silent as my staff;
> Up the sea's massy floor
> I saw the skaters pass.
>
> Long like the wind, as light
> I flowed upon their track
> Until at evening's edge
> I marked their breathless flocks.
>
> I sped among them then
> Like light along its lands —
> Love wreathed their lips, and speed
> Stiffened their tissue limbs. . . .

Half vision, half nightmare, the poem closes in on a note of
lost personal focus. The speaker discerns in the stars the image
of "one obsessing face," with which he comes into a precarious
sympathy or relationship while caught up in the swirling skaters'
movement that controls the curve of the poem. But finally,
abandoned and abandoning, he is whirled into "the abyss":

> But the iron's dazzling ring, the roar
> Of the starred ice black below
> Whirl our dazed and headlong strides
> Through the whirling night into
>
> The abyss where my dead limbs forget
> The cold mouth's dumb assent;
> The skaters like swallows flicker
> Around us in the long descent.

These motifs of coldness and distance, and of a fantasy realm
that is only a heightening of desolate reality, persist throughout
Jarrell's career. It is hard not to see "The Skaters" as a suicidal
projection of the symbolic search for the irretrievably lost
mother:

> The million faces flecked
> Upon my flickering gaze

> Bent to me in the stars
> Of one obsessing face . . .

A hopeless distance, a bewildering cosmos. Another poem in the volume, "The Bad Music," is addressed to "Anna" and uses the same pattern of symbolic imagery as "The Skaters" without reaching the glitteringly impersonal final set of that poem. Here the speaker sits by a window watching students as they return home from caroling. They carry candles that "wink out and on and out, like mixed-up stars," and

> I sit here like a mixed-up star:
> Where can I shine? What use is it to shine?
> I say; and see, all the miles north inside my head,
> You looking down across the city, puzzling.
> . . . .
> High over the millions who breathe and wait and sparkle . . .

"The Bad Music" makes almost embarrassingly explicit the buried reference, which is not the literal meaning, of "The Skaters." In its first stanza, the speaker blurts out his accusation of abandonment to Anna:

> The breast opening for me, the breaths gasped
> From the mouth pressed helplessly against my wrist
> Were lies you too believed; but what you wanted
> And possessed was, really, nothing but yourself:
> A joy private as a grave, the song of death. . . .

Poetically, what is interesting in the relation of the two poems is the similarity of their *process*. Each starts in a state of passive melancholy and moves into active despair. Under surface differences of tone and theme, they share a configuration of feeling and imagery. The "mixed-up star" symbolism in both poems projects the speaker's relation to the elusive object of his love. Faces appear as part of a subjective constellation in which confusion reigns, and it is all but impossible to sort out lover from beloved (son from mother) or either one from the shifting mass of other people or, indeed, from the whole objective universe. The pattern of movement is characteristic of Jarrell: a static initial state of sadness; then a phase of confusion that lets deeper depression flood into the poem; and then a final bitter thrust. We see it working in the famous five-line war poem "The Death of the Ball Turret Gunner":

> From my mother's sleep I fell into the State,
> And I hunched in its belly till my wet fur froze.
> Six miles from earth, loosed from its dream of life,
> I woke to black flak and the nightmare fighters.
> When I died they washed me out of the turret with a hose.

This poem is "impersonal." The speaker is not the poet himself but a dramatic character, a soldier who has been killed in the war. Yet the ironic womb imagery recalls the earlier mother theme, as of course the word *mother* itself does. We begin with the abstract yet unhappy assertion in the first line, an assertion that the young man received into the military world from the dreaming family world of childhood has hardly had time to emerge from fetal unconsciousness before he is in a new womb, that of war. Attention shifts in the next line to the chill, metallic character of that new womb. Suddenly then, the next two lines transport us to the gunner's moment of "waking" into nightmarish vision, at the moment his plane is hit by flak in the sky. The image is fetal; a note by Jarrell in *Selected Poems* stresses the fact that, "hunched upside-down in his little sphere," the gunner "looked like the foetus in the womb." The scene itself here is close to the confused cosmos of the two poems already discussed. Life is seen as only a "dream," whereas death is the reality into which the protagonist is born. In the harshly distorted womb images of this poem, we have once again the motif of love betrayed.

What Jarrell forces on our imaginations through his grotesque symbolism is the obscenity of war, its total subversion of human values. In highly compressed form, he has summoned up his subconscious preoccupations and the dynamics of poetic association they generate to make a poem that gets outside his own skin. The conversion process was not simple, though the result is emphatically clear in its narrative movement and in its succession of tones and intensities. Instead of the anapests that launch the first two lines, a suddenly lurching hovering-accent gets the third line off to a wobbling start that helps shake the poem open to let in wider ranges of felt meaning. (Effects of confusion and ambiguity, in rhythmic shifts as in the literal suggestions of language, often have this function in poems.) The brutal nastiness of the closing line refocuses the poem sharply, yet the final effect is not abrupt. The line is hexameter, longer by a foot than any of the preceding lines. It has the impact of a final "proof" of war's nature as a mockery of all that is life-giving.

It is easy to see how such a poem was prefigured in *Blood for a Stranger*. If we think of that book as comprising a definite unit of sensibility, we shall perceive it as, in large part, a complaint against loss of the world of childhood. (Jarrell specialized in psychology as an undergraduate at Vanderbilt University and was, in his omnivorous way, a reader of Freud; he is very likely to have "psychoanalyzed" himself to some degree at least.) The unresolved discontents of childhood are certainly present, but the real complaint is against separation, against initiation into adulthood, against the loss of an insufficiently discovered and savored life of innocence. "What we leave," mourns the opening poem ("On the Railway Platform"), "we leave forever." Another poem, "90 North," makes explicit the contrast between the secure childhood where

> At home, in my flannel gown, like a bear to its floe,
> I clambered to bed

and the present, "meaningless" moment where

> all lines, all winds
> End in this whirlpool I at last discover.

True enough, a bear climbing onto its floe is not the most secure of beasts; but the nightmares of childhood, in Jarrell's poem, do end in "rest" and a "warm world" of dependable certainties where "I reached my North and it had meaning." Of the poems in *Blood for a Stranger* specifically about childhood and separation, the most poignant is "A Story," a monologue by a boy sent away to school. It has none of the portentous phrasing that mars "90 North" and other poems of this volume. Its thoughts are always appropriate to the speaker. "I liked home better, I don't like these boys" is more to the point than the generalizations in "90 North" about "wisdom" and "pain."

Not to linger overlong with this first book, it has other, though related, points of interest besides this central one of the child soul's vulnerability. In "Children Selecting Books in a Library," for instance, Jarrell meditates charmingly, if slightly pedantically, on the value of reading fairy tales. Another piece, "The Cow Wandering in the Bare Field," has been praised by Allen Tate, who remembers seeing it when Jarrell, then a freshman at Vanderbilt, was seventeen. Its beginning at least is slightly reminiscent of Hart Crane's "Black Tambourine," the details at once starkly literal and accusatory:

> The cow wandering in the bare field,
> Her chain dangling, aimless, —
> The Negro sitting in the ashes,
> Staring, humming to the cat. . . .

Jarrell rarely again tried this kind of distanced yet incisive presentation. Indeed, he loses track of it later on in this very poem; he was after a faint modulation toward a theme of social protest, perhaps, and he did think of himself as a "radical" in his youth. But that side of him is seen in poems strongly indebted to Auden and Spender, with such titles as "The Machine-Gun," "The Refugees," "A Poem for Someone Killed in Spain," and "For an Emigrant." Part I of the last-named poem, with its final stanza greatly altered, was salvaged for the *Selected Poems* and retitled there as "To the New World." It was interesting as showing special sympathy for the victims of the Nazis and for its insight into the life of exiles:

> Free — to be homeless, to be friendless, to be nameless,
> To stammer the hard words in the foreign night. . . .

"For an Emigrant" shows, also, Jarrell's early realization that, ultimately, the refugee condition is universal; the balm of America is only a salve:

> You escaped from nothing; the westering soul
> Finds Europe waiting for it over every sea. . . .

"For an Emigrant," despite its political clichés and its ser-
monizing, meant something for Jarrell's future development.
Much of it has to do with the effect of anti-Semitism and fascism
on a *child's* life in Europe, and it attempts to assimilate the politi-
cal lessons of the thirties in such a way as to bring the poet's
childhood-obsession into a wider, more adult context of aware-
ness. The poem anticipates, as well, Jarrell's later tendency to
assume a European consciousness and graft it onto his American
personality — a tendency for which Pound and Eliot had doubt-
less provided models. Jarrell, however, differed from them by
playing the role of an exile in his own land, if far more modestly
than they and with a lesser genius though a real, and kindred,
sense of cultural mission.

Jarrell served in the Army Air Force between 1942 and 1946.
"In the first months of the War," Robert Lowell writes in an
"appreciation" appended to the 1966 paperback edition of *The
Lost World*, "Jarrell became a pilot. He was rather old for a be-
ginner, and soon 'washed out,' and spent the remaining war
years as an aviation instructor. Even earlier, he had an expert's
knowledge. . . . Nine-tenths of his war poems are air force
poems, and are about planes and their personnel, the flyers,
crews, and mechanics who attended them. No other imaginative
writer had his precise knowledge of aviation, or knew so well
how to draw inspiration from this knowledge." His mind was
similar to Hardy's and to Owen's in its fusion of informed objec-
tivity with a compassion as close to sentimentality as intelligence
and taste would allow. Of course, the world of which he wrote
was very far from Hardy's, and he lacked Owen's combat ex-
perience. But in his war poetry he was like Hardy in bringing to
bear on it his whole, extraordinarily literate intelligence — an
intelligence of the kind that feels imaginative literature as the
distillation of considered experience, the usable treasure of a
contemplative mind. And he was like Owen in the way the pres-

sure of his empathy with the pilots he knew made him envision their war experience in a vivid, accurate manner unmatched by most of his writing having to do with civilian life. The poetry of their condition lay for him, as for Owen, "in the Pity." For both poets this is a sort of passionately apprehended disproportion between the young soldiers' ultimate innocence and the terror they both suffer and inflict. It is realized not in sentiment but in action.

Jarrell's war poems are found mainly in his *Little Friend, Little Friend* and *Losses* volumes, which came directly out of the war years, and there are a few more in *The Seven-League Crutches*. His vision of the soldier as betrayed child is clearly epitomized in "The Death of the Ball Turret Gunner," a poem strategically placed at the end of *Little Friend, Little Friend*. As with most American and British poets of the second world war, the ultimate implied attitude is an ambiguous, or at any rate a tentative, one. The shock, horror, and questioning that mark the poetry of the first world war were the discovery of a generation, a discovery crystallized on the run, in the midst of death — the discovery that war *was* the trenches, the barbed wire, the humanly pointless slaughter while, in Owen's words, "God seems not to care." Jarrell and his contemporaries had been teethed on that earlier work; for them it was the definition of war experience. All later war poetry is in an important sense informed by the World War I "tradition." However, there are at least two significant differences for Jarrell's generation. First, they felt a far greater initial detachment from official rhetoric and from the assumptions of the social system. And second, though there was a good deal of old-fashioned combat in the later war, the over-all organization and the far greater importance of the air forces and long-range technology and communication made the involvement of most soldier-poets far less immediate than before.

These differences may be overstressed, but I am trying to suggest that the poetry of Jarrell's generation feels the impact of war with a double awareness. It is still in touch with the original shock of World War I, but is further away from the almost tribal sense of participation in a ritual gone wrong. Herbert Read's

poem "To a Conscript of 1940" is a bridge between the two
positions in time. The ghost of a soldier of 1914–18 speaks to the
poet, a survivor who now faces the new war situation:

We think we gave in vain. The world was not renewed.
There was hope in the homestead and anger in the streets
But the old world was restored and we returned
To the dreary field and workshop, and the immemorial feud

Of rich and poor. Our victory was our defeat.
Power was retained where power had been misused
And youth was left to sweep away
The ashes that the fire had strewn beneath our feet.

But one thing we learned: there is no glory in the deed
Until the soldier wears a badge of tarnish'd braid;
There are heroes who have heard the rally and have seen
The glitter of a garland round their head.

Theirs is the hollow victory. They are deceived.
But you, my brother and my ghost, if you can go
Knowing that there is no reward, no certain use
In all your sacrifice, then honour is reprieved.

To fight without hope is to fight with grace,
The self reconstructed, the false heart repaired. . . .

   Basically, this is the position — acceptance of the war (presum-
ably because of the policies and aggression of the Nazi govern-
ment) but without any chivalric or apocalyptic illusions. The his-
tory of the between-wars governments was too well known; cer-
tain Marxian and pacifist conceptions, admittedly contradictory,
had irrevocably entered Western sensibility; and the fact that
military victory would not solve the great social problems of the
age was widely understood. Jarrell's way of encompassing all this
was, on the whole, to adopt an existential approach. Here were
men — *child*-men, really — in circumstances beyond their con-
trol or even their comprehension. It was not existential*ist* —
neither a revolutionary perspective, nor a challenge to men to be
as fully and heroically human as possible in the circumstances of
limited choice open to them, is implied. Jarrell's emphasis is on
the saving innocence of those whom these circumstances have

after all made, as he says in "Eighth Air Force" (*Losses*), "murderers." That is a bitter word, yet Jarrell uses it a bit lightly and ironically. Because the young American airmen also run the risk of death, as he himself does not, he compares them with Christ. The comparison has some validity. Whitman, in "A Sight in Camp in the Daybreak Gray and Dim," had used it for the soldier as *victim*; and even when the soldier is constrained to kill he is in some sense still a victim. Pressed too hard, though, the argument is obviously forced and sentimental. Could one have put the case otherwise about young German soldiers in the same situation? Hardly. And if not, must not one say also that the most hardened killer is ultimately an innocent victim, a Christ crucified on the cross of his particular fate? But Jarrell did not follow the logic through:

> The other murderers troop in yawning;
> Three of them play Pitch, one sleeps, and one
> Lies counting missions, lies there sweating
> Till even his heart beats: One; One; One.
> *O murderers!* . . . Still, this is how it's done:
>
> This is a war. . . . But since these play, before they die,
> Like puppies with their puppy; since, a man,
> I did as these have done, but did not die —
> I will content the people as I can
> And give up these to them: Behold the man!
>
> I have suffered, in a dream, because of him,
> Many things; for this last saviour, man,
> I have lied as I lie now. But what is lying?
> Men wash their hands, in blood, as best they can:
> I find no fault in this just man.

In these lines Jarrell makes explicit the prevailing social assumption about war: that men cannot be held responsible for what history compels them to do, especially when they are on the "just" side of the struggle. But he tries, too, to make a subtly paradoxical argument to get past the objections to this assumption, and his style turns to putty in the process because the thought is too contrived. The reality of the situation requires the most relentless intellectual toughness and unwillingness to be an apologist for war mentality. Otherwise, the paradoxical fact that one can, in a sense, be good and innocent while behaving murderously becomes merely another sophistical argument for further mass murder. Jarrell himself recognizes this problem by his play on the word *lie*, but self-irony does not always purge a speaker of the error he confesses by it. Indeed, Jarrell's note on this poem, given in his introduction to *Selected Poems*, has no self-irony at all: "'Eighth Air Force' is a poem about the air force which bombed the Continent from England. The man who lies counting missions has one to go before being sent home. The phrases from the Gospels compare such criminals and scapegoats as these with that earlier criminal and scapegoat about whom the Gospels were written."

The limitation in Jarrell's war poetry is not, however, political or intellectual. It is a matter of energy. He focuses on the literal data of war — their irreversible actuality, and the pity of the human predicament implicit in that actuality. The poems stop short of anger, of programs, of anything that would constitute a challenge to soldiers or to their commanders or to the statesmen who make policy. Letting the facts of war experience speak for themselves, Jarrell sank all his real poetic imagination into primary acts of empathy; ordinarily he resisted any obvious political rhetoric. In "Eighth Air Force" we have a rare instance of his swinging out of his usual orbit to deal with the moral issues of mass bombing. His failure to handle the problem poetically lay in inadequate resources of emotional complexity and intellectual power.

But within the narrower limits of its engagement, Jarrell's war poetry is often superb. In poems like "A Front," "A Pilot from the Carrier," "Pilots, Man Your Planes," and "The Dead Wingman" — the last of these a dream poem, but one that presents the essence of a familiar situation: a pilot searching for a sign of a shot-down wingman — the poet's entire effort is to project the sense of men and machines in action, from the viewpoint of a participant. In all the poems just named, Jarrell has a double aim. First, he wishes to get the technical and atmospheric details in coherent order (a bombing plane whose radio has gone bad, so that the pilot cannot be diverted from a closed landing field to another still open and therefore crashes; a plane that has been hit and is burning, from which the pilot parachutes; a carrier under attack from a Japanese torpedo plane; the situation of the airman hunting for a lost comrade). And second, he desires to make the perspective that of a living, suffering man. "A Pilot from the Carrier" and "A Front" are in the same volume, *Little Friend, Little Friend*, as "The Death of the Ball Turret Gunner." They carry a kindred birth-death motif, though less explicitly. The pilot in the plane from the carrier, "strapped at the center of his blazing wheel," tears himself loose from that womb of death and is reborn via parachute

> Into the sunlight of the upper sky —
> And falls, a quiet bundle in the sky,
> The miles to warmth, to air, to waking:
> To the great flowering of his life . . .

The pilot in "A Front" cannot be wrenched free in time, and perishes. In *Losses*, the men on the carrier in "Pilots, Man Your Planes" are sleeping "hunched in the punk of Death" until awakened into their own literal deaths unless they escape in time. The pilot in "The Dead Wingman" searches in his dream over that same amniotic sea into which so many figures of "Pilots, Man Your Planes" have disappeared, but he never finds the dreadful evidence of the birth into death that he seems to need for deep inward confirmation of his own reality:

> The plane circles stubbornly: the eyes distending
> With hatred and misery and longing, stare
> Over the blackening ocean for a corpse. . . .

I have not really meant to labor this womb referent, which appears and disappears, usually very fleetingly, in Jarrell's shifting float of associations. His creation of an ambience of confused details, a dream of total self-loss, before a final note of profound sadness is equally important in all the poems I have just mentioned. What gives them more authority than the poems of *Blood for a Stranger* is not only the precision within the confusion, but also the definiteness of the military setting within which the lost, childlike psyche of Jarrell's soldiers (with the poet's voice standing in for them, as it were) speaks its pain. Several times in the two "war" books the persons spoken for are women or children. The title of *Little Friend, Little Friend*, which evokes just the childlike psyche to which I have referred, is taken from a phrase used in the book's opening poem, "2nd Air Force." Here, as Jarrell's note tells us, a "woman visiting her son remembers what she has read on the front page of her newspaper the week before, a conversation between a bomber, in flames over Germany, and one of the fighters protecting it: 'Then I heard the bomber call me in: "Little Friend, Little Friend, I got two engines on fire. Can you see me, Little Friend?" I said, "I'm crossing right over you. Let's go home."'"

The woman of this poem might just as well have been the mother of the ball turret gunner in the closing poem. Her son — this is the whole burden of the poem — has indeed fallen from her womb into that of the state. The barren and dangerous world of the air base appears amid "buses and weariness and loss," with its "sand roads, tar-paper barracks," and "bubbling asphalt of the runways." A specific womb image dramatizes what has happened to her transplanted son: "The head withdraws into its hatch (a boy's)." This alien world — "The years meant *this*?" — is her and our bleak introduction to what the war means for the soldiers as Jarrell understands them. Between "2nd Air Force" and "The Death of the Ball Turret Gunner," then, the volume makes its journey through a wasteland of deadly machinery and pathetic soldiers who "pass like beasts, unquestioning," through their new life where "the bombers answer everything."

Both *Little Friend, Little Friend* and *Losses* contain many closeups and vignettes of soldiers: men being classified, a soldier whose leg has been amputated, prisoners, a soldier being visited in the hospital by his wife and baby, men being discharged from service, a field hospital. Politically and historically, the war may have been unavoidable, but for Jarrell this is more an existential than a moral reality. He does, of course, recognize the monstrousness of the Nazis in "A Camp in the Prussian Forest" (*Losses*) —

> Here men were drunk like water, burnt like wood.
> The fat of good
> And evil, the breast's star of hope
> Were rendered into soap.

Yet it is the pointlessness and cruelty of war that emerge as the poet's repeated insight. Each soldier, as the mother sees in "2nd Air Force," is "heavy with someone else's death" and a "cold carrier" of "someone else's victory." The poem "Losses," in the earlier book but clearly the source of the later one's title, utters a complaint on behalf of all the young *and* of their victims. Although its speaker does not explore the moral dilemma involved, he does raise an ultimate question:

> In bombers named for girls, we burned
> The cities we had learned about in school —
> Till our lives wore out; our bodies lay among
> The people we had killed and never seen.
> When we lasted long enough they gave us medals;
> When we died they said, "Our casualties were low."
> They said, "Here are the maps"; we burned the cities.
>
> It was not dying — no, not ever dying;
> But the night I died I dreamed that I was dead,
> And the cities said to me: "Why are you dying?
> We are satisfied, if you are; but why did I die?"

It is interesting that World War II produced no great poem at once absolutely ruthless in its fidelity to the realities of human experience in the war and encompassing in its understanding of all their complex contradictions: particularly, the crushing choice seemingly thrust on the most advanced spirits between pure pacifism and accepting the need to destroy the Nazi power. The rhetorical questions at the end of "Losses" — slightly confused because of the ambiguous use of the word "I" in the closing line — suggest the epic psychological exploration needed, but not furnished, to give body to their meaning. At a pragmatic and popular level the questions were certainly answerable by reference to recent history. The answers were both moral and practical, involving the fate of nations and of ethnic groups as well as of political and economic systems. The contradiction lay,

as Malraux perceived in an only slightly different context, the
Spanish Civil War, in the fact that the methods of war compel
imitation of the enemy and indeed outstripping him in his own
methods. It is indeed possible to present the voice of an innocent
and ignorant soldier asking "Why?" Yet even the boys Jarrell
wrote about had more of a sense, however inarticulately they
might express themselves, of "why" than he quite gives them
credit for. As for the poet himself, a number of the pieces show
the usual intellectual's grasp of the economic and historical as-
pects of modern war. Of the American poets who emerged im-
mediately after the war, only Robert Lowell was keyed to the
demands of the materials, but on the other hand he had neither
the literal experience nor the inclination to work on *the* war
poem. Perhaps Pound and Eliot, by their keen location of the
inner contradictions of Western culture, had rendered a large
effort of this sort redundant for later poets.

   That Jarrell wanted to suggest large historical and mythologi-
cal considerations is clear from "The Wide Prospect," which
comes just before "The Death of the Ball Turret Gunner" at the
end of *Little Friend, Little Friend*, and from the two poems that
close *Losses*: "In the Ward: The Sacred Wood" and "Orestes at
Tauris." The influence of Marx via Auden is obvious in the
opening stanza of "The Wide Prospect":

>Who could have figured, when the harness improved
>And men pumped kobolds from the coal's young seams
>There to the west, on Asia's unrewarding cape —
>The interest on that first raw capital?
>The hegemony only the corpses have escaped?

The poem ends, after a determinedly sustained exposition along
these lines, with an imagery of ritual sacrifice that links Marxian,
Freudian, and myth-and-ritual oriented motifs:

>the man-eaters die
>Under the cross of their long-eaten Kin.

>All die for all. And the planes rise from the years
>. . . . .

When men see men once more the food of Man
And their bare lives His last commodity.

The poems at the end of *Losses* are superior in being free of
the long, expository sections, with a forced liveliness of imagery
but without driving energy, of "The Wide Prospect." "Orestes at
Tauris," the closing poem, was according to Jarrell an early
composition written before any of the poems from *Blood for a
Stranger* included in the *Selected Poems*. Very different in charac-
ter from anything else in the war books, it shows Orestes arriv-
ing in Tauris after being pursued relentlessly by the Furies,
under compulsion "in expiation for his crime, to bring back to
Greece that image of Artemis to which the Tauri sacrificed the
strangers cast up on their shores" (Jarrell's note in *Losses*). This
long, partially surrealist narrative poem imagines the sacrificial
beheading of Orestes by his sister Iphigenia, now a priestess,
instead of their triumphant escape. Jarrell's recasting of the
myth, in a well-sustained unrhymed pattern of four- and
five-stress lines that focuses on the succession of impressions,
states of feeling, and sensations that Orestes experiences, makes
for an effect of terror amidst psychological confusion and bar-
baric splendors. The condition of Orestes and Iphigenia at the
end then becomes a perfect mythic embodiment of Jarrell's vi-
sion of war as the sacrifice of driven innocents for the sake of a
savage, mindless determinism inherent in our natures:

> The people, silent, watching with grave faces
> Their priestess, who stands there
> Holding out her hands, staring at her hands,
> With her brother's blood drenching her hands.

"In the Ward: The Sacred Wood," which precedes "Orestes at
Tauris," is perhaps Jarrell's most determined effort to give
mythic dimensions to his theme of the sacrificed innocent in war.
His own description of the poem, in his introduction to *Selected
Poems*, goes: "The wounded man has cut trees from paper, and
made for himself a sacred wood; with these, the bed-clothes, the
nurse, the doctor, he works his own way through the Garden of

Eden, the dove and its olive-leaf, the years in the wilderness, the burning bush, the wars of God and the rebel angels, the birth and death and resurrection of Christ." This account, and the style of the poem, somewhat recall the symbolic distortions of thought and syntax of Lowell's early poems —

> Is the nurse damned who looked on my nakedness?
> The sheets stretch like the wilderness
> Up which my fingers wander, the sick tribes,
> To a match's flare, a rain or bush of fire. . . .

But Jarrell's movement does not rip free into Lowell's frenzied piling up of associations and allusions. He does not achieve that state of passionate intensity of speech which makes the whole language an electric field of highly charged, crackling movements of realization. In this poem, however, he surpasses Lowell in one important respect. At each point along the way, as the wounded soldier ponders the symbolic analogies with Christ implicit in his condition, he nevertheless at the same time maintains a basic simplicity and a distance from the mental game he is playing. Unlike "Eighth Air Force," this poem does not press an identity between the dying soldier and Christ. The dominant tone is one of a real man, without hope, letting go though aware of a dream of divinity incarnate — a tone corresponding to the progress of negative heroism in Read's "To a Conscript of 1940." Negation is accepted quietly; this is one of Jarrell's most touching and thoughtful poems:

> And beneath the coverlet
> My limbs are swaddled in their sleep, and shade
> Flows from the cave beyond the olives, falls
> Into the garden where no messenger
> Comes to gesture, "Go" — to whisper, "He is gone."
>
> The trees rise to me from the world
> That made me, I call to the grove
> That stretches inch on inch without one God:
> "I have unmade you, now; but I must die."

Earlier, in discussing "The Death of the Ball Turret Gunner," I ventured a description of the characteristic structural dynamics of Jarrell's poems as involving a static initial state of sadness, then a phase of confusion that lets deeper depression flood into the poem, and then a final bitter thrust. Most lyric-contemplative poetry since the early Romantics has, in fact, a comparable structure. That is, an initial state of unease or depressed feeling is followed by the introduction of complicating matter for contemplation: any of a number of contexts of awareness that enlarge and, very likely, confuse the original perspective. The final "resolution" of the poem is a reorientation of the speaker's initial attitude in the light of the intervening complication. It may take the form of acceptance or reconciliation though at the same time what is being "affirmed" is defeat of a sort — what we might call "depressive transcendence." Needless to add that shifts of style, rhythm, intensity, and level of diction are as important as the literal statements.

Without forcing the point, we can say that Jarrell's whole poetic career follows a similar pattern of movement. After the early poems of childhood desolation, the speaking psyche confronts three bodies of material external to itself: war experience, the world of myth and folk legend (to which are added, often, the associations of music, painting, and literature), and individual human suffering. In the final phase of his career, the poet objectifies himself, in relation to his childhood life, as one of the sufferers over whom his attention has hovered with such empathy. That is, he has brought back his earliest preoccupations into the center of his work, but in a focus altered by the discipline through which he has passed and the knowledge he has accumulated. He has learned to isolate the pity of the irrecoverable and, therefore, of the irredeemable in existence and is free to present sharp, concrete memories and to play with them in a number of ways.

In *Losses*, we see the three bodies of "external" material (war, myth and legend, and suffering individual people) already present. War is of course the overwhelming major subject. But there are other myth-involved poems besides the two we have already examined, among them "The Märchen" and "The Child of Courts"; Jarrell's fascination with the German *Märchen*

(folktales, in this case those of the brothers Grimm) is at this
point related to the historical fatalism induced by his response to
the war. The dreams and terrors of primitive life foreshadowed
those of the modern age with its discovery of the limitations of
man's hopes and prospects:

> Listening, listening; it is never still.
> This is the forest: long ago the lives
> Edged armed into its tides (the axes were its stone
> Lashed with the skins of dwellers to its boughs);
> We felled our islands there, at last, with iron.
> The sunlight fell to them, according to our wish,
> And we believed, till nightfall, in that wish;
> And we believed, till nightfall, in our lives.

These are the opening, and on the whole the best, lines of
"The Märchen," a somewhat preciously proliferative poem
which nevertheless shows Jarrell's characteristic wit, ingenuity,
and sympathy with the common lot. He had learned, in his war
poems, how to write with economy, but there is no economy in
this poem of over a hundred lines of moderately roughened
blank verse. Jarrell luxuriates in the way the *Märchen* bring folk
motifs and folk wisdom, simple and often comic materials re-
lated to the life of peasants, together with the symbolic and
archetypal motifs of religious or mythical tradition: Christ and
the old gods, Hell, "the Scapegoat," "Paradise," and "the Cross,
the Ark, the Tree." The perspective he introduces has to do with
primitive man's desire, never fulfilled but never forgotten or
relinquished either, even in our time, to make reality conform to
his wish. Herein, for Jarrell, lies the inescapable pathos of the
human condition, of which the vulnerable innocence of children
is the most obvious embodiment. The *Märchen* show that it is not
so much our inability to make wishes come true as the paltriness
of the wishes themselves that is defeating. In Romantic tradition
generally, it is the disparity between desire and reality, between
subjective and objective "truths," with which the poet is obsessed
— ultimately, the pity that we cannot stamp our own images on
nature. In Jarrell there is a curious turn of emphasis: the inade-

quacy of imagination, driven as it is already by conditions im-
posed on it by nature, is the heart of the problem —

> Poor Hänsel, once too powerless
> To shelter your own children from the cold
> Or quiet their bellies with the thinnest gruel,
> It was not power that you lacked, but wishes.
> Had you not learned — have we not learned, from tales
> Neither of beasts nor kingdoms nor their Lord,
> But of our own hearts, the realm of death —
> Neither to rule nor die? to change, to change!

"The Child of Courts" (reprinted in *Selected Poems* as "The
Prince") presents the ambivalent night-terror of a child who
fears that the ghost of a buried man has come up out of the
grave toward him but who then is disappointed: "I start to weep
because — because there are no ghosts." The poem at first am-
biguously suggests a prison atmosphere. But the child calls out
"Mother?" — in an equally ambiguous context, however — and
thus there is a suggestion not so much of a prison as of a castle or
palace in which there is intrigue and insecurity. One thinks of
Young Prince Edward after Henry's death, a thought mildly
encouraged by the two titles. The situation of this brief and
simple poem suggests, at one and the same time, the well-known
situations of Edward and other English princes, the grisly cir-
cumstances of certain folk legends, and the excited imagination
of any sensitive child at certain times.

> After the door shuts, and the footsteps die,
> I call out, "Mother?" No one answers.
> I chafe my numb feet with my quaking hands
> And hunch beneath the covers, in my curled
> Red ball of darkness; but the floor creaks, someone stirs
> In the other darkness — and the hairs all rise
> Along my neck, I whisper: "It is he!"

Many years after *Losses*, in his 1965 volume *The Lost World*,
Jarrell published "A Hunt in the Black Forest," which begins
exactly as "The Child of Courts" does, except for a shift to the
third person that heralds a new, or at least a redirected, point of
view toward the same situation:

> After the door shuts and the footsteps die,
> He calls out: "Mother?"

The speaker now, however, is not the child but an omniscient
narrator. The circumstances, like the title, suggest the world of
the *Märchen*, projected in a Freudian nightmare fantasy. A king,
out hunting, comes to a hut in the forest where a deaf-mute
feeds him a stew that poisons him while a red dwarf watches
through the window. At the end of this poem, whose every stage
is brilliantly and dramatically clear and sinister, there is a blend-
ing of supernatural and psychologically pointed details that
brings us all the way over from the climax of the king's death to
the further, greater climax of the child sensibility underlying the
entire story.

> Then a bubbled, gobbling sound begins,
> The sound of the pot laughing on the fire.
> — The pot, overturned among the ashes,
> Is cold as death.
>
> Something is scratching, panting. A little voice
> Says, "Let *me*! Let *me*!" The mute
> Puts his arms around the dwarf and raises him.
>
> The pane is clouded with their soft slow breaths,
> The mute's arms tire; but they gaze on and on,
> Like children watching something wrong.
> Their blurred faces, caught up in one wish,
> Are blurred into one face: a child's set face.

The mute, the dwarf, and the child thus share horrified, guilty
fascination; they are three facets of innocence, despite their in-
volvement in a primal tragic scene. It would not be difficult to
"interpret" the story as one in which the child (into whose face
the other faces blend at the very end of the poem) is both the
victim — the stew that the king his father ate — and the killer
who destroys his father through the very act of being devoured
by him. If we put "The Child of Courts" and "A Hunt in the
Black Forest" side by side and consider each a gloss on the other,
it becomes clear that the addition of the third-person narrator
enabled Jarrell to fill out the symbolic context of the original

poem's conception. But he added to it the distanced understanding of an adult voice presenting the unresolved anguish of one kind of disturbed childhood. "A Hunt in the Black Forest" brings both its psychological and its archetypal motives directly to bear on the tale it has been telling by a final refocusing of elements present in the story from the start. It represents, as do the more literally autobiographical poems of the final volume, an achieved objectification of the speaking self and an achieved clarity as well. Thought is presented experientially, with sharply sketched action and description that leave room for shadows, depths, and implied complexities.

One poem in *Losses*, "Lady Bates," especially foreshadows Jarrell's turn, after the war period, to poems centered on suffering individual persons, often women. The Lady Bates of the title is, says Jarrell in his notes to *Selected Poems*, "a little Negro girl whose Christian name is *Lady*." The child has died, and the poem is addressed to her as an epitome of everything helpless and betrayed in human existence. Viewed unsympathetically, the poem is an example of sophisticated sentimentality, a humanitarian southerner's attempt to speak to his knowledge of the hurt done to Negroes in a language appropriate to both. "Lady Bates," significantly, comes first in *Losses*, the only poem quite of its kind in this book, preceding all the war pieces. A certain oversimplification of the meaning of ordinary people's lives, comparable to that we have seen in the war poems, comes through in "Lady Bates" despite its genuinely touching aspects. The worst of Jarrell is concentrated into parts of this poem that mercilessly expose both his condescension and the presumptuousness of his spokesmanship for the girl:

> Poor black trash,
> The wind has blown you away forever
> By mistake; and they sent the wind to the chain-gang
> And it worked in the governor's kitchen, a trusty for life;
> And it was all written in the Book of Life;
> Day and Night met in the twilight by your tomb
> And shot craps for you; and Day said, pointing to your soul,
> "This *bad* young colored lady,"
> And Night said, "Poor little nigger girl."

"Lady Bates," with its weaknesses, continues Jarrell's development toward the objectification of the speaking self that I have suggested is the chief triumph of *The Lost World*. Like the many soldiers who are his subjects in the war volumes, the little black girl in this poem serves two functions in this development. First and most obviously, she is one of the many figures in his poems whose reality he seeks to repossess as persons outside himself. Secondly, though, she and the other figures are the beneficiaries (or victims) of an empathy that enables him to project onto them certain basic features of the child psyche familiar in his earlier poems — its confusion, innocence, and betrayal by life. It would be accurate to say that each of these figures is at once himself or herself *and* Randall Jarrell; not, of course, Jarrell the wit, translator of Rilke, and edgily competitive poet, but the essential Jarrell whose sensibility defines itself in his poems in the way we have been tracing.

This essential sensibility enters many of the speaking voices in Jarrell's next volume, *The Seven-League Crutches*. In fact, reading through this volume, one is pierced by the realization of how completely possessed by it his writing is and what a chilling desolateness he coped with. It is not only the specific *child* minds he presents that make the realization so forcible, though indeed this volume gives us several such characterizations to add to "Lady Bates." The one closest to "Lady Bates" in tone is "The Truth," in which, Jarrell explains in *Selected Poems*, "the little boy who speaks . . . has had his father, his sister, and his dog killed in one of the early fire-raids on London, and has been taken to the country, to a sort of mental institution for children." This poem has none of the cultural overlay of "Lady Bates," the treacherous sense of "understanding" the black child's world that cuts across Jarrell's finer sense of her as one abandoned by life in her own idiosyncratic way. "The Truth" is stripped down to the essential anguish and bewilderment:

> When I was four my father went to Scotland.
> They *said* he went to Scotland.
>
> When I woke up I think I thought that I was dreaming —

I was so little then that I thought dreams
Are in the room with you, like the cinema.
That's why you don't dream when it's still light —
They pull the shades down when it is, so you can sleep.
I thought that then, but that's not right.
Really it's in your head.

And it was light then — light at *night*. . . .

And yet, as with the play of thought in "Lady Bates," one can
well ask of this poem whether the anguish and bewilderment are
really the little boy's or Jarrell's. All that charming talk about a
child's notion of what dreams are is really in Jarrell's grown-up
voice, reminiscing about his own memories. Naturally, these
thoughts about dreams being like the cinema might occur to any
child, and my only point is that Jarrell is using this kind of
situation, so close to his own constant preoccupation, as a suita-
ble instrument on which to play. He is a virtuoso of pity, and the
form his virtuosity takes is to work his own voice into his materi-
als so as to bring out their intrinsic pathos and his active insight
simultaneously.

In "The Black Swan," a poem about another child, this fusion
of sensibilities works superbly. The preface to *Selected Poems* tells
us that this poem was "said, long ago, by a girl whose sister is
buried under the white stones of the green churchyard." "The
Black Swan" and a number of other poems in *The Seven-League
Crutches* mark a considerable advance in the artistic isolation and
redirection of Jarrell's deepest motifs. The loneliness, the sense
of a chaotic universe, and the lost focus of identity (expressed as
a shared or confused identity) of his best later work are all pres-
ent at the very start of "The Black Swan":

When the swans turned my sister into a swan
  I would go to the lake, at night, from milking:
The sun would look out through the reeds like a swan,
  A swan's red beak; and the beak would open
And inside there was darkness, the stars and the moon. . . .

This beginning, a decisive act of empathic imagination, opens
up a world of associations to the end of recovering the stab of

primal pathos. The swan images proliferate, and the mad or nightmare-ridden speaker becomes a swan herself as, out of the realm of heartless nature and death, her sister responds to her call. This poem alone would make it clear that Jarrell's poetic control had grown enormously by 1951. He could now deal purely and forcefully with psychological and mythic or archetypal materials and could write his own thoughts directly without overintellectualizing and without superciliousness. "The Orient Express" opens *The Seven-League Crutches* on a note of unpretentious intimacy that combines his ever-present child-mindedness with his adult intelligence:

> One looks from the train
> Almost as one looked as a child. In the sunlight
> What I see still seems to me plain,
> I am safe; but at evening
> As the lands darken, a questioning
> Precariousness comes over everything. . . .

All of Jarrell is there, as simply apparent as possible. But the form itself has a new sort of interest when compared to much of Jarrell's earlier work. The ease and grace of movement, the sustained clarity of speech, and the engaging, concrete thoughtfulness keep the reader listening and moving along with the speaker. The lines of this passage, as in the poem as a whole, tend toward a three-stress unit but often — here in the two opening lines — depart from it. Rhyming effects (an exact rhyme in lines one and three, the echoing of *-ing* in lines four, five, and six, the repetitions of "look" and "one," and the sequence of the monosyllabic verbs "look" and "looked" and "see" and "seems" and "comes") are introduced lightly yet saturate the sound structure as in the even richer "The Black Swan." One finds a similar felicity and immediacy in the two poems that close the book, "The Venetian Blind" and "Seele im Raum" — poems which both recall, the former in its literal theme and the latter in its title, a poem of Rilke's. "The Venetian Blind" does indeed present its protagonist as a "Seele im Raum" or "soul in space."

He is lost in himself forever.

And the Angel he makes from the sunlight
Says in mocking tenderness:
"Poor stateless one, wert thou the world?" . . .

The bars of the sunlight fall to his face.

And yet something calls, as it has called:
"But where am *I*? But where am *I*?"

Rilke's "Seele im Raum," written in 1917, has as its literal subject the condition of a soul torn from its body and suddenly become pure potentiality in a realm of pure being. The soul feels stripped of comforts, exposed, and tremulously fearful in its ignorance of its own destiny. Jarrell's "Seele im Raum" has in part the same theme, but the central situation of his poem is that of a woman who once had the grotesque illusion that an eland was present wherever she was. The woman's pathetic obsession would be hilariously absurd were it not, as her monologue shows, symptomatic of her sense of being a lost self despite the fact that she was a wife and mother. Her period of madness is now over; but in an important way she misses the eland, which was so tangibly and oppressively present to her and yet was the only thing that was hers alone: her soul's embodiment of its own misery —

Today, in a German dictionary, I saw *elend*
And the heart in my breast turned over, it was —

It was a word one translates *wretched.*
. . . .

— It was worse than impossible, it was a joke.

And yet when it was, I *was* —
Even to think that I once thought
That I could see it is to feel the sweat
Like needles at my hair-roots, I am blind

— It was not even a joke, not even a joke.

Yet how can I believe it? Or believe that I
Owned it, a husband, children? Is my voice the voice
Of that skin of being — of what owns, is owned
In honor or dishonor, that is borne and bears —
Or of that raw thing, the being inside it

> That has neither a wife, a husband, nor a child
> But goes at last as naked from this world
> As it was born into it —
>
> And the eland comes and grazes on its grave. . . .

The passage I have just quoted takes us from the punning proof that the eland had been for the speaker a projection of her soul's *elend* condition, its misery, to the bitter sense she has now of all that she has lost and then, finally, to that sense of being stripped of a human past and utterly out in space of which Rilke writes. Jarrell's absorption in Rilke was one of his great passions; it must have been of tremendous importance to him in the progress of his art that I have described. He immersed himself in the greater poet, whose themes were so close to his own. The sensibilities of children and of women dominate the attention of both poets. Both are in search of points of directive contact with chaotic reality — both are "souls in space." Both, incidentally, had noncombatant military service involving a certain disillusionment, and there were temperamental affinities as well (as in their mixture of endearing traits with ruthless critical attitudes).

Rilke's essential influence on Jarrell seems to have been to encourage him to widen his poetic thought and to reach for a more concentrated and evocative imagery, a more personal and vital poetic speech and rhythmic movement, and a style both natural to him and in touch with European cultural tradition. It is interesting that *The Seven-League Crutches* begins with a section called "Europe" — poems with European settings to which Jarrell attaches his American awareness. The displacement of context enables him to convert old sets of thought into deepened historical and philosophical musings. Looking out from the Orient Express, he can see that the whole world (not just his own empirical life) is unassimilable to the soul in space and yet has its own aesthetic magnetism we cannot avoid:

> It is like any other work of art.
> It is and never can be changed.
> Behind everything there is always
> The unknown unwanted life.

One could conceivably make the same observation looking from an American train, but just that kind of consideration is involved in the implied comparison. It is just the sensed history behind the fields, people, houses, and villages that makes the feeling of an essential changelessness of existence such a powerful one. In "A Game at Salzburg," the same principle is at work. Jarrell's explanation in *Selected Poems* shows how much he relishes the knowledgeableness behind the poem, the kind of Europeanized wit its subject enables him to cultivate: "I put into 'A Game at Salzburg' a little game that Germans and Austrians play with very young children. The child says to the grown-up, *Here I am*, and the grown-up answers, *There you are*; the children use the same little rising tune, and the grown-ups the same resolving, conclusive one. It seemed to me that if there could be a conversation between the world and God, this would be it." And so, in the poem, the whole style is delightfully relaxed until the very end. The poet (during the year in which he was a participant in the Salzburg Seminar in American Civilization) is seen passing lazy, happy days amid the innumerable tokens not only of an old civilization but also of the recent war. One notices with some surprise and interest that his juxtapositions of a modern American intelligence like his own with all these surrounding signs and symbols, under circumstances at once so congenial and so poignantly and volatilely suggestive, have led him into a tone and rhythm that must have influenced Robert Lowell's style in *Life Studies*:

> A little ragged girl, our ball-boy;
> A partner — ex-Afrika-Korps —
> In khaki shorts, P. W. illegible.
> (He said: "To have been a prisoner of war
> In Colorado iss a *privilege*.")
> The evergreens, concessions, carrousels,
> And D. P. camp of Franz Joseph Park;
> A gray-green river, evergreen-dark hills.
> Last, a long way off in the sky,
> Snow-mountains.

These are the social and political and historical realities, all within the unchanged ancient landscape. When, later on, the poet finds himself playing the little game of *Hier bin i'* — *Da bist du*, with a three-year-old, there is an inevitably ironic echo from that opening scene. Reality is intractably itself, and the fact is softly underlined in the persistence of a language and a ritual even in a tiny girl "licking sherbet from a wooden spoon" as she engages the poet in the game. Later still, he moves "past Maria Theresa's sleigh" and the statues, mostly broken, in the garden where "the nymphs look down with the faces of Negroes." The two worlds suddenly related in this image are one world after all, as is the prewar world that became the one at war and then the postwar one. At the end, Jarrell's old, persistent insight is thrust into the foreground, but the voice adopted is a European one recalling the "dreamy" American to the imponderable:

> In anguish, in expectant acceptance
> The world whispers: *Hier bin i'*.

We cannot pursue all the examples of Jarrell's "Europeaniza-tion" in *The Seven-League Crutches*. One further instance is the translation of Corbière's "Le Poète Contumace." Corbière's tough-mindedness and scathing but funny self-characterizations show up the sentimental limits of Jarrell's own work. Neverthe-less, Jarrell admired Corbière and aspired to his kind of mental-ity.

Jarrell's one novel, *Pictures from an Institution*, bears extended analysis because so much that was important to him is packed into it, and also because it is an extremely clever work of satire as well as a humanely intelligent book. It is set in a progressive women's college not altogether unlike Sarah Lawrence College, and its pictures of the academic and personal life of all con-cerned remain extremely amusing. I shall discuss it only very briefly, in relation to Jarrell's poetic development. It represents, I think, a completion of his attempt to assimilate his own frame of thought to that of cultivated and sensitive Europeans. The novel is written in the first person, from the viewpoint of a poet who has been teaching at Benton College for a number of years. The real hero, though, is an Austrian-Jewish composer named

Gottfried Rosenbaum through whose eyes the provincialism, complacency, and emptiness of much of American education are made, somewhat lovingly, clear, while certain genuine American strengths and potentialities are seen as goods after all. Dr. Rosenbaum's mind is razor-keen, though he does not ordinarily use it to slash people. That role is taken by a visiting novelist, Gertrude Johnson, whose analytical savagery has no kindness in it and who is often malignantly inventive in her sizing up of people, all grist for her novels. She is going to do a novel about the college, and it will be merciless — presumably far more so than *Pictures from an Institution* itself. Yet this necessary comparison gives one to think. Gertrude, as it were, discharges the hostile and supercilious side of Jarrell's critical intelligence, while Gottfried represents a more genial ideal. John Crowe Ransom, in his contribution to *Randall Jarrell, 1914–1965*, notes the indications that Gertrude undergoes something like a "conversion" to a more humane attitude in the course of the novel, and I would suggest that the improvement of Gertrude is something in the nature of a purgation for Jarrell himself. The "I" of the novel, the poet who is ready to leave the limited campus scene at the end of the year, has been close to both Gertrude and Gottfried. Gottfried, with his elderly Russian wife who shares his cultivation and his sense of tragic history, will remain after the writers have left. With them will stay the talented and loyal Constance Morgan, who in her life embodies the best of American openness and possibility as Gottfried and Irene embody the living tradition of European art with which we must remain in vital touch. Constance, an orphan, is thus one of four figures who represent ideals or characteristics of Jarrell himself. The book reaches a certain serenity and insight into the best qualities of each of the characters, despite the fun at the expense of most of them along the way.

What an injustice I have done to this novel, with its marvelously amusing passages that Jarrell wrote in an ecstasy of acerbic release. It is his most balanced work, done not long after his marriage to Mary von Schrader in 1952, and it helped him gain a precarious personal balance. It was also a self-deceptive balance, a standoff between barely repressed total revulsion and sentimental voting for the triumph, in any one person, of decency over stupidity and mean-spirited worldliness. A variety of sexual repression is involved as well. In the novel, as in Jarrell's poetry, sexuality in itself seems hardly present as a factor in his own thought and emotions or in those of his characters. His attitude toward women is a little like his attitude toward unhappy children and a little like Sophocles' toward "the Mothers": awe, mystification, and, sometimes, a cozy sympathy with a bitter edge nevertheless. The sense of a life ridden by despair that comes through in his last two books of poems is linked with that bitter sympathy. The balanced feeling of control of the mid-1950s dissolves into something harsher, more convincing finally, and at its best more brilliant.

The three poems that open the 1960 volume, *The Woman at the Washington Zoo*, are rather precise examples of Jarrell's feeling for women. He thinks about them a great deal, and passionately, but in the ways I have suggested. The title poem is one of a number written from the point of view of a woman, usually aging, who feels that, as she says, "The world goes by my cage and never sees me." (Jarrell discusses the composition of this poem brilliantly in one of his essays in *A Sad Day at the Supermarket*, 1962). The poem begins with a tone of quiet desperation and in a sometimes banal cadence of a sort occasionally cultivated by Eliot, but rises to a hysterical pitch at the end — an accusation against fate and an appeal to be transformed. The woman's outcry is directed toward a vulture, both real and symbolic. She wants to be devoured and transformed, and her language suggests that the bird of prey to which her protest and prayer are addressed embodies the male principle:

Vulture,

When you come for the white rat that the foxes left,
Take off the red helmet of your head, the black
Wings that have shadowed me, and step to me as man:
The wild brother at whose feet the white wolves fawn,
To whose hand of power the great lioness
Stalks, purring. . . .

You know what I was,
You see what I am: change me, change me!

It is the first time in his poems that Jarrell speaks so fiercely through a woman's voice. In the next poem, "Cinderella," he does so again, but here, for once, female toughness — and even hardness — of spirit comes through. Both Cinderella and her fairy godmother are presented as coolly anti-male. Cinderella, on her very wedding day, under the "pulsing marble" of her wedding lace, "wished it all a widow's coal-black weeds." Later she became "a sullen wife and a reluctant mother." The god-mother is sophisticated into an archetypal "God's Mother" who comes into her own whenever her son is away. At these times she invites Cinderella into the "gold-gauzed door" of her Heaven that exists only in the flames of the male-created Hell, and they gossip comfortably apart from male ideas, ideals, and laws. This poem is far more effective than the long, rather involved, and precious one that follows: "The End of the Rainbow." In this latter poem, about a woman "old enough to be invisible," Jarrell's proliferating details carry a certain pathos but, even more, suggest the poet's extraordinary identification with his protagonist.

After these opening poems of human sensibility gratingly out of phase come the four most striking pieces of the book — poems that, together with those in the title sequence of *The Lost World*, complete Jarrell's work by closing in on intimate realities of his own actual life and memory. Again we have an interesting parallel to Lowell, for both poets were moving into their confes-sional period at the same time. Lowell's *Life Studies* had appeared the year before, an enormous gathering of concentrated neu-rotic energy centered on his childhood and the personalities of his parents as somehow symptomatic of America's and the world's malaise. Although Jarrell's confessional poems are less ambitious formally and symbolically than Lowell's, they are in many ways closer to the anomie and the disturbances that mark the common life in our day.

Jarrell is in his own way as much an exotic as Lowell. The

strains of his boyhood are as atypical as those of the privileged
Bostonian, and the adult lives of both men have been atypical
too. But often in these poems he summons up the world of
plain-living, laboring souls and of the hardships and pleasures
of ordinary life. The confusing images of his beloved grand-
mother wringing a chicken's neck, and of the already dead bird
still running about in circles, recur, for instance, in a number of
the poems. Each is an image of the brutal nature of existence
and cannot be separated out from the meaning of love. Millions
of ordinary folk know the experience described in "A Street off
Sunset" (in *The Lost World*):

> Mama comes out and takes in the clothes
> From the clothesline. She looks with righteous love
> At all of us, her spare face half a girl's.
> She enters a chicken coop, and the hens shove
> And flap and squawk, in fear; the whole flock whirls
> Into the farthest corner. She chooses one,
> Comes out, and wrings its neck. The body hurls
> Itself out — lunging, reeling, it begins to run
> Away from Something, to fly away from Something
> In great flopping circles. Mama stands like a nun
> In the center of each awful, anguished ring.
> The thudding and scrambling go on, go on — then they fade,
> I open my eyes, it's over . . . Could such a thing
> Happen to anything? It could to a rabbit, I'm afraid;
> It could to . . .

The details here are as plain, and as hideous, as, say, those in
John Clare's "Badger." Where Jarrell differs from a true *naïf*,
though, is in his superimposed notes of observation, themselves
simple in tone but implying meditative and informed intelli-
gence: "righteous love" (a note of psychological insight, for the
woman's look is a gesture both of self-encouragement and of
apology and self-justification); "away from Something" (a note
to underline the presence of universal terror); "like a nun"
(again, the note of reaffirmed innocence, which is yet "the center
of each awful, anguished ring"); and at last the deliberate point-
ing up of the child's reactions. The easily colloquial iambic pen-

tameter lines run on quite naturally; one hardly notices the al-
ternating rhymes that help rock the movement into hysteria —
that is, into the child's momentarily traumatized hypnosis by the
impossible thing that is happening. Jarrell uses this pattern
throughout the "Lost World" sequence. It makes for a slightly
relaxed, anecdotal tone that drags boringly at times but provides
a frame at others for effects such as this one. This weakness, in
itself, is a reflection of Jarrell's desire to keep his form open to
common speech and common psychology — something he
much admired in Robert Frost's work.

Returning to *The Woman at the Washington Zoo* and the four
poems there that I have noted, we can see that "In Those Days"
and "The Elementary Scene" are both exceedingly simple in
form. "In Those Days" consists of four quatrains with the sim-
plest of rhyme schemes, *abcb*, and is in a basic iambic tetrameter
with much variation for naturalness and dramatic immediacy. It
reads, except for the deliberate avoidance of smoothness of
meter, like an afterbeat from Heine, particularly in the last
stanza:

> How poor and miserable we were,
> How seldom together!
> And yet after so long one thinks:
> In those days everything was better.

Almost doggerel — but this ending shrugs off a painful nos-
talgia for a past love, the whole adolescent atmosphere of which
has been evoked, with all its bittersweet frustration and sense of
wintry isolation of the two young people, in the preceding stan-
zas. The poem strikes a new personal key for Jarrell, and serves
as an overture to the further exploration of the speaker's lost
past. Then come "The Elementary Scene" and "Windows," still
quite simple in their diction and the scenes they envision: the
first a rural elementary school at Hallowe'en, the second the
home of dead elders who once loved and cherished the speaker.
Jarrell's ability to suggest, with utmost economy, a milieu at once
provincial and inarticulate and yet full of unmet challenge — the
reality of an irretrievable folk past that might have led to a far

different life for the speaker, one less to be regretted, perhaps
— is his greatest strength.

> The thin grass by the girls' door,
> Trodden on, straggling, yellow and rotten,
> And the gaunt field with its one tied cow . . .

— the lines recall his very early "The Cow Wandering in the
Bare Field" and the curious persistence of images demanding
clarification again and again during a poet's lifetime. The self-
reproach at the end of "The Elementary Scene" — "I, I, the
future that mends everything" — is the final evidence that this is
one of his purest poems, a poem of unearned but heavily felt
depression, in which the speaker takes upon himself the guilt of
time's passing. So also in "Windows," it is the unbearable ir-
revocability of the past that the speaker lives with and endures
(in this respect a true heir to Frost and E. A. Robinson). The
beloved dead, imagined alive in their time, are compared in
their vivid presence to "dead actors, on a rainy afternoon," who
"move in a darkened living-room" on a television screen.

> *These* actors, surely, have known nothing of today,
> That time of troubles and of me. Of troubles.
> . . . .
> They move along in peace. . . . If only I were they!
> Could act out, in longing, the impossibility
> That haunts me like happiness!

Sentimentality is held at a distance in this poem by the sheer
force of illusion: the construction of a moment of the recaptured
past so keenly present to the speaker's desire that it goes beyond
imagination —

> It blurs, and there is drawn across my face
> As my eyes close, a hand's slow fire-warmed flesh.
>
> It moves so slowly that it does not move.

The poem "Aging," which follows, does not have the fine
sensuous conviction of "Windows" and does lapse into sentimen-
tality. When, in the "Lost World" sequence and in "Remember-

ing the Lost World," literal memory again picks up these motifs,
the intensity and concentration are sacrificed for the anecdotal
colloquialism we have seen. These are poems banking on total
rather than on selected recall and striving to hold their recov-
ered, or reimagined, reality intact against the poisonous fact of
elapsed time. Theirs is an opposite method, allowing room for
something like a novelistic play of mind over bizarre contradic-
tions of a child's life in Hollywood, a life at once disciplined by
good gray work and indulged by an almost sensually remem-
bered aunt and her friends, one of whom owned the MGM lion.
It is a bath of charming, touching, and heartbreaking memory in
the new open mode that Jarrell had discovered. The new mode
seems to have freed him from a vision too sharp to be endured,
and to have taken him over the line of belief in the present
reality of the past. "Thinking of the Lost World" ends:

> LOST — NOTHING. STRAYED FROM NOWHERE. NO REWARD.
> I hold in my own hands, in happiness,
> Nothing: the nothing for which there's no reward.

"I felt at first," writes John Crowe Ransom in the essay I
quoted from earlier, "that this was a tragic ending. But I have
studied it till I give up that notion. The NOTHING is the fiction,
the transformation; to which both boy and man are given. That
World is not Lost because it never existed; but it is as precious
now as ever. I have come to think that Randall was announcing
the beginning of his 'second childhood.' There is nothing wrong
about that, to the best of my knowledge." Perhaps, but what Mr.
Ransom is describing is the letdown, or failure of nerve, in the
face of the issues (which Jarrell nevertheless did to a certain
important extent face) that often takes the form of a paradoxi-
cally melancholy complacency in writers just below the energy
level of genius. Jarrell himself approaches the issue wryly in the
quoted lines, and also in the self-ironically named poem "Hope,"
which takes us into the poet's grown-up life with all its gaiety,
fears, and gallant playing of roles. It is almost as though he had
given the tragic its due in "The Elementary Scene," "Windows,"
and the very dark-spirited Rilke translations of *The Woman at the*

Washington Zoo and then turned his back on the discipline of greatness.

But this would be too harsh a judgment. At fifty-one, Jarrell was still expanding his range of technique and of personal sympathies. He might well have reversed his direction once more and made another fresh start as he had done in the war poems and again in *The Seven-League Crutches* and the last books. With all the intelligence and openness to varied literary influences reflected in his criticism and his translations during the two postwar decades, he was surely capable of a great deal of further development despite a deep formal conservatism. Our poetry — and it is Jarrell's *poetry* almost exclusively that we have been concerned with — is today struggling in a new way with the question of the role of an active, many-sided intellectuality in essential poetic structure. Jarrell might conceivably have contributed something of interest to this exploration. Meanwhile, he remains a force among us as a poet of defeat and loneliness who nevertheless does not allow himself to become less spirited. He is like that ex-P.W. in his poem "A Game at Salzburg" who says, "To have been a prisoner of war in Colorado iss a *privilege*."

John Berryman

$\mathbf{D}$espite career-long unevenness in the quality of his work, John Berryman has become a major American poet, has achieved a permanency that places him in a group with Theodore Roethke and Randall Jarrell. Berryman, it seems to me, has taken on the whole modern world and has come to poetic terms with it. At the same time he has taken on himself, and has come to poetic terms with that too. He has seen the wreck of the modern world (or, better, the modern world insofar as it is a wreck) and the wreck of his personal self in that world. He is not a pessimist but has, rather, what we would have to call a tragic view of human life — with good reason for holding it. Yet, not surprisingly, the tragic view finds its complement in a comic view, his wild and so often devastatingly effective sense of humor. He is preeminently a poet of suffering and laughter.

To understand his achievement it is necessary to look first at the life of the man, for his poetry will emerge as strongly autobiographical, and the intensity of his personal suffering must be understood. He was born October 25, 1914, in McAlester, Oklahoma, and grew up in Anadarko, Oklahoma, a town of 3000. His father was the town banker, his mother was a schoolteacher, and he had a younger brother. His upbringing was strict Roman Catholic, which was the faith of both his parents,

171

and, though in his last years he attended mass only occasionally, he remained a Catholic in spirit, religiously questing. Until he was ten he spent summers on a farm, throughout the year fished and hunted, and was from the beginning a bright boy in school rather than a young rebel. When he was ten the family moved to Tampa, Florida, where his mother and father had severe marital difficulties. His father, fearing that his wife was about to leave him, repeatedly threatened to drown himself and John with him. Lack of money was not the problem; in fact, young John had an allowance of $25 a week, all of which he spent on his stamp collection. His relationship with each of his parents was, moreover, close. His father, a captain in the National Guard, even took the boy with him occasionally when he went on maneuvers to Fort Sill, Oklahoma, as well as on hunting and fishing trips. But when John was twelve he suffered an ultimate trauma — his father shot himself right outside his son's window. The father was buried in Oklahoma, but the son never returned to his grave.

After the death of the father, the family settled in New York. John's mother then married a Wall Street banker named John Angus McAlpin Berryman, who formally adopted John and his younger brother. (John's father's name had been John Allyn Smith.) His mother and stepfather were divorced after ten years of marriage, but whatever the strains of their relationship the children were not adversely affected, and Berryman was good to his adopted children. John was sent to South Kent School in Connecticut, which his mother chose for him. South Kent was, in John's later words, "very muscular," that is, devoted to athletics, and very high-church Episcopalian. Though he came to feel friendly toward it later, at the time John hated South Kent with heart and soul. He was much bullied there, had many fights — usually with stand-off results — began to have literary ambitions, and rebelled because he was an intellectual and the school, as he saw it, was not sympathetic to intellectuals. At South Kent the boys were beaten regularly with a paddle, upon the command "Assume the angle." But the experience of the school was partly redeemed for John by two masters, one in

English and one in history, who were sympathetic to him personally.

Following four years at South Kent, he attended Columbia, from which he took his B.A. in 1936. The teacher who inspired him was Mark Van Doren, all of whose courses he took. His development as a writer probably began at about the age of nineteen under the close personal influence of Van Doren, whose book of poems *A Winter Diary* he reviewed, and then Van Doren got him going on other poets. He flowered at Columbia despite dismissal for half a year for flunking one of Van Doren's courses because he read only seventeen of forty-two assigned books. He returned to make A's and be elected to Phi Beta Kappa.

Following graduation from Columbia, a traveling fellowship took him to Cambridge, England, for two years. There he wrote poetry all the time and was known as a poet though he was not actually publishing at the time. He took a B.A. from Clare College in 1938 and returned to New York, where he became a close personal friend of Delmore Schwartz, then poetry editor of *Partisan Review*, a friendship renewed when both were teaching at Harvard, Berryman from 1940 to 1943 and Schwartz from 1940 to 1947. Berryman's long teaching career had begun at Wayne State in 1939. He taught at Princeton intermittently from 1943 to 1949, held a fellowship there in 1950–51, and received a Guggenheim Fellowship in 1952–53. He had been rejected for service in World War II on medical grounds. His eyesight was poor and he had recurrent serious nervous difficulties.

He married for the first time in 1942. The marriage lasted eleven years. One of the love affairs he had during this time became the basis of his *Sonnets*. It was this affair that brought him to the point of suicide, with thoughts of killing both himself and his mistress because she flatly refused to leave her husband and to marry him. His wife, who was ignorant of the affair, persuaded him to undergo psychoanalysis, and he stayed under analysis from 1947 to 1953. The analysis relieved his suicidal depression and led him to renounce the affair; thereafter he still saw his analyst occasionally. At the time of his separation from his wife in 1953 — his heavy drinking and the tensions accompanying the writing of *Homage to Mistress Bradstreet* acting as causes — both were hoping for reconciliation.

In 1955 he moved to the University of Minnesota, where he remained, and became a professor of humanities. He remarried in 1956, had a son by this marriage, and was divorced in 1959. Again heavy drinking and disorderly behavior acted as causes, as well as the tensions accompanying his writing, this time, of the Dream Songs. He married once more in 1961. He and his third wife Kate, who was twenty-five years younger than he, had two daughters, Martha and Sara. Like her husband, Mrs. Berryman was also a Catholic living outside the Church because of their marriage. In his last years John Berryman was evangelistically opposed to adultery. On Friday, January 7, 1972, he jumped to his death from a bridge over the Mississippi River, landing on the west bank about a hundred feet below.

Formal honors for his poetry were awarded to Berryman throughout his career. These include the Shelley Memorial Award in 1949, the Harriet Monroe Poetry Prize in 1957, the Pulitzer Prize for poetry in 1965, the Bollingen Prize in 1968, and the National Book Award for poetry in 1969.

Throughout his career — and underlying the unevenness in the quality of his work — Berryman was beset by the problem of style. It is as if he wrestled with artistic agonies at the same time as with personal ones, or that the former were perhaps a deep reflection of the latter. Although it is safe to say that he arrived at widespread and qualitatively certain recognition with his 1968 volume, *His Toy, His Dream, His Rest*, his earlier reviewers show great consistency in recognizing the problem of style. Going back to 1948 and Berryman's first important collection of poems, we find Dudley Fitts writing that it is "somehow without the excitement that attends the transformation of a craft into a completely realized art," and Randall Jarrell saying, "Doing things in a style all its own sometimes seems the primary object of the poem, and its subject gets a rather spasmodic treatment." Stanley Kunitz, with language strongly in mind, called *Homage to Mistress Bradstreet* a failure "worth more than most successes."

John Ciardi wondered whether the same poem was "a thing literary and made," and John Holmes thought that it would "fascinate the intellectuals." Louise Bogan responded to *77 Dream Songs* with the incisive phrase "this desperate artificiality." Even Berryman's biography of Stephen Crane revealed the problem of style. As Morgan Blum acutely observed, Berryman's trouble in the biography "apparently resides in an inability to reduce his insights to reasoned discourse." One could as easily say that in the biography Berryman so insisted on style, on being his own man, that he paid a price for it. Blum's summary judgment, "Flawed and distinguished," has the force of an epithet summarizing a central reaction to Berryman. But implicit in the reaction is the fact that there is only one Berryman, the Berryman of tension, agony, and struggle.

The biography of Crane, which appeared in 1950, is almost a tour de force. It is as if nothing but tension, agony, and struggle could have produced it. The closer one looks at its organization, the more one realizes the truth of Morgan Blum's comment. Despite the fact that it must be granted in advance that the art of writing biography is extraordinarily challenging — in my own opinion the most difficult of all literary writing — there is hardly an excuse to be found for the diffuseness Berryman's work displays. Even when Berryman comes to a climactic chapter on the all-important subject of Crane's art, he seems unable to pull his materials together, despite the fact that in a cumulative way, as the reader by that time knows, he has the basic resources to do it. What makes matters even more frustrating for the reader is that Berryman's purpose is clearly to make an intelligent and balanced attempt at a fair evaluation of Crane. He obviously wants to do what the academically oriented critic normally does do. He is also too honest to make excuses. Although he remarks with casualness in his preface that it is a "psychological biography," he does not use that fact as a device to mitigate his own responsibility as a critic to make judgments when judgments are called for. And yet he persistently falls short of doing what he is telling himself that he must do.

The biography of Crane represents, then, Berryman's inability to reduce his insights to reasoned discourse or, to give the matter another emphasis, a values choice of passion over reason. Trite as it sounds, the poet in him wins out. His style is vigorous and vivid, and his eloquence is the kind found in only the very finest biographies. His eye for detail, his sensitivity to the selection of detail, is acute. One of the best parts of the book, for example, is his description of Crane's childhood, as when he describes the young Stephen's contact with the color red or the boy's terror when his hands brush a handle of his father's coffin. In broad terms Berryman communicates sympathy for his subject by means that are often poetic. He leaves the reader with a vivid picture of Crane, a man who had teeth among the worst those who knew him had ever seen, an artist dead at twenty-eight of tuberculosis. It should be emphasized, however, that the biography is a far cry from being merely a poetic outpouring. Some of its vigor of thought, which relates ultimately to a poetic talent of forceful expression and projection of a speaker's character, is similar to that distinguishing the best academic writing. Berryman wisely sees, for example, that our own period of literature has developed toward increasing absorption in style, and he emphatically sees Crane as a great stylist, particularly as an impressionist, mentioning, as one of Crane's friends recorded it, Crane's assertion that impressionism was truth. Berryman also sees Crane as a writer of will, and comes to the very sensible conclusion that the world emerging from some of Crane's early sketches was one of "perfect aloneness." Sympathy and insight give the biography a unity that counters its diffuseness. There is a pattern here, I would suggest, that anticipates Berryman's experience with "The Dream Songs," but by that time he is all poet and whatever his organizational problems with the poem, he is also far beyond the possibility of any flirtation with a tour de force.

Berryman's poetic output divides into what might conveniently and after the familiar pattern be called the early Berryman and the later Berryman. The early Berryman, whose work began appearing in such journals as *Southern Review, Kenyon*

Review, Partisan Review, Nation, and *New Republic* in the late 1930s, publishes twenty poems in 1940 in the New Directions book *Five Young American Poets* and a pamphlet called *Poems* in 1942. Then in 1948 he publishes the important *The Dispossessed,* which collects, often in revised form, many previously published poems. He also writes a sonnet sequence in the 1940s but this is not published until 1967. The later Berryman publishes *Homage to Mistress Bradstreet* in 1956, *77 Dream Songs* in 1964, *His Toy, His Dream, His Rest,* which completes the poem "The Dream Songs," in 1968, and *Love and Fame* in 1970; the posthumous *Delusions, Etc.* appears in 1972. The 1958 *His Thought Made Pockets & the Plane Buckt* is a group of thirteen poems which may be regarded as an extension of *The Dispossessed,* and the 1967 *Short Poems* merely brings together *The Dispossessed, His Thought Made Pockets,* and a rather ineffectual poem called "Formal Elegy" written in 1963 on the occasion of the death of President John F. Kennedy.

So much for orientation to the poet's life and output. The immediate basis for the division between early Berryman and later Berryman is a striking contrast in style. Indeed, *Homage to Mistress Bradstreet* is rightly regarded as a breakthrough for Berryman, though the early Berryman obviously meshes with the later Berryman and the later Berryman does not hold, as it were, to the style of his breakthrough. Always conspicuously conscious of his identity as a poet, he provides us in Sonnet 47 with the perfect epigraph for his contrasting styles when he refers to "Crumpling a syntax at a sudden need." The early Berryman tends not to crumple his syntax but to write "normal," or we could say "traditional," verse sentences such as these:

> Images are the mind's life, and they change.
> "A POINT OF AGE"

> We must travel in the direction of our fear.
> "A POINT OF AGE"

> An ultimate shaking grief fixes the boy
> As he stands rigid, trembling, staring down
> All his young days into the harbour where
> His ball went.
> "THE BALL POEM"

I hope you will be happier where you go
Than you or we were here, and learn to know
What satisfactions there are.
                            "FAREWELL TO MILES"

How could you be so happy, now some thousand years
disheveled, puffs of dust?
                            "NOTE TO WANG WEI"

But in *Homage* a crumpling of syntax is typical and will be recognized as an element of the stream-of-consciousness or shift-of-association technique so common in the twentieth century — and also harking back to Gerard Manley Hopkins' sprung rhythm — that it too must be called "normal":

So squeezed, wince you I scream?   (19.1)

Pioneering is not feeling well,
not Indians, beasts.   (23.2–3)

This technique is, of course, larger than the crumpling of the syntax of a single sentence; since it is basically a device to dramatize the condition of the mind the crumpling in *Homage* is also a movement, often abrupt or rapid, from sentence to sentence, from thought to thought, or emotion to emotion. Quantitatively speaking, there are numerous normal verse sentences in *Homage*, but the steady effect of the poem is one of associational shift. Consider now a few examples of crumpled syntax from the Dream Songs:

Maybe but even if I see my son
forever never, get back on the take,
free, black & forty-one.
                            NUMBER 40

The course his mind his body steer, poor Pussy-cat,
in weakness & disorder, will see him down
whiskers & tail.
                            NUMBER 49, "BLIND"

              Henry — wonder! all,
when most he — under the sun.
                            NUMBER 52, "SILENT SONG"

But it must be said that this syntax, conspicuous as it is, does *not* dominate the Dream Songs, which are replete with normal English verse sentences. At the same time the first 77 Dream Songs do, like *Homage*, have a steady shift-of-association effect. Their crumpled language tends to be an untraditional drunken lurching consonant with the central character, Henry, and the psychic or dream world which he inhabits. To simplify a complicated matter we may say for the moment that the later Berryman writes in a style, or styles, directed toward dramatic immediacy. The early Berryman writes in a style that is ultimately dramatic but he tends to be a "speaker" of individual poems who does not become a developed character such as, for example, Frost's mythic New England Yankee or, in identity closer to the real-life poet, the Roethke who journeys to the interior in "North American Sequence." We could easily imagine the later Berryman — Mistress Bradstreet and Henry — on a stage in some kind of performance, but not the early Berryman. Clearly the early Berryman was searching for a poetic identity which could only be found by an experiment in style.

Style, however, can be a false light to follow. The preeminent question to ask about the early Berryman is, I think, whether or not he creates a substantial number of poems that establish not so much a style as the fact of his talent and particularly that talent as it identifies itself in terms of essential subject and theme. The question is, What does the Berryman of *The Dispossessed* care about? Though he is an individual speaker of poems rather than a developed character, is there nevertheless a certain unity to his early work, does the speaker of his poems take on a singleness of character? And to suggest the answers to these questions is naturally to anticipate his later development.

The most essential thing to say about the Berryman of *The Dispossessed* is that he offers a subjective response to the objective reality of the modern world. His early poems typically do not encounter objective reality in terms of an elaboration of the facts of that reality. He thus forgoes what we might call pure or external subject interest in favor of a focus on the individual as the individual responds to his world. It is most decidedly not an egocentric emphasis, but rather a steady and a dynamic relationship between the individual, the sensitive individual, and the world to which he *must* respond. The speaker of his early poems is typically anxious to generalize about humanity from a variety of specific experiences, but to proceed from a specific experience is not the same as to detail the specifics. The persistent concern is broad, and distinctly in the humanistic tradition. It would be fair to say that the basic character of the speaker in *The Dispossessed* is that of a sensitive and rather desperate humanist — we think too of the man who has abandoned his Catholic faith. What he cares about, broadly speaking, is our common humanity and its survival in the face of terrible threats. He cares about caring. His poetic attempt, his subject, is *how it feels* to be in a certain kind of world.

The pivot point of the world he finds himself in is World War II, the beginning of which he regards as a dark time for mankind, and as reason for feeling hatred and bitterness. It is a dark time because he finds fascism so evil and committed to destroy precious individual freedom. He sees the state as a monster of oppression, "At Dachau rubber blows forbid" ("Letter to His Brother") — this written in 1938. Or consider the terror and bitterness in these sensitive lines:

>   The time is coming near
> When none shall have books or music, none his dear,
> And only a fool will speak aloud his mind.
>   "THE MOON AND THE NIGHT AND THE MEN"

He looks out and sees "tortured continents" ("Boston Common") and becomes inwardly tortured by what he sees. His reaction to the world of the 1930s and 1940s is to take its burdens upon himself — much as Robert Lowell was shortly to do — and, as a result, to enter into the abyss of himself, which, as Yeats remarked, may show as reckless a courage as those we honor who die on the field of battle.

The early Berryman as a speaker of poems interests us, then, as a sensitive individual meditating upon and absorbing the shocks of a grim time. His perspective is broad in the sense that besides the state he sees other threats to human freedom: materialism, for example, as he calls out, "Great-grandfather, attest my hopeless need / Amongst the chromium luxury of the age" ("A Point of Age"). In a poem called "World-Telegram" he even catalogues the ordinary events of the day, and masks his horror with this reportorial matter-of-factness:

> An Indian girl in Lima, not yet six,
> Has been delivered by Caesarian.
> A boy. They let the correspondent in:
> Shy, uncommunicative, still quite pale,
> A holy picture by her, a blue ribbon.

At the end of the same poem he speaks in desperate understatement to dramatize the condition of civilization as he sees it: "If it were possible to take these things / Quite seriously, I believe they might / Curry disorder in the strongest brain." To take upon oneself the horrors of such a world as the *World-Telegram* reports is clearly to go mad. Berryman knows that we are saved, if we can be saved, by the strength of rational awareness and perhaps a final necessary refusal to accept burdens which are beyond our capacity as individuals to endure.

The Berryman of *The Dispossessed* also emerges in the poignant terms of more personal experience, as, for example, this reference to the loss of his father: "The inexhaustible ability of a man / Loved once, long lost, still to prevent my peace" ("World's Fair"). Or the reader can look at the fine poem "Farewell to Miles" on the simple subject of saying good-bye and the "ultimate loss" which that involves. But it must be said that the pessimism, the despair, and the bitterness which characterize the early Berryman are balanced by hope and such affirmation as these lines from "Letter to His Brother": "May love, or its image in work, / Bring you the brazen luck to sleep with dark / And so to get responsible delight." And he affirms especially the life of nature, "natural life springing in May," with a healthy sense of man's mortality, "Those walks so shortly to be over" ("The Statue"). Or the reader may wish to look at another fine early poem, "Canto Amor," which tells us "Love is multiform" and sings to the end of joy.

It is clear that the early Berryman creates a substantial number of poems that establish the fact of his talent as it identifies itself in terms of essential subject and theme, or in terms of the singleness — the sheer interestingness — of the character of his speaker. What, then, qualifies praise of *The Dispossessed*? The answer to this is probably as obvious as it could be. Vagueness, obscurity, a failure to project a clear dramatic situation, characterize a number of the poems in the volume. We hear, too often, a flat academic voice, given to a kind of punchless abstraction:

> Cold he knows he comes, once to the dark,
> All that waste of cold, leaving all cold
> Behind him hearts, forgotten when he's tolled,
> His books are split and sold, the pencil mark
> He made erased, his wife
> Gone brave & quick to her new life.
> "SURVIVING LOVE"

Even the grammar — "leaving all cold / Behind him hearts" — fails. Or we encounter a dreadful triteness, as in these opening lines: "The summer cloud in summer blue / Capricious from the wind will run" ("Cloud and Flame"), suggesting a verse exercise, an unauthentic voice. It is worth noting that any poet who lets himself become so sloppy in his craft is sure to irritate his critics, especially if it is obvious that he is intelligent and should know better.

But what is really intriguing about *The Dispossessed* is not so much its obvious weakness as a phenomenon involving the relationship between what Fitts calls *craft* and *art* and Jarrell calls *subject* and *style*. I refer to poems that are very appealing in their rhythms — and generally speaking expert in their craft — but nevertheless do not finally work as poems, or fulfill the treatment of subject. "Winter Landscape," for example, transcribes skillfully from the Brueghel painting "Hunters in the Snow" but does not realize a meaningful theme about it or, as Berryman intended, about something else. Or consider the following from the title poem, "The Dispossessed":

> That which a captain and a weaponeer
> one day and one more day did, we did, *ach*
> we did not, *They* did . . cam slid, the great lock
>
> lodged, and no soul of us all was near was near, —
> an evil sky (where the umbrella bloomed)
> twirled its mustaches, hissed, the ingenue fumed,
>
> poor virgin, and no hero rides. . . .

Not even notes or a rationalization of context can rescue lines like these from their lack of exact, or exactly suggestive, imaginative coherence. It is relatively easy to dismiss egregious verse, but here we are frustrated by a sense of talent going to waste. What is not so apparent, though perhaps hardly hidden, is that the early Berryman is seeking to find himself as a poet. His bent, I think, is toward impressionism, but in *The Dispossessed* he does not readily shape impressions into the final imaginative world we call the poem. "Winter Landscape," the first poem in the chronologically arranged volume, and the title poem, the last, are different aspects of the same problem. The general movement of the book, in terms of style, is toward a loosening of form, a syntax crumpling that distinctly anticipates *Homage to Mistress Bradstreet*. This movement is particularly apparent in sections IV and V. The temptation, at first, is to see Berryman's development as linear from traditional to modern, but this would be exactly to miss the point. His basic problem as a young poet is not so much stylistic development, important as that is, but rather discovering *how* or *to what* style is best applied. His bent toward impressionism was to become the impressionism of the mind of *Homage* and the Dream Songs. This, I believe, is the basic reason why *Homage* and the Dream Songs do not look imitative, though there is obviously nothing startling in the twentieth century about their technique. Both have their roots in the active soil of the early Berryman's struggle for poetic identity.

That struggle produced a good number of successful poems, some mellifluous misses, and a forgivable amount of weak verse. It was also a period in which Berryman produced two short stories which relate importantly — partly because they *are* short stories — to his early development. The first, and his first, "The Lovers," appeared in the Winter 1945 *Kenyon Review* and is reprinted in *The Best American Short Stories 1946.* "The Lovers," which recalls Joyce's "Araby," tells of the discovery that adolescent first love cannot last. Like "Araby" it is told from the point of view of the mature man looking back over his past experience, but it is not a powerful story, chiefly because it is more expository than dramatic. It does, however, contain this comment from the narrator which implies strong awareness of personal development: "Purity of feeling, selflessness of feeling, is the achievement of maturity. . . ." Viewed as an aspect of the struggle of the early Berryman, this statement both defines his basic problem as an artist and points to his later achievement. His second story, "The Imaginary Jew," also appeared in *Kenyon Review* (Autumn 1945) and won first prize in the *Kenyon Review*–Doubleday Doran story contest. Although superior to "The Lovers," it is a cross between a fairly good short story and a beautiful essay. The speaker is a man who has gone through the harrowing experience in the late 1930s of being mistaken for a Jew. The story ends: "In the days following, as my resentment died, I saw that I had not been a victim altogether unjustly. My persecutors were right: I was a Jew. The imaginary Jew I was was as real as the imaginary Jew hunted down, on other nights and days, in a real Jew. Every murderer strikes the mirror, the lash of the torturer falls on the mirror and cuts the real image, and the real and the imaginary blood flow down together." Berryman did not go on to become a short-story writer, though he wrote other stories yet unpublished. Poetic language and firm subject matter, such as may be seen in "The Imaginary Jew," were not enough to make him a wholly successful short-story writer. He needed to escape from his own intellect, his academic intelligence, in order to achieve selflessness of feeling, or the power of the truly dramatic. Mistress Bradstreet and Dream Song Henry were to become his challenge to selflessness.

Our descriptive definition of the early Berryman completes itself as we examine *Berryman's Sonnets*. Except for their number, 115, they could easily be construed as a section, perhaps a later section, of *The Dispossessed*. They give us a greater sense of dealing with an objective as well as a subjective reality than is characteristic of *The Dispossessed*, probably for the obvious reason that behind them lies the story of a love affair, illicit, between "the poet" and a Danish-American blonde named Lise, but their subject, paralleling *The Dispossessed*, is preeminently *how it feels* to love, which is to say, how it feels to respond to a personal situation as opposed to more general world conditions. The singleness of situation of the sonnets and the fact that the speaker is talking directly to his lady love doubtless helps to give them a somewhat greater dramatic immediacy than the poems of *The Dispossessed*, but they fall far short of creating a speaker who is also a developed character in a developed situation, in what we would recognize as a good plot. Nevertheless, as with the speaker of the poems in *The Dispossessed*, the speaker of the sonnets does take on a singleness of character and further suggests a certain unity in Berryman's early work.

The sonnets — apparently written over a period of several months in 1946 — are a sequence of emotions hinged on the ecstasy and the pain of a particular love. The speaker's epithet for himself is "The adulter and bizarre of thirty-two" (105), but the sonnets hardly make us feel much about his guilt. What they do make us feel is his energy, his humor, and his exuberance. He coins an appropriate epigraph for the affair as "knock-down-and-drag-out love" (97). But this is, of course, rhetoric for an old ideal, elsewhere simply stated, "without you I / Am not myself" (94), "you are me" (27), or love's goal is "To become ourselves" (45). Though somewhat repetitious in theme, the sonnets are appealing in their sheer erotic exultation, their reveling in sex — breasts, blonde hair, soul kisses, biting and kissing, even an orgasm compared to a rumbling subway train. But the speaker, fortunately, never takes himself too seriously and can see their quarrels as funny, as when his lady breaks her knuckle in smashing objects. He has a quick wit: "In the end I race by cocky as a comb" (52), ". . The *mots* fly, and the flies mope on the food" (53). He speaks to his lady with tender and somewhat formulaic but delightful irony: "You, Lise, *contrite*, I never thought to see" (18), or laughs wryly, laughs inside: "My glass I lift at six o'clock, my darling, / As you plotted . . Chinese couples shift in bed" (13), a reference, of course, to the renowned particulars of Oriental lovemaking. He loves to kid his lady about her drinking, and to kid himself — "we four / Locked, crocked together" (33). What the sonnets best accomplish is finally to sing assuredly of joy: "What I love of you / *Inter alia* tingles like a whole good day" (86). The spirit of E. E. Cummings is here.

As with *The Dispossessed* there is an unevenness in the quality of the sonnets as poems. The following, for example, is conventional to the point of being banal: "I feel the summer draining me, / I lean back breathless in an agony / Of charming loss I suffer without moan, / Without my love, or with my love alone" (59). As is rhyming like this: "I grope / A little in the wind after a hope / For sun before she wakes . . all might be well" (68). But the amount of this kind of writing over the span of the sonnets is relatively small. More difficult to assess is the difference between the sonnets that really work as poems and those that, though they may have outstanding qualities or lines, do not. In any case, style as the primary object of the poem does not characterize the sonnets, for they always have subject and are, moreover, seldom "difficult" in the sense that the poem "The Dispossessed" is difficult. But their technique often shows signs of strain, or tends to be nonfunctional, and thus they have a certain link to Berryman's preoccupation with style, his straining for effect at the price of poem quality. Berryman's typical devices in the sonnets are ellipsis and variations of normal sentence structure. He often omits connectives, such as prepositions, relative pronouns, and conjunctions, and secures an elliptical effect by an omission of punctuation, an omission which when it works

creates a functional ambiguity of syntax. His variation of normal
sentence structure takes such form as wide separation of a verb
from its direct object, sudden interruptions and shifts from one
sentence pattern to another, and inversion both for rhythmic
effect and to aid in speeding the movement of the speaker's
thoughts. The net intent of such technique, healthily, is better
dramatization, and there is, of course, an obvious anticipation of
what he is to do some years later. But the question, as always, is
not what technique is used — including devices and conventions
as traditional as his Petrarchan rhyme scheme or as modern as
rapid shift of association — but whether or not a chosen tech-
nique works.

A contrast will serve us well in evaluating Berryman's
achievement as a sonneteer. Consider the opening octave of
sonnet 71:

> Our Sunday morning when dawn-priests were
>   applying
> Wafer and wine to the human wound, we laid
> Ourselves to cure ourselves down: I'm afraid
> Our vestments wanted, but Francis' friends were crying
> In the nave of pines, sun-satisfied, and flying
> Subtle as angels about the barricade
> Boughs made over us, deep in a bed half made
> Needle-soft, half the sea of our simultaneous dying.

Although at first glance this might look fluid and controlled, the
opening metaphor is both strained and vague. It functions to set
the time of the lovers' action as simultaneous to a communion
service, with an obvious ironic contrast between the sacred and
the profane, the familiar Donnean paradox that profane love
may be sacred. But what precisely is a "dawn-priest"? If merely a
priest who gives communion at dawn, then the speaker is forc-
ing us to make an association that offers no more than short
literal mileage. Why are the priests "applying" wafer and wine?
The word is ill chosen. Why "the human wound"? Such a phrase
tells us nothing about the communicants and has a gravity sug-
gesting that the speaker is a prig. Is the tongue, moreover, in
some meaningful sense suggestive of "wound"? Why even

bother to say "human" wound? With such a start there is little hope for the poem, but craft gets worse. The device of separating the adverb "down" from its verb "laid" helps the rhythm of the line at the price of creating a dull academicism. By line 3 we are, moreover, scarcely ready to believe that the lovers really have anything wrong with them that needs to be cured. If sin, original or recent, the premise is just too much to accept. In line 4 the reference to "Our vestments" merely belabors a contrast already made. By the time we come to the periphrasis "Francis' friends" for "birds" we suspect — perhaps with a groan — that the speaker is not only a bore but also a sentimentalist, especially if the birds are "crying" tears as well as just crying out, and it is useless to argue that since the birds are "sun-satisfied" the context excludes the suggestion of crying tears since the context is established too late for such exclusion. The phrase "Subtle as angels" is meaningless as description of how the birds are flying, nor is it, even if accepted in some metaphysical way, a phrase to which the speaker has established his right. And then, why does the speaker describe the boughs about which the birds are flying as a "barricade"? The description is arbitrary rather than in relation to the feeling of the presence of some enemy, real or imagined. Finally, the metaphor of the bed, half "Needle-soft" and half "sea," fails, for the two halves do not relate to suggest the total quality of the lovers' experience. Even the final phrase, "simultaneous dying," dying used in the Elizabethan sense of orgasm — with now a groan from English teachers — is too much. Since these are lovers, dare we not assume their simultaneity? At the end of the octave we feel nothing about either the sacred or the profane, and the sestet, which includes such miserable phrases as "shivering with delight" and "Careless with sleepy love," is more of the same.

Here by contrast is a Berryman sonnet (9), that works:

> Great citadels whereon the gold sun falls
> Miss you O Lise sequestered to the West
> Which wears you Mayday lily at its breast,
> Part and not part, proper to balls and brawls,
> Plains, cities, or the yellow shore, not false

Anywhere, free, native and Danishest
Profane and elegant flower, — whom suggest
Frail and not frail, blond rocks and madrigals.

Once in the car (cave of our radical love)
Your darker hair I saw than golden hair
Above your thighs whiter than white-gold hair,
And where the dashboard lit faintly your least
Enlarged scene, O the midnight bloomed . . the East
Less gorgeous, wearing you like a long white glove!

The general reason why this sonnet works is that the character of the speaker is interesting, not boring, not sentimental, not priggish, but instead honest, tender, sensuous, erotic, realistic, acutely aware, and wittily self-ironic. But there is a touch of circularity in this argument, since the character works because the craft succeeds, and the craft works because the character is well conceived — such paradox is poetry's way. The first line of sonnet 9 is fatuously conventional and toneless, but the poet immediately establishes a personal tone that frames the impersonality in an ironic way. By line 3 he is calling his love a "Mayday lily," which ordinarily might be fatuously conventional but here has sincerity because it is touched with irony. Lovers, we feel, ought to have a sense of humor, especially about sex, because ironic self-awareness is part of love's delight. In a similar way, the bawdy pun on "balls" in line 4 falls within the frame of the speaker's irony. He earns the right to call his love a "Profane and elegant flower," a phrase which also refers back ironically to the epithet "Mayday lily." By the end of the octave we feel something about the sacred and the profane, something about delight. The sestet becomes its vivid, erotic, profane, and yet humorously sacred example. "O the midnight bloomed."

Such a fine poem as sonnet 9 represents Berryman's achievement as a sonneteer. Many others of the 115 could be named. As a sample, I would suggest these: 12, 13, 32, 33, 37, 53, 67, 75, 104, and 115. The unevenness in the quality of *Berryman's Sonnets* seems to me patent, though opinion on individual sonnets will naturally vary. What is important is the high quality of those that succeed, which leads us to conclude that a good number of high-

quality poems from *The Dispossessed* combine with a good number
of high-quality poems from *Berryman's Sonnets* to establish the
fact of Berryman's talent, and particularly that talent as it identi-
fies itself in terms of *how it feels* to respond to his world. Such talent
is always rare and makes us hope that it will flower into new
achievement. It is, however, a talent that is distinguished only in
the narrow sense of basic ability. It is a talent that typically car-
ries a poet to a plateau of challenge. The early Berryman, at the
not surprising age of approximately forty, had to make a new
turn or fall back with the talented nondescript. Turn he did, and
with his turn came 456 lines, fifty-seven eight-line stanzas, called
Homage to Mistress Bradstreet.

Homage is a poem that requires definition. It is basically an
interior monologue narrative, with Anne Bradstreet revealing
the story of her life in the early colonies. Born Anne Dudley in
England in 1612, she married Simon Bradstreet at sixteen,
crossed the Atlantic in the *Arbella* in 1630, had the first of her
eight children in 1633, became the first woman in America to de-
vote herself to writing poetry, and died in 1672 (her husband be-
came colonial governor of Massachusetts in 1679). But *Homage*,
though it functions to tell a story, is primarily concerned with a
sensibility, with *how it feels* to be a sensitive individual in a certain
kind of world. It is the voice of Anne that we hear, for example
in a moment of peace following the delivery of her first child:
"Blossomed Sarah, and I / blossom" (21.7–8). Her voice is, how-
ever, a voice that we hear only in relationship to the voice of the
poet, for the poem opens with the poet rather than Anne as
speaker. He imagines her in her grave:

> The Governor your husband lived so long
> moved you not, restless, waiting for him? Still,
> you were a patient woman. —
> I seem to see you pause here still:
> Sylvester, Quarles, in moments odd you pored
> before a fire at, bright eyes on the Lord,
> all the children still.
> 'Simon . .' Simon will listen while you read a Song.

Because of the tenderness of the speaker toward his subject, *Homage* immediately defines itself as a poem of personal caring, and the poet takes on the character of the caring self. To this — implying, as it does, that human relation is the ultimate reality — all else, it seems to me, is eventually subordinated. As a poem of personal caring, with consequent emphasis on personal identity, *Homage* also immediately defines itself as a poem distinctly and appealingly modern in subject and in theme. But the personal identity is the *combined* identity of the poet and Anne, the union, if you will, of past and present. Although the voice of the poet opens the poem and thus provides a framing point of view for what follows, the two voices blend, modulate from one to the other, and, though often distinct, are finally one voice, a voice of passion and caring, which is the final identity sought, and an emblem of our common humanity.

This identity — emerging from a technique appropriately called fluid characterization — has to be set forth in terms that seem faithful to the complexity of human experience. To the dramatic immediacy of voice must be added substance, detail. In this respect the first stanza is particularly instructive, and reveals the later Berryman's extraordinary mastery of economy of means — sonnets were good practice. In one stanza is established (1) the character of the poet, his tenderness, his caring, his distinctive tone, (2) the character of Anne, wife, mother, intensely religious person, and would-be poet, and (3) a sense of relationship between them. In fact, it is not going too far to say that the sexual love of the sonnets is transmuted into the poet's caring for Anne, as in the simple and direct "Lie stark, / thy eyes look to me mild" (2.8–3.1), or in the question "How do we / linger, diminished in our lovers' air" (3.4–5). Or as in this explicit expression of the caring theme: "We are on each other's hands / who care" (2.7–8). Moreover, this caring later becomes a love dialogue directly between the poet and Anne, which is to say, a symbolic marriage or consummation of identity. The first stanza introduces the identity of poet as the specific link between the two. In the accurate words of the notes on the poem, Sylvester and Quarles were "her favourite poets; unfortunately." Despite her prolific output, Anne was not much of a poet at all, a fact of which Berryman makes us acutely aware. She is "mistress neither of fiery nor velvet verse" (12.8); her poems are "bald / abstract didactic rime" (12.5–6), and are "proportioned" and "spiritless" (42.6). Through her Berryman seems to be expressing by implication his own fear of not succeeding as a poet. What it means to be a poet is obviously an important theme of the poem, not, however, in the contemporary mode of self-conscious artiness but rather as an aspect and epitome of what it means to be a person.

Neither the first stanza nor the other examples thus far cited suggest that the language of *Homage* presents us with a problem, but it does. In general terms the problem is, How is the poem to be read? More specifically, the reader encounters a good deal of speech that is stylized or mannered. This is not in itself a fault. On the contrary, it is an acceptable device and even, for both Anne and the poet, an acceptable premise of character. The problem is rather one of degree.

Ciardi refers, for example, to Berryman's eccentricities in *Homage* and observes as chief among them "a constant queer inversion of normal word order." "Can be hope a cloak?" (40.8) asks Anne, and the reader rightly asks why this is not simply, "Can hope be a cloak?" One could argue from the negative and say that the latter, with its lightly accented rapid syllables between two long o's, sounds like doggerel and thus has to be avoided. But when poetry modifies actual speech for the sake of rhythm or meter, it usually manages to retain the quality of speech, as Frost does so beguilingly when his New England Yankee speaks an iambic pentameter that no new England Yankee ever spoke, or as Hopkins does when, to quote Kunitz, "however radical his deflections from the linguistic norm," he "keeps mindful of the natural flow and rhythm of speech, which serves him as his contrapuntal ground." So the question is whether or not the inversion "Can be hope a cloak?" has some relation to a quality of speech or thought that is Anne's. It would, I think, be merely a formal rationalization to say that she is a would-be poet, or even a bad poet, and thus reflects that fact in her mannered speech. But I do not think it merely a formal rationalization to relate this inversion to the meditative quality of her mind. If the short sentence is read very slowly, the inversion functions to heighten its questioning power, whereas this is not true in the doggerellike noninverted version. My example, to be sure, is rather extreme, and if *Homage* were permeated with such extremes I suspect it would be a freak or at least would break down as a poem. But the following inversions, by contrast, are more representative of this aspect of the language of the poem and even out of context reveal a "contrapuntal ground":

> Out of maize & air
> your body's made, and moves. I summon, see,
> from the centuries it.   (3.1–3)

> Winter than summer worse   (9.1)

> The shawl I pinned
> flaps like a shooting soul
> might in such weather Heaven send   (11.2–4)

> Brood I do on myself naked.   (27.4)

> so shorn ought such caresses to us be   (30.5)

> Once
> less I was anxious when more passioned to upset
> the mansion & the garden & the beauty of God.
> (49.7–8, 50.1)

The reader's response to such lines depends desperately on how they are read. *Homage* becomes a poem that demands to be read aloud; it requires, moreover, a willingness not only to be in but to participate in a reflective or a meditative mood, to join the perceiving spirit. Whenever it seems not to be reading smoothly, the reader may find that all that is necessary is a change of pace, or a pause (sometimes a short pause, sometimes a very long one), or an accent for emphasis. There is of course a limit to how much of this kind of demand a poem may make on us, for a poem must draw us into an imaginative world, not shut us out. The reader's response is finally dependent upon his orientation to a paradox. Every poem stands lifeless on the page until the reader gives it life by interpreting it, and yet every poem stands on the page only with the life that it inherently contains. In *Homage* Berryman has extended the typical twentieth-century shift-of-association device to a stylizing or mannering of speech, the intent of which is to create a new dynamics of language. As Kunitz remarks, "the peculiar energy of language compels attention." In compelling attention the language also succeeds in compelling our sympathetic involvement in character, and all that that implies. In *Homage* Berryman modifies natural rhythms of speech to suggest, which is to say to dramatize, the dynamics of human thought and emotion. In doing so he often sacrifices some but far from all of the quality of natural speech, leading critics to use such terms as *peculiar* and *queer*. To this I can only say that today's "peculiar" and "queer" may become tomorrow's standard, though *Homage* is the kind of poem that may require the reader to become an amateur actor to know its rewards.

Critics have tended, I think, to make too much of the language of *Homage* and as a consequence to ignore its structure, which combines with its language and characterization to give it hard dramatic impact. Berryman takes just four stanzas to establish the character of the poet as the caring self, ending with quietly powerful lines that declare the feeling of universal brotherhood poised with an awareness of our mortality (4.2–8). We then hear the voice of Anne, who describes the ocean crossing and early hardships in the New World with cinemato-graphic immediacy — sleet, scurvy, vermin, wigwams, a tidal river, acorns, brackish water. The controlling sensibility is that of a pioneer spirit, as shown in this religious affirmation discreetly couched in lyrical understatement: "Strangers & pilgrims fare we here, / declaring we seek a City" (8.4–5). The word *city* is charged with biblical echo, "holy city," "city of God," "they of the city shall flourish like grass" (Psalms, 72:16), "Glorious things are spoken of thee, O city" (Psalms, 87:3), "he shall build my city" (Isaiah 45:13). Specifically the reference seems to be to Hebrews 11:13–16: "These all died in faith, not having received the promises but having seen them afar off, and were persuaded of *them*, and embraced *them*, and confessed that they were strangers and pilgrims on the earth. For they that say such things declare plainly that they seek a country. . . . But now they desire a better *country*, that is, an heavenly: wherefore God is not ashamed to be called their God: for he hath prepared for them a city." This is echoed in Anne's own meditation 53: "We must, therefore, be here as strangers and pilgrims, that we may plainly declare that we seek a city above and wait all the days of our appointed time till our change shall come." Here we should note that in *Homage* Anne speaks from a point of view that both is and is not the poet's point of view. It is not the poet's point of view in the sense that he is specifically a Christian believer. It is his point of view in the sense that his humanistic fervor is a religious phenomenon. The "city" which the poet seeks is, we feel, a heart's union, an existential consciousness of the human reality as it suggests a divine reality; it is a spiritual meaning in life urgently lived as human relationship. Such a comparison and contrast, uniting and yet separating past and present, is integral to the dramatic impact of the poem. This is another aspect of fluid characterization functioning to dramatize the dynamics of human thought and emotion.

At 12.5 the voice of Anne is interrupted by the voice of the poet, and their dialogue continues until 39.4. But the focus continues to be on Anne's description of her experiences and feelings. The distinctive characteristic of that description is that it unites soaring religious and metaphysical concerns with the raw reality of the pioneer experience. Although Anne's final concern as a Puritan woman of the seventeenth century may be for a divine reality, she is also — though the terms are not hers — an existential consciousness in the act of searching for meaning in life. Religion, for her, is not a pat answer to anything. At fourteen she was carnal, and knew it. She states flatly, "Women have gone mad / at twenty-one" (15.7–8). "O love, O I love" (18.6), she exclaims, and that love is multifarious in its quality, carnal, erotic, marital (one flesh and one spirit), motherly, religious, universal, what Goethe called eternal womanly. Her consciousness is epitomized now in a long passage on the birth of her first child. It is a time of mixed emotion, of horror combined with

joy, of pain and shame, until "it passes the wretched trap whelm-
ing and I am me / drencht & powerful, I did it with my body"
(20.8, 21.1). Identity: "I am me." Anne — as any psychiatrist
would say — is healthily not alienated from her own body. The
childbirth becomes her symbol for what it means to be human,
the ultimate symbol of the caring self; also, of the continuity of
past and present, and of a sense of our mortality and immortal-
ity. Everything that she is or could be seems beautifully sum-
marized in a single line: "Mountainous, woman not breaks and
will bend" (21.5).

The childbirth passage marks the end of the first third of the
poem. The second third is the remainder of the love dialogue
between the poet and Anne, with dialogue as dialogue receiving
more emphasis and becoming quite explicit. Kunitz — in a reac-
tion parallel to that of Jarrell commenting on an early Berryman
poem called "At Chinese Checkers" — feels that it "tends to col-
lapse into bathos somewhat reminiscent of Crashaw's extrava-
gant compounding of religion and sex." He finds that Berryman
lapses into the incongruous when the poet interrupts·Anne's
flights with, for example, such lines as "I miss you, Anne" (25.3),
or "I have earned the right to be alone with you" (27.6). Berry-
man himself says that the latter line belongs to Anne, and we
should also notice that it completes a couplet: "A fading world I
dust, with fingers new. / — I have earned the right to be alone
with you." The general point, however, still has to be reckoned
with. Kunitz cites, for example, Anne in reply to the poet: "I
know. / I *want* to take you for my lover" (32.4–5). But this, it
seems to me, is to read out of context. Out of context in two
senses; first, the immediate, for Anne, as is typical with her, is in
a moment of self-recognition: "I am a sobersides; I know. / I
want to take you for my lover." I think too that a long reflective
pause, a dramatic turning to the poet, at the end of the first line
charges the lines with a quality that is anything but bathos. Sec-
ondly, the larger context should not be ignored. When Anne,
whom, following the childbirth passage, we know as a woman,
not a girl, speaks of such desire, it is not a cliché of romantic
youth but an earned truth. What is true, of course, is that such

lines as "I *want* to take you for my lover" could be out of a soap opera. In addition to context, the question is one of proportion. A powerful context has to be created; if every other line is a cliché, it never will be. Berryman's use of such lines seems to me distinctly sparing. They fall, I think, well within the framework of the poem's fidelity to the complexity of human experience, a fidelity which, of course, a soap opera never wants to have and never can have.

The dialogue following the childbirth passage functions to unite the poem's two caring selves, a marriage, symbolizing the fact that life finds its meaning in terms of human relationship. This is naturally a complement to rather than a denial of Anne's concern with obedience to the will of God. The last third of the poem is the voice of Anne except for the final three stanzas, in which the poet says his farewell. Anne continues her story, but the tones of passion, appropriately, subside. Her spirit in these last stanzas is essentially one of reconciliation. "I lie, & endure, & wonder" (51.3). We have the sense of reflecting on a whole life and all that it has meant and could mean. When the poet says farewell, we, I think, say it too. "I must pretend to leave you" (56.1). The experience of the poem has, finally, been the experience of love:

> still
> Love has no body and presides the sun,
> and elfs from silence melody. I run.
> Hover, utter, still
> a sourcing   whom my lost candle like the firefly loves.
> (57.4–8)

And so with *Homage to Mistress Bradstreet* the early Berryman becomes the later Berryman. The move is made, at approximately the age of forty, from talent to talent best applied. With *Homage* Berryman achieves poetic maturity and becomes a poet of the first rank. The process harkens back to, of all places, his short stories. *Homage*, after all, is a modern narrative, and Berryman has the narrative bent. In his short stories, moreover, he uses poetic language, and in *Homage* he is language's daring master. In *Homage* he combines in narrative form the vivid detail of American history with the sensibility of the present. But in the short stories he does not live up to his own excellent dictum: "Purity of feeling, selflessness of feeling, is the achievement of maturity," for in the short stories he remains an academic personage. But in *Homage* he achieves purity and selflessness of feeling, he creates the caring self, paradoxically retaining his academic intelligence while yet losing it. In *Homage* he is not expository, but dramatic. And in *Homage* he combines the best elements of his early self. His language is original and his musicality, his sound, is not less than marvelous. He has depth of feeling, passion, and humane concern, combined, all, in an authentic voice, or voices, with a fidelity to the complexity of human experience that only really mature poets can show. In *Homage* he is, moreover, not really "difficult," as he is in a number of his early poems, though *Homage* requires a certain careful attention if the reader is to feel its power. In American poetry following World War II, only two long poems emerge as great. Roethke's "North American Sequence" is one, and *Homage* is the other. Allen Ginsberg's "Howl" would be a third except for the fact that it is based on a false premise, that the poet, as he says in the first line of the poem, saw the best minds of his generation destroyed by madness, whereas in fact no best minds in any sense are then forthcoming, despite the poet's elaborate and passionate effort to describe them. But from premise to dramatic power Berryman in *Homage* and Roethke in "North American Sequence" are true. With *Homage* Berryman is indelible on the American scene.

The inevitable question of what was to follow *Homage* was answered eight years later by the Pulitzer Prize–winning *77 Dream Songs*, the first installment, parts i, ii, and iii, of the very long poem called "The Dream Songs," and four years after that by *His Toy, His Dream, His Rest*, the second and final installment, parts iv–vii. The total number of Dream Songs, each one eighteen lines long, is 385, thus making a poem of 6930 lines, or nearly twice the length of *Hamlet*. The arithmetic alone prompts the question, Does it all hang together? Is it finally a poem in the

ideal sense of a final imaginative coherence? Does it have a single
dramatic impact similar to that of *Homage*? The answer is flatly
no. In plain terms, it lacks plot, either traditional or associative.
In fact from an artistic point of view the Dream Songs parallel
the sonnets. It is altogether appropriate that they are collected
and numbered as a single poem, for as a sequence they are
distinctly homogeneous, but this is not the same as to say that
they have an organic structure (plot in its ultimate sense). What
distinguishes them from the sonnets, however, is the range and
quality of their imaginative power. They are even in their matur-
ity, their purity and selflessness of feeling, in some ways an
achievement beyond *Homage*, which is no light compliment. But
they are not a poem that takes the logical step beyond *Homage*,
the creation of a new masterpiece with *Homage*'s exciting single-
ness of effect and yet in every way deeper and richer.

By what standard, then, are we to judge Berryman? If
we compare "The Dream Songs" as poetic structure to *Hamlet* —
that is, to any impressively long and tightly knit poetic work
recognized as great — "The Dream Songs" comes off a poor
second. We may ask whether or not Berryman's flaws fall
reasonably within the framework of a distinguished achieve-
ment. For "The Dream Songs" the answer would, I believe, be
yes, not merely because many of them are brilliantly successful
as individual poems but, more important, because there is a
cumulative impact, a wholeness that is distinctly short of a fully
realized organic structure and yet participates in some of the
final effect that organic structure is known to yield. I would say
that Berryman made a serious mistake in not culling the Dream
Songs more carefully, in not ruthlessly discarding those that are
inferior. But even if this were done, we would end by talking
about cumulative impact as opposed to organic structure.

Not that such a matter as judging a poem as long and complex
as this will be settled in a day, for critics may well be puzzling
over it for years to come. But even Berryman himself attests to
the crucial nature of the problem of its structure: ". . . so to
begin Book VII / or to design, out of its hotspur materials, / its
ultimate structure / whereon will critics browse at large . . ."

(293). But this is, I think, essentially Berryman the academic man — and a very good one at that — assuring himself of success merely by recognizing the existence of the problem. His assertion about structure doubtless relates to his terrible unrest over the possibility that he might not succeed wholly, in final terms, as a poet. In a word, he hungers for fame, "his terrible cry / not to forget his name" (266). This all too human hunger relates, in turn, to the depths of his own personal insecurities, as might be suggested, for example, by his repeated references to mere sexual conquests, which imply great insecurity and immaturity of personality, not that he does not recognize, simultaneously, the grief of it all and seek, as always, a mature understanding of it. Put another way, there is a strong element of defensiveness in his personality, but since this is coupled with piercing honesty he emerges as a poet who delves into life and takes us with him rather than yielding to what the critic would come to judge as tired formulas.

At the heart of the Dream Songs is the character of Henry, who, according to Berryman, "refers to himself as 'I,' 'he,' and 'you,' so that the various parts of his identity are fluid. They slide, and the reader is made to guess who is talking to whom." In a somewhat defensive note to *His Toy, His Dream, His Rest* he adds that the poem "is essentially about an imaginary character (not the poet, not me) named Henry, a white American in early middle age sometimes in blackface, who has suffered an irreversible loss. . . ." This raises the important question of how imaginary is Henry and how much the real-life John Berryman he is. This in turn raises another question, which is that of the relationship between *77 Dream Songs* and *His Toy, His Dream, His Rest*. The answer to this latter question, in general terms, is that "The Dream Songs" becomes increasingly autobiographical. But its more specific terms involve an aspect of technique, a description of which is necessary to an understanding of the relationship between imaginary Henry and the real-life poet.

In technique *77 Dream Songs* is clearly an extension or variant of *Homage*, with a movement, however, from a relatively ordered consciousness, Anne's, to a relatively disordered (dream) consciousness, Henry's. But we immediately confront the problem of the relationship between Henry's life as reality and his life as dream. It is a problem that prompts recall of Jarrell's comment, "Doing things in a style all its own sometimes seems the primary object of the poem, and its subject gets a rather spasmodic treatment." *77 Dream Songs* certainly shows us a style (mainly Henry's way of speaking) all its own and, like the sonnets, has a clear subject, Henry, or more broadly the modern world. Nevertheless, these Dream Songs not only are difficult but remain difficult in spite of the reader's sympathetic acceptance of their dramatic situation, of their intent, and of their technique, whereas *Homage* by contrast does not remain difficult for long. What, then, is the best way to define the problem of these Dream Songs remaining difficult? Frederick Seidel calls it withdrawing "into abstraction," and "disguised personal allusion," but it is, I think, more than both of these things. It is essentially what Edmund Wilson was talking about when he made this comment in *Axel's Castle* on symbolism: ". . . what the symbols of Symbolism really were, were metaphors detached from their subjects — for one cannot, beyond a certain point, in poetry, merely enjoy color and sound for their own sake: one has to guess what the images are being applied to." In *77 Dream Songs* Berryman persistently takes the risk of detaching metaphor, broadly construed, from subject. That he is talking about psychic reality does not change this fact. The strange thing is that any poem in the volume may seem to have the quality of simultaneously being a metaphor detached from its subject and yet realizing its subject, giving it a treatment that could not be called spasmodic. If, on the whole, the first 77 Dream Songs emerged as metaphors detached from their subjects they would be incomprehensible and fail as poems. If, on the whole, they emerged as metaphors that fully realized their subjects (and as a structure created a world) they would probably constitute the first installment of the finest long poem in the twentieth century. Instead they tend to exist in a perilous balance which puts an extraordinary demand on the reader and holds both frustration and reward.

But the Dream Songs of *His Toy, His Dream, His Rest*, as if in acknowledgment of this problem and in a desire to do something about it, tend to drop the extraordinary demand and move in the opposite direction, often becoming such flat and explicit statement that a child, or at least a young adult, could hardly mistake their meaning, their clarity as metaphor in a broad sense. Style, in other words, is distinctly no longer the primary object of the poem. Louise Bogan could never use the phrase "this desperate artificiality" in reference to *His Toy, His Dream, His Rest* as she did with *77 Dream Songs*. What this all means in simple terms is that "The Dream Songs" grows increasingly and plainly autobiographical, though aspects of the earlier technique do persist. We become, that is, increasingly aware that Henry is indeed John Berryman struggling with his own life, with the whole problem, human, spiritual, call it what you will, of his own identity. We become increasingly aware that Henry is an imaginary character simply in the sense of serving as an alter ego, a device whereby the poet may look at himself, talk about himself, talk to himself, and be a multifarious personality. But, just as with the early Berryman, it is not an egocentric emphasis but rather a question of "how I feel" (120) in the sense of how a sensitive individual feels in response to his own psyche and to the world he inhabits. Henry is John Berryman saying, Here I am as a man, as the particular implies the universal. In this he succeeds. Henry is interesting. He has sheer interestingness, which is of course not to say that every Dream Song succeeds by this standard. That the poetic technique of "The Dream Songs" tends to shift from *77 Dream Songs* to *His Toy, His Dream, His Rest* is, it seems to me, a weakness, and this is true despite the flexibility gained by the device of fluid characterization. For a shift in technique must be functional, must be, in fact, part of the organic character of the poem as a structure. Henry, in sum, is a brilliant but insufficient unifying device. The question of how imaginary he is, and of how much the real-life John Berryman he is, is important only insofar as the poem creates a nonfunctional tension between the two. Who would object if Henry were wholly imaginary and one were hardly able to see or to care about a reference to the real-life John Berryman in the poem?

Who would object if Berryman deliberately wrote an autobiographical and perhaps even a confessional poem? What we care about is only that the poem exists beautifully as a poem, and yet in the final analysis the device *is* the poem, and so it is unsettling to lose our sense of the fictional Henry in favor of the quasi-fictional Berryman.

In *77 Dream Songs* Henry is essentially a picaresque hero in the ironic mode, a comic type who begins as a stereotype from vaudeville and ends as distinct in his humanity and suffering. He is described as "a human American man" (13), "free, black & forty-one" (40), a man whose basic problem is clearly to bear the slings and arrows of outrageous fortune, particularly the outrageous fortune of being black in white America, though fluid characterization does enable us to accept Berryman's later statement that Henry is white, which is to say, for dramatic purposes, a white man who imagines how it feels to be black. Henry is described, often in an ironic context, by such words as *bewildered, horrible, desolate, bitter, industrious, affable, subtle, somber, savage,* and *seedy.* Or in a somewhat more extended way: "hopeless inextricable lust, Henry's fate" (6), "with his plights & gripes / as bad as achilles" (14), and "savage and thoughtful / surviving Henry" (75). The words used to describe him in *His Toy, His Dream, His Rest* are quite consistent with those found in *77 Dream Songs: disordered, obsessed, stricken, sad, wilful, sympathetic, lively, miserable, impenetrable, mortal, joyous, perishable, anarchic, apoplectic,* and *edgy.* But in *77 Dream Songs,* although we have a visual, a concrete sense of what he is, he is not detailed in the sense that Mistress Bradstreet is detailed. When we finish *Homage* we can recall the facts of a biography, but when we finish *77 Dream Songs* we can recall only the existence of a man. The Henry of *77 Dream Songs* is a character in a mode perhaps best described as impressionistic or mildly surrealistic. The Henry of *His Toy, His Dream, His Rest* is in the realistic mode. Although there is certainly a strain of the picaresque hero in the later Henry, Henry *as* picaresque hero gives way to the quasi-fictional John Berryman. There is a great deal of consistency in this, but significant inconsistency too.

The complexity of the problem of responding to "The Dream Songs" as a whole poem inheres, finally, in the relationship between the conception of the character of Henry and the degree of success of the individual Dream Song. It will be instructive to select a fairly representative Dream Song from *77 Dream Songs* for commentary, and then to put it next to a fairly representative autobiographical passage from *His Toy, His Dream, His Rest.* Here is Dream Song 76, "Henry's Confession":

> Nothin very bad happen to me lately.
> How you explain that? — I explain that, Mr Bones,
> terms ǫ' your bafflin odd sobriety.
> Sober as man can get, no girls, no telephones,
> what could happen bad to Mr Bones?
> — *If* life is a handkerchief sandwich,
>
> in a modesty of death I join my father
> who dared so long agone leave me.
> A bullet on a concrete stoop
> close by a smothering southern sea
> spreadeagled on an island, by my knee.
> — You is from hunger, Mr Bones,
>
> I offers you this handkerchief, now set
> your left foot by my right foot,
> shoulder to shoulder, all that jazz,
> arm in arm, by the beautiful sea,
> hum a little, Mr Bones.
> — I saw nobody coming, so I went instead.

For purposes of analysis we can disregard the fact that the character of Henry has been previously defined and ask how this poem handles the key problem of characterization. It opens with Negro dialect, the voice of Henry, who is speaking with Mr. Bones, a friend, a vaudeville stereotype, an alter ego, a mere name suggesting death. Both characters are comic, with the comedy springing from Henry's premise that he normally expects something very bad to happen to him every day. We are at once in the world of the vaudeville skit. It is a charming and disarming world, and in its way a fit place to discuss the nature of man. But at the end of the first stanza the voice of

Henry — and the vaudeville skit — is dropped, and the poet's voice enters. The handkerchief sandwich motif at the end of the first stanza continues the vaudeville joke but some of the tone of the joke is abandoned. There is nothing particularly funny in the second stanza about the death of a father or a bullet on a stoop, especially if it is read as a reference to the suicide of Berryman's father. But at the end of the second stanza we return to the voice of Henry, though the poet is also speaking the line "You is from hunger, Mr Bones." In the first line of the third stanza we return to the voice of Henry in his conversation with Mr. Bones, but the voice that follows seems to be more that of the poet than that of Henry, and the vaudeville humor is but slightly sustained. But if the poem is to realize its subject, which I take to be man's mortality or his isolation in the universe, then the handkerchief and the sea must become unifying symbols, must take us into the subject. This they do not do in a complete way. A fuller situation for the handkerchief offering is needed, and the relationship between the popular song phrase "by the beautiful sea" and "a smothering southern sea" is not at all clear — metaphor is detached from its subject. Part of the problem is that the reference to "a smothering southern sea" (with *bullet, stoop, island,* and *knee*) is itself vague. The referent of lines 9–11 is too personal to the speaker to have universal meaning. The "smothering southern sea" happens to be the Gulf of Mexico, but knowledge of this fact does not improve the poem as a poem. And yet the poem as a whole does have singleness of effect. ". . . hum a little, Mr Bones" becomes Henry's sprightly understatement, right from a vaudeville skit, of self-persuasion and universal affirmation, not to mention the suggestion of darker agony as we hear the line as the poet's voice, or one could say a nonvaudevillian Henry. And the last line seems particularly effective as a summary of the human condition that the poem has been defining: "I saw nobody coming, so I went instead."

Consider now these lines from Dream Song 143 on the subject of the father's suicide:

He was going to swim out, with me, forevers,
and a swimmer strong he was in the phosphorescent Gulf,
but he decided on lead.

That mad drive wiped out my childhood.

It might aid our appreciation of these lines to recall the biographical fact that Berryman's father had threatened to drown himself and John with him, but the lines stand well as they are. What is being said is perfectly plain, and this plainness, this direct treatment of subject, is typical of *His Toy, His Dream, His Rest*. There are poems in *77 Dream Songs* that also treat subject directly — such as the rather conventional and quite unsuccessful 18, "A Strut for Roethke," the perfectly successful 35, "MLA," and the moving 37-39, "Three around the Old Gentleman," honoring Robert Frost — but these are more the exception than the rule.

What we have in *His Toy, His Dream, His Rest*, then, is the mature Berryman grappling in a straightforward way with the meaning of his life. One is prompted to recall the dictum of F. Scott Fitzgerald that if you begin with an individual you create a type, but if you begin with a type you create nothing. Berryman sees himself as a dying man, "in love with life / which has produced this wreck" (283). With a discreet sense of mortality he affirms his individual dignity and worth: "If the dream was small / it was my dream also, Henry's" (132). The life he looks back on is one full of wives and rages, though with typical humor he comments, "The lust-quest seems in this case to be over" (163). Though often angry and protesting, he celebrates many things, a democratic society, the sheer mystery of love, the birth of his daughter, the success of his third marriage, autumn, which seems so much to be an American season and "comes to us as a prize / to rouse us toward our fate" (385), his old friends, particularly, and elegiacally, Delmore Schwartz, the poet's ideal of perfection, "to craft better" (279), anything and everything which out of suffering he can emerge to affirm.

Taken as a whole the Dream Songs are a panoramic meditation on life and death. The title of the second volume sums them up best of all. His toy is life as a game we play (and the stakes are not less than everything), his dream is life in its psychic aspects and the poet's goal of fame, and his rest is an infinite sense of man's mortality and immortality, and finally death itself. He proclaims the value of life as a thing lived: "No, I want rest here, neither below nor above" (256), and we believe him when in Dream Song 83 he writes, "I know immense / troubles & wonders to their secret curse."

Following *His Toy, His Dream, His Rest,* John Berryman was to publish three additional volumes. The first was a volume of poems, *Love and Fame,* in 1970. The remaining two were published posthumously, a volume of poems, *Delusions, Etc.,* in 1972 and an incomplete novel, *Recovery,* in 1973. Of these I regard only *Love and Fame* as vital to an overview and final judgment of his poetic career. *Recovery,* an unfinished novel or quasi-autobiographical account of rehabilitation for alcoholism, reminds us that Berryman's imaginative power did not lie in the area of fiction. He is, for example, unable in *Recovery* to write convincing dialogue or to build to points of persuasive dramatic intensity. However sensitive his exploration of the problem of alcoholism, of its "feelings of inferiority" and its "delusions," he remains in this as in his previous fiction an academic personage. The novel is complete enough for us to know that no additional chapters could have made it succeed. *Delusions, Etc.,* though not as weak as *Recovery,* is not Berryman at his best. But *Love and Fame* is a different matter. It is, in my judgment, a beautiful work.

Love and Fame, plainly autobiographical, represents, as is the case with Berryman's Dream Songs, an achievement beyond the excellent *Homage to Mistress Bradstreet.* But at the same time we also sense in *Love and Fame* that something continues to be wrong with Berryman's art. That something is, in my opinion, that Berryman's terrible unrest is not finally made dramatically functional, is not transmuted into the kind of truth which we expect of art. More specifically, the intense feelings of ambivalence which he had toward his parents, particularly toward his father, are not absorbed into his biographically oriented art. This ambivalence, as I see it, takes the form in his later poetry of two antithetical qualities that tug at each other simultaneously and with approximately equal strength. One is dramatic integrity and fidelity to the complexity of human experience; the second is strain, unconvincing exaggeration, phoniness, rationalization, unpersuasive self-justification. We are inclined to read Berryman in *Love and Fame*, which brings the problem to a point of summation, now the one way, now the other, and often both ways at once. On the subject of his life, his sufferings, he is generally convincing, except that, strangely, there is always at least a faint suggestion of a sense in which he threatens not to be convincing at all. It is tempting to say that his later poems seem bent on serving the purpose of self-justification, but this idea is too simple. I look rather for a clue to the real problem in the fact that he is not convincing on two subjects, sex and politics. His fervent political statement strikes me as skin-deep. Sex is the subject really important to him, and my guess is that his persistent theme of sexual engagement, foul and fair but mostly fair, is a mode of bragging that in turn relates to a theme of secondary impotence which he ultimately could not come to terms with in his poetry. He was not in final terms — both as man and artist — sure of himself. Our reaction to *Love and Fame*, and to his later poetry generally, is mixed because his uncertainty sometimes carries us into the depths and other times keeps us on the surface of life, and typically does both at once. But John Berryman's gifts, however much the product of a strong will, were rare. My judgment of his work as a whole is that he earned a place in the history of American poetry but that a finer immortality eluded him.

Robert Lowell

F or all the horrors of this age, and for all the attractions of others . . . I'd rather be alive now than at any other time I know of. This age is mine, and I want very much to be a part of it," Robert Lowell remarked in 1965. Though deeply, irredeemably, involved in the present, Lowell characteristically approaches the present through the perspective of the past. This is hardly surprising. Born on March 1, 1917, into a family whose history was mingled with New England's, Lowell was personally obliged to acknowledge the importance of his lineage and forced to recognize the influence on him of what he inherited. The first woman to step off the *Mayflower* was one of Lowell's ancestors; another was twice elected governor of Plymouth. The earliest Lowell in America, Percival, became a merchant in Massachusetts in 1639. John Lowell served in the provincial and federal congresses and founded Boston's first United States Bank. Other distinguished Lowells included the builder of the Lowell cotton mills, the founders of the Lowell Institute and the Lowell Observatory, and two poets, James Russell Lowell and Amy Lowell. Rebels against tradition, yet forebears of traditions, the Lowells were energetic, curious, and inventive — but also conservative; individualistic — but also formal and ceremonious.

In Robert Lowell these paradoxes would be sharpened into a poetry equally remarkable for a sense of the apocalyptic present and a knowledge of past history, for force and control, for richness and restraint. Under the pressure of such a system of contraries, Lowell's poetic manner has changed drastically during the last thirty years. His earliest verse was characterized by a tone of baroque exaltation — for instance, in "The Drunken Fisherman" (1944):

> Wallowing in this bloody sty,
> I cast for fish that pleased my eye
> (Truly Jehovah's bow suspends
> No pots of gold to weight its ends);
> Only the blood-mouthed rainbow trout
> Rose to my bait. They flopped about
> My canvas creel until the moth
> Corrupted its unstable cloth.
>
> A calendar to tell the day;
> A handkerchief to wave away
> The gnats; a couch unstuffed with storm
> Pouching a bottle in one arm;
> A whiskey bottle full of worms;
> And bedroom slacks: are these fit terms
> To mete the worm whose molten rage
> Boils in the belly of old age?

By the sixties, Lowell's poetry had experienced many modifications. No longer oratorical and less pointedly symbolic, it might be dramatic — as in "The Drinker" (1964):

> The man is killing time — there's nothing else.
> No help now from the fifth of Bourbon
> chucked helter-skelter into the river,
> even its cork sucked under.
>
> Stubbed before-breakfast cigarettes
> burn bull's-eyes on the bedside table;
> a plastic tumbler of alka seltzer
> champagnes in the bathroom.
>
> No help from his body, the whale's
> warm-hearted blubber, foundering down

> leagues of ocean, gasping whiteness.
> The barbed hooks fester. The lines snap tight.

Or intensely personal, even confessional — as in "Fourth of July in Maine" (1967):

> We watch the logs fall. Fire once gone,
> we're done for: we escape the sun,
> rising and setting, a red coal,
> until it cinders like the soul.
> Great ash and sun of freedom, give
> us this day the warmth to live,
> and face the household fire. We turn
> our backs, and feel the whiskey burn.

Despite such striking external shifts, all of Lowell's work exhibits the same preoccupations. His basic subject has always been the fate of selfhood in time, and his basic method the examination of the convergence in man of past history and present circumstance. Much that seems contradictory in Lowell's development becomes clear when we understand that he imaginatively projects a system of tensions and contrasts which is designed to express both his will to believe and his capacity for doubt, his necessary reverence toward man or God as well as his inevitable irreverence toward the universe. Like the skeptical satirists of the Renaissance or the encyclopedists of the seventeenth and eighteenth centuries — Montaigne, Burton, Rabelais, Diderot — Lowell is essentially an ironist, interested in enigma rather than certitude, in awareness more than in knowledge. The critic of Lowell, then, must trace out the stages and varieties of his development in order to show the unity of his work and describe the nature of his achievement.

Robert Lowell's youth was characterized, he has said, by "the anarchy of my adolescent war on my parents." His mother "did not have the self-assurance for wide human experience; she needed to feel liked, admired, surrounded by the approved and familiar." As for his father, "By the time he graduated from Annapolis . . . he had reached, perhaps, his final mental pos-

sibilities. He was deep — not with profundity, but with the
dumb depth of one who trusted in statistics and was dubious of
personal experience." For the "morose and solitary" young
Robert, "hurting others was as necessary as breathing." Since he
was uncertain of his own identity he concluded that his heritage
was not precisely the one he wanted and that he would need to
reshape it if he were ever to accept it.

It was in poetry that he sought principles upon which to base
an education, and to define himself and his vocation. Around
the age of seventeen he wrote a metrical epic about the Crusades
which he showed to Robert Frost. ("You have no compression,"
Frost said.) Richard Eberhart, who was then on the faculty of
Lowell's prep school, St. Mark's, remembers that Lowell brought
him about sixty poems, "shyly placing [them] on my desk when I
was not there." These included "Madonna," Lowell's first pub-
lished poem ("Celestial were her robes: / Her hands were made
divine; / But the Virgin's face was silvery bright / Like the holy
light: Which from God's throne / Is said to shine"), "Jericho,"
"New England," "Death," "Easter, an Ode," "Jonah," and "Pho-
cion." Written in difficult Latin forms, these poems mixed
Catholic with Puritan materials ("When Cotton Mather wrestled
with the fiends from Hell"), bewailed the conflict between the
poet and society ("Most wretched men / Are cradled into poetry
by wrong"), and emphasized mystical awareness ("A sight of
something after death / Bright Angels dropping from the sky").
Eberhart remembers that "a heavy driving force and surd of
prose which would bind the lyric flow in strict forms" were al-
ready evident in them.

At Harvard between 1935 and 1937, Lowell attempted to find
"new life in his art" and shed "his other life." He rebelled against
the pedantry of the Harvard English Department and scorned
the *Advocate* — which refused to print his violent poems. He put
Leonardo and Rembrandt prints on his walls and Beethoven
on his phonograph, and collected "soiled metrical treatises
. . . full of glorious things: rising rhythm, falling rhythm,
feet with Greek names." Aided by these, he "rolled out

Spenserian stanzas on Job and Jonah surrounded by recently seen Nantucket scenery. Everything I did was grand, ungrammatical and had a timeless, hackneyed quality." In 1937 his discovery of William Carlos Williams's work unsettled his convictions about the necessity for exotic meters, intricate style, and elaborate diction and left him still longing for guidance, while rebelling against the negative identities which America, his parents, Harvard, and Boston tradition threatened to impose upon him.

At this crucial moment he defined himself through another series of writers. On the strength of a casual invitation from Ford Madox Ford, he drove to Monteagle, Tennessee, to visit him at the house of Allen Tate and Caroline Gordon. Ford had not yet arrived. But Tate immediately offered himself as friend, magisterial teacher, and literary father — exactly what Lowell was seeking. "Stately yet bohemian, leisurely yet dedicated," Tate learnedly maneuvered Lowell through the English, Greek, and Latin classics, while "blasting" most "slipshod" modern poets. His unequivocal declaration that "a good poem had nothing to do with exalted feelings" convinced Lowell that a poem "was simply a piece of craftsmanship, an intelligible or cognitive object," and that he might master its techniques. After completing the Harvard term, Lowell returned to Monteagle. With "keen, idealistic, adolescent heedlessness," he camped for three months on Tate's lawn and sweated out a series of "grimly unromantic poems — organized, hard and classical as a cabinet."

That fall, with Tate's encouragement, Lowell transferred to Kenyon College, where John Crowe Ransom set the self-consciously Aristotelian, anti-Romantic, ceremonious, and politically orthodox intellectual tone. Lowell was to be permanently affected by the influences exerted on him at this time — Ransom's New Critical emphasis on wit and paradox, Tate's "attempt to make poetry much more formal . . . to write in meters but to make the meters look hard and make them hard to write," contemplative religious literature, Hart Crane, the classics, and criticism like William Empson's *Seven*

Types of Ambiguity. Attempting to synthesize all these, he found each poem he wrote "was more difficult than the one before, and had more ambiguities." To make matters more difficult, Lowell was experiencing a spiritual crisis which ended in his rejection of the secularistic accommodations of his Protestant heritage and his conversion to Catholicism. His personal crisis resounded in his poems. Though regarding them as "forbidding and clotted," Ransom accepted two Lowell poems for *Kenyon Review* in 1939.

During the year following his *summa cum laude* graduation from Kenyon in 1940, Lowell and his new wife, Jean Stafford, lived with the Tates. While their wives hummed along on fiction, the two poets studied, talked, and wrote slowly; Lowell completed only a handful of poems in this year. Still, the creative energies released by Lowell's education, conversion, marriage, and poetic apprenticeship finally took form in a slim first volume, *Land of Unlikeness* (1944).

Strengthened by what Tate called "a memory of the spiritual dignity of man," Lowell writes in this book as an avowed Christian, with T. S. Eliot and G. M. Hopkins as his conscious models. Reviewing Eliot's *Four Quartets* in 1943, he argued that *"union with God* is somewhere in sight in all poetry." A 1944 "Note" on Hopkins shows Lowell interested in the way Hopkins's "unique personality and holiness" flowered in poetry. Certainly, much of the turbulence of Lowell's early poetry comes from his conscious struggle to approach Christian perfection. "According to Catholic theology," he wrote, "perfection demands a *substantial transformation* which is called first 'sanctifying' grace and then beatitude, it involves the co-working of grace and free will." His effort to order his language and perfect his verse was analogous (as he saw it) to the discipline of contemplation, the achieved aesthetic experience of a poem analogous to spiritual illumination. But Lowell's way with poetry would be neither Hopkins's nor Eliot's. In the American romantic tradition, he not only merged poetry with religion but equated both with culture, and thus attempted to be oratorical and satirical, exalted and apocalyptic, visionary and prophetic, idealistic and pessimistic, hortatory and violent. Yearning for a civilization in which men bear a likeness to God, he finds in the modern world only St. Augustine's *regio dissimilitudinis* — capitalism, war, secularized consciousness.

Lowell had learned much from his soiled metrical treatises — most of all from Bridges's *Study of Milton's Prosody.* His poetic techniques in *Land of Unlikeness* are carefully calculated to convey strain and tension. "There is not," R. P. Blackmur commented, "a loving metre in the book." The use of thud-meter with sporadic substitution and hard, short runover lines, often with strong caesuras immediately preceding the final stress, clogs the rhythms and hints at an agonized consciousness, able only to stab itself into language. Short, heavily stressed lines and jangling rhymes shatter the harmony, as if mellifluousness were a disease which threatened to infect him. Strained verbs call attention to the harshness of being. Repetition is the basis of his style: repeated symbols (instead of narrative development), serious puns, frequent allusions, parallelism, formal recurrence, lack of transitions, and repeated assonantal and alliterative sound devices all suggest astonished concentration on the same matter, taken up from different aspects. In losing his perception of his eternal soul's likeness to God, man is lost in time. "The Park Street Cemetery" begins the volume; "Leviathan," an apocalyptic poem of the future, ends it. Between them is a senseless present. Secular man cannot see that he is the "ruined farmer" Cain, that the Charles River is the Acheron, that war renews Christ's crucifixion, that King Philip's severed head is John the Baptist's, that the Puritans are Dracos. Such equivalences, literally understood, were basic to Lowell's imaginative conviction that history is reiteration. They necessarily kept his poems from developing: there are no climaxes in them, only the momentary shutting down of vision.

"The Boston Nativity" typifies Lowell's effects and themes. A child stillborn on Christmas Eve parallels Christ, whose redemption of man is also abortive since men at the "spun world's hub"

celebrate a secular Christmas, forgetting their likeness to God
and their kinship to Christ. "Progress can't pay / For Burial," the
poet admonishes this Christ / child:

> Child, the Mayflower rots
> In your poor bred-out stock. Brave mould, here all
> The Mathers, Eliots and Endicots
> Brew their own gall . . .

He concludes by symbolizing in this child the apocalyptic anti-
Christ whose nativity — World War II — signalizes the con-
summation of this pagan civilization: "Soon the Leviathan / Will
spout American."

"The Park Street Cemetery," "On the Eve of the Immaculate
Conception, 1942," and "Christ for Sale" are similar. There may
be hope, the poet suggests in the last — "Us still our Savior's
mangled mouth may kiss / Although beauticians plaster us with
mud" — but only for the kiss of death, the boon of extinction.
The true analogue for these poems is not mystic contemplation,
but the desperation of Tashtego's last act in *Moby Dick* — spiking
the sky-hawk to the mast and so taking down a form of divinity
with the damned *Pequod*. Lowell is fully aware of its many echoes
in his concluding "Leviathan":

> Great Commonwealth, roll onward, roll
> On blood, and when the ocean monsters fling
>   Out the satanic sting,
> Or like an octopus constrict my soul,
> Go down with colors flying for the King.

Although Lowell retained ten poems from *Land of Unlikeness*
for *Lord Weary's Castle* (1946), he dropped the outraged, Chris-
tian poems that Tate pointed to as the core of *Land of Unlikeness*,
and kept only those which could be rewritten with dramatic and
elegiac points of view. *Lord Weary's Castle* studies the dulled con-
sciousness of modern man, weary of morality and responsibility,
indifferent to crime, numb to punishment, ungrateful and pur-
poseless. Like the Lord Wearie of the ballad, man has neglected
the payment due Lambkin, Christ, the architect of his salvation.
The prophet of conscience, who had taken the epigraph for

Land of Unlikeness from St. Bernard's sermon on the Song of Songs, shifted to the poet of consciousness, who found in a traditional ballad and a humanistic use of Christian myth vehicles to express the new concerns of his imagination.

These are best indicated by Lowell's revisions of the earlier "Christmas Eve in the Time of War: A Capitalist Meditates by a Civil War Monument." "Tonight," the capitalist bitterly remarks in the original version, "the venery of capital / Hangs the bare Christ-child on a tree of gold"; hysterical, he cries "for Santa Claus and Hamilton / To break the price-controller's stranglehold." At the conclusion, the avenging Christ answers his bawling:

> "I bring no peace, I bring the sword," Christ said,
> "My nakedness was fingered and defiled."
> But woe unto the rich that are with child.

Thoroughly rewritten, reduced from five to three stanzas, and retitled "Christmas Eve under Hooker's Statue," the *Lord Weary's Castle* version dramatizes man's historic infidelity to himself in war and usury. An anonymous speaker compares the Civil War to his own disillusion; both his nation and he have been stung by knowledge. He is answered not by an apocalyptic Christ, but by Herman Melville — and not the Melville of *Moby Dick*, but of *Battle-Pieces*, a book ruled by conciliation and forgiveness. Thus Lowell hints at a stage beyond vengeance, a promise of reconciliation:

> "All wars are boyish," Herman Melville said;
> But we are old, our fields are running wild:
> Till Christ again turn wanderer and child.

Awakened to the dramatic possibilities of restoration, Lowell can end his poems climactically instead of catastrophically. Irony had resulted from his earlier method of contrasting doubt and faith, affirmation and rejection, synthesis and disintegration: now their interaction results in drama.

The first poem in *Lord Weary's Castle*, "The Exile's Return," announces and defines the principles of this shift. At the end of *Land of Unlikeness* Lowell had pointed to the consequences of man's disobedience: "When Israel turned from God's wise fellowship, / He sent us Canaan or Exile." But the exile has returned. He can, Lowell suggests in Shelleyan imagery of the seasons, have spring, a return from exile, by enduring the winter of his death. Lord Weary's destroyed castle — specifically the broken buildings and "torn-up tilestones" of occupied Germany — might be rebuilt. But man is still "unseasoned," unchanged. Lowell's symbol for contemporary man in "The Exile's Return" is Thomas Mann's Tonio Kröger, torn between nineteenth-century serenity and twentieth-century Armageddon. Thus, the poet, pointing hesitantly toward a revivification of European Christianity ("already lily-stands / Burgeon the risen Rhineland, and a rough / Cathedral lifts its eye"), considers man's renewal unlikely. "*Voi ch'entrate*, and your life is in your hands," he ambiguously concludes.

"The Exile's Return" is Lowell's inscription to the hell of his volume. Subsequent poems poise man in the Purgatorio of his indecision. "The year / The nineteen-hundred forty-fifth of grace," he writes in the second poem ("The Holy Innocents"), "Lumbers with losses up the clinkered hill / Of our purgation." "Colloquy in Black Rock," which follows, dramatizes the dialectics of indecision central to the first two poems. In its first and second sestets, locating the poem in an industrial section of Bridgeport, Connecticut, Lowell parallels the technological "jack-hammer" hell of machine society to the frenzied human heart beating jack-hammer-like toward death, breaking down into elemental "Black Mud." But the quatrain connecting these sestets, alluding to "the martyre Stephen, who was stoned to death," reminds the reader that Lowell took his epigraph for *Lord Weary's Castle* from the Secret of the Mass for St. Stephen, the first martyr for his faith. The second quatrain develops this theme: even though Stephen "was broken down to blood," his heart was the "House of our Savior" and his death a "ransom," salvation. Resolved to mud, man might escape the mire of flesh; then, mud "Flies from his hunching wings and beak — my heart, / The blue kingfisher dives on you in fire." Although this final image recalls the "dove descending" of *Little Gidding* and

Hopkins's "The Windhover," it provides a violent, and success-
ful, epiphany. By developing ordered moral connections be-
tween the Black Rock of civilization (hell), the Black Mud of
death (purgatory), and the blue kingfisher-Christ (salvation),
Lowell created an image of salvation as powerful as his images of
destruction. The poem which investigates their connections
coheres and develops.

Asked to comment on his poetry, Lowell said he was "essen-
tially in agreement" with Randall Jarrell's review of *Lord Weary's
Castle*. Lowell's poems, Jarrell argued, "understand the world as
a sort of conflict of opposites": there is "the cake of custom," the
realm of inertia, complacence, and necessity, everything that
blinds or binds: "the Old Law, imperialism, militarism, capital-
ism, Calvinism, Authority, the Father, the 'proper Bostonians,'
the rich . . ."; against this grinds "everything that is free
or open, that grows or is willing to change." Lowell's earliest
poems moved toward the closed world — from unfulfilled pos-
sibility to the necessity of apocalypse. Now he moves them from
necessity toward intimations of liberation.

The major poem of the second mode is "The Quaker
Graveyard in Nantucket." New England's whaling industry,
based on the greedy exploitation of nature; Ahab's arrogant
vengeance in *Moby Dick*; modern war, resulting in the death at
sea of Lowell's cousin Warren Winslow; and modern politics,
Hobbes's Leviathan, the state, are all analogues of each other.
Constricting human possibility, all hint at the way that modern
men prey on each other and point to the "promised end" de-
scribed in *King Lear* as the result of violations of the cosmic
order.

Sections I to V of the poem are generally pervaded by
images of the closed world, all that is wrecked and de-
stroyed — Winslow himself, the shipwreck described in Thor-
eau's *Cape Cod*, the doomed *Pequod*, and, at last, secular Amer-
ica. But in this poem Lowell works from the apocalyptic to
the elegiac tradition — the obvious model for his prosody,
themes, and organization coming from Milton's "Lycidas." Like
Milton, Lowell asserts that disaster can be averted and the moral

order restored through Christ. The apocalyptic analogies are balanced by a redemptive series: the design of Creation announced in Genesis; Quaker traditions of pacificism; the traditional symbolization of Christ as a whale, "IS, the whited monster"; Father Mapple's warnings in *Moby Dick* about the neglect of gospel duty; St. Matthew's claim (12:40) that Jonah's imprisonment in the whale's belly for three days prophesied Christ's resurrection; the Jewish mystical tradition that (as summarized in Jessie L. Weston's *From Ritual to Romance*), "at the end of the world, Messias will catch the great Fish Leviathan, and divide its flesh as food among the faithful"; and, at last, the Virgin's shrine at Walsingham, destroyed in the Reformation and recently restored. By section VI, these suggest a cosmic arc of liberation, the promised end of salvation — for Winslow and "the world [that] shall come to Walsingham" to contemplate the Unknowable "expressionless / Face" standing above the world of profane action. At first associated with the closed world, Winslow is finally identified with the liberating re-creation. Lowell's last line, "The Lord survives the rainbow of His will," alludes to God's covenant with Noah after the flood wiped away a corrupt world, as well as to Shelley's famous conclusion to "Adonais." Like Keats, trampled to fragments in life, Winslow is transfigured in the image of the rainbow, the "dome of many-colored glass" of a renewed genesis and covenant with man. The self — of Winslow or of the poet who meditates on his death — is defined by its absorption into suprapersonal structures of behavior and belief.

Elsewhere in the volume Lowell employs the opposite method — defining the ego by its separation from coherent spiritual guides. In poems of this mode, he mixes psychological, naturalistic, and clinical with phantasmagoric images and perspectives. "I lean heavily to the rational, but am devoted to surrealism," he has said. The utterly rational man, he implies, can be described only by surrealist techniques; the self locked in itself is nightmarish, and makes surrealism "a natural way to write our fictions."

The major poem of this mode is "Between the Porch and the Altar." Its contemporary hero "thinks the past / Is settled. It is honest to hold fast / Merely to what one sees with one's own eyes." For past affirmations of social, political, or religious communities, he has only "awed contempt." Separated from these, he has only a lost self talking and dreaming itself into existence, and he must conclude: "Never to have lived is best." The final section of the poem is his death fantasy. At a Boston nightclub called "The Altar" he and his mistress watch an ice-skating floor show. Driving home, he dreams he has an automobile accident near a church where his funeral mass is being performed. Self-contained, his existence has had no meaning except the numbed agony of self-consciousness; his birth and death are one wheel of fire — "The bier and baby-carriage where I burn."

Yet, submerged in his unconscious reflections, dreams, and memories are suprapersonal archetypes by which the hero might have been more than a Meredith and enter ancient passion even through modern love. The title of the poem is derived from Joel 2:17, the epistle read in the mass on Ash Wednesday, and hints at the whole of sacred history between genesis (the Porch), and apocalypse (the Altar). The fall of Adam is recreated in the speaker's failure. Images of idols, serpents, and dragons writhe in his mind from Ezekiel and Revelation. Even his dream that he has raced "through seven red-lights" is a phantasmagoric overflow of his suppressed guilt over committing the seven deadly sins. Unable to acknowledge these beliefs, which torment him into guilty nightmare, the speaker is tragic, his poem a drama of consciousness.

The major modes of *Lord Weary's Castle* are (1) the definition of the individual through suprapersonal structures and (2) the dramatization of the self's terrifying alienation from these through the divorce of observation from feeling and of sensibility from culture. "In Memory of Arthur Winslow" combines these modes. In a well-defined theological tradition of New England writing — Mrs. Stowe's *The Minister's Wooing* is an earlier example — this poem, a meditation on Winslow's death outside the religious community, raises basic questions concerning the relation between belief and salvation. Winslow, section ı suggests, is conducted "Beyond Charles River to the Acheron" and hell (a greater Boston) by "longshoreman Charon," damned because he had no faith. He contrasts to earlier New England's "Pilgrim Makers," in whose lives politics were united with belief in God's Holy Will for his people in America. In the family cemetery where Winslow is buried (section II), the tombstones of the early settlers "are yellow," "sunken landmarks," echoing unheeded "what our fathers preached." Their faith had made the Pilgrims "point their wooden steeples lest the Word be dumb"; now, dwarfed pines (instead of steeples), "the first selectman of Dunbarton," a "preacher's mouthings," and a dying sun symbolize the dwarfed civilization (the "shell of our stark culture") of which Winslow has been a part. He "must have hankered for our family's craft," Lowell writes in III. But lacking his ancestors' sense of permanency, he has not attached himself to anything permanent. His modern "craft" substitutes capitalistic for communitarian accomplishments and allows him to lose in Boston real-estate speculations the gold hosed out from Colorado.

In section IV, "A Prayer for My Grandfather to Our Lady," the poet defines his own permanent attachments. He will not unsay his judgments of the "painted idols" adored by his grandfather, but he musters the faith to pray for him: "Mother, run to the chalice, and bring back / Blood on your finger-tips for Lazarus who was poor." His prayer is a collage of his two modes. Imitating the stanzaic form of Matthew Arnold's "The Scholar Gypsy" and recalling the "sea of faith" in "Dover Beach," Lowell symbolizes in Winslow the closed world, "Beached / On . . . dry flats of fishy real estate," sterile even at the edge of the sea. But the poet is in the sea striking for shore. Denouncing modern degradation, he yet achieves a dramatic ecstasy of awareness; and mediating between the closed and open worlds, he speaks for himself.

Lord Weary's Castle brought Lowell, barely thirty, a Pulitzer Prize, praise from T. S. Eliot, Conrad Aiken, William Carlos Williams, and George Santayana, and appointment as the consultant in poetry at the Library of Congress. His third volume, *The Mills of the Kavanaughs* (1951), showed further development of his technical range. Having explored Puritan and Catholic

Christian humanism in his first two books, he now gave up orthodox affiliation with any church and proceeded to use Western civilization and his personal crisis as material for his poetry. This new work showed the increasing influence of Ransom rather than Tate; of narrative poets like Chaucer, Dryden, Milton, Browning, Hardy, E. A. Robinson, and Conrad Aiken rather than of the metaphysicals or Hart Crane; and of prose writers like Henry Adams, James, Tolstoi, Chekov, and Faulkner. Earlier, Lowell's language had been characterized by its tension, a straining to push to and beyond the capacities of language. In *The Mills of the Kavanaughs* he moved toward the language of urbanity, where the strain exists in the sensibility and consists in the attempt to conceal the strain which periodically leaps through the conversational surface. Lowell reined his tendency toward generalization and accusation and developed single-mindedly his talent for complex plots, conversational ease, and vivid characters. While his verse shows a marked decrease in religious fervor it correspondingly increases in sensuous observation, interest in sexual passion, preoccupation with individual yearning and frustration, and emphasis on particularized character.

Love and morality are the central themes of *The Mills of the Kavanaughs*. The speaker of each of the seven poems has experienced a crisis of belief which arises from his involvement with morality and love. In "Falling Asleep over the Aeneid" an old man dreams that at the funeral of Pallas he is Aeneas. He remembers that years before, his aunt called him away from reading the *Aeneid* — "'Boy, it's late. / Vergil must keep the Sabbath'" — to prepare for his Uncle Charles's funeral, attended by "Phillips Brooks and Grant," the cultural and military heroes of the American Civil War. The *Aeneid* and the Civil War merged in the boy's mind and affected his life. Now the old man, missing church for Vergil and using his uncle's sword for a crutch, comes to understand the meaning of his uncle's death as a heroic aspect of American history by redreaming it through the perspective of the Roman epic of man and nation. Though Lowell's technique is borrowed from *Sweeney Agonistes*, his old

man achieves stature denied to Sweeney by asserting the power
of memory over habit and of perspective over the present.
Though outwardly pathetic, the old man himself is a hero in
emphasizing, like Vergil, the enduring powers of morality and
love and celebrating them imaginatively.

Lowell's longest consecutive poem, "The Mills of the Kavan-
aughs" brings cultural memory together with psychological
analysis through the mode of drama. Based on the principles
of mythic literature that Eliot defined in reviewing *Ulysses*, the
poem manipulates "a continuous parallel between contem-
poraneity and antiquity," as "a way of controlling, or ordering,
or giving a shape and a significance to the immense panorama of
futility and anarchy which is contemporary history." Anne
Kavanaugh, suddenly faced with a crisis of memory and self,
plays solitaire with the Douay Bible as her partner and "dummy"
opponent. But, irresistibly, she finds her analogue not so much
in Christian myth as in Ovid's account of Persephone in
Metamorphosis, V. Four-parted, in imitation of Persephone's cir-
cle of seasons, her reverie details her life in relation to her
husband's. Beginning in spring, when she meets Harry (stanzas
1–7), and continuing through the summer of their courtship
(8–15), the autumn of marriage (16–22), and the winter of
Harry's manic depression and suspicion (23–38), her recollec-
tions join myth and fact in daydreams and nightmares. Harry,
the Demeter-Pluto to her Persephone, turns "whatever brought
one gladness to the grave."

As characters in his poems find secular stability through su-
prapersonal forms of belief, myth, or meditation, so perhaps
Lowell himself turned to drama as a way of achieving poetic
objectivity and personal stability during the breakup of his first
marriage. His crisis of self prompted him to portray people at
critical moments. That he did not yet dare express personal
emotions directly, but concealed them in myth and dramatic
monologue prompted William Carlos Williams to complain that
he preferred "a poet of broader range of feeling" than that
shown in *The Mills of the Kavanaughs*.

Still, this volume points directly to Lowell's development in his subsequent work, in which three strains predominate: (1) imitations, disconnected from the mythic method, however "repoeticized" (as in *Imitations*, 1961, and *The Voyage and Other Versions of Poems by Baudelaire*, 1968); (2) drama, associated either with the mode of imitation (as in *Phaedra*, 1961, and *Prometheus Bound*, 1969), or with Lowell's efforts to dramatize the history of culture (as in *The Old Glory*, 1965); and (3) poems exploring the central character of the poet himself (as in *Life Studies*, 1959, *For the Union Dead*, 1964, and *Near the Ocean*, 1967).

An important influence on *The Mills of the Kavanaughs* was Chaucer, whom Lowell called "our one English poet to tell stories in a clear, distinguished, witty, absorbing style." For Lowell, Chaucer provided not only an example of narrative clarity; Chaucer's contemporaries called him the "great translatour" in recognition of the skill with which he freely rendered foreign tales into English poetry. Already interested in translation, Lowell in the fifties began seriously to write what he would call "imitations," repoetizations of European authors. In the fall of 1949 Lowell went with his second wife, Elizabeth Hardwick, to teach at the Writer's Workshop of the University of Iowa and promptly announced a course called "Five Poets in Translation" (Rimbaud, Baudelaire, Valéry, Rilke, Horace), soon adding others to these (Foscolo, Leopardi, Vigny, Musset, Verlaine, Mallarmé, Gautier, and Hugo). Inevitably led to study the heritage of these poets, he next offered a "Greek Poetry Workshop" in Homer (his favorite poet) and Pindar. His critical method, as recalled by one of his Iowa undergraduates, is illuminating. After reading a poem in the original and loosely translating it, he proceeded to commentary: "He would describe a phrase in terms of another phrase, another poet, a group of people, a feeling, a myth, a novel, a philosophy, a country. . . . He would compare and contrast, describe." Such teaching, followed by three years' residence in Europe, led to Lowell's imitations. Imitation became his way of discovering himself in poetic tradition. But he also regarded the act of translation as an act of culture — the retrieval or the preservation of a heritage of sense and sensibility, for the sake of contemporary life. He said that because "no [earlier] translator [had] had the gifts or the luck to bring Racine into our culture," he attempted to translate *Phèdre*, a play adapted by Racine from Euripides' *Hippolytus*. By doing so, he hoped, some of the concerns shared by classical and enlightenment culture would be made available to modern men. He also claims contemporary relevance for his rendering of *Prometheus Bound*: "I think my own concerns and worries and those of the time seep in." As Americans have often learned their Americanism abroad, Lowell sharpened his American vision through classical and European poetry. Williams had warned Lowell not to remain in Europe. His imitations brought him back by showing him how best to possess Europe as an American.

Lowell rewrote, shortened, lengthened, or otherwise altered others' poems with Jamesian boldness, as if revising his own earlier work according to his mature perspective, designing *Imitations* to be read as a sequence of original poems. Finding "something equivalent to the fire and finish of [the] originals" involved, Lowell remarked, "considerable re-writing." Stressing the unity of his selections by rendering all in the same style, he also ordered them in a continuous sequence which breaks chronology in order to repeat and interweave themes. Not at all an eclectic collection of European poems, *Imitations* resembles many modern long poems based on the principle of *Song of Myself* in developing through a sequence of insights, investigations, images, and observations.

In *Imitations* a single mode of the imagination predominates: the poet confronts and understands himself through engagement with all that is not-the-self — others' selves, as in "For Anna Akmatova"; historical objects, as in "A Roman Sarcophagus"; other poets, as in the Gautier elegies; myth, as in "Helen." But the self confronts itself chiefly through what Lowell calls the "mania" in man and physical nature. The first poem is Lowell's description (from Homer) of the killing of Lykaon by Achilles. "Sing for me, Muse," he begins, "the mania of Achilles." Rich in the imagination of atrocity, the speech of Achilles is indeed manic. In his last poem (Rilke's "Pigeons," dedicated to Hannah Arendt, who has written of the manias of modern man) Lowell reminds us of the persistence in modern times of the ancient Achillean way, closing the volume with an image of mania's eternal return:

> Over non-existence arches the all-being —
> thence the ball thrown almost out of bounds
> stings the hand with the momentum of its drop —
> body and gravity,
> miraculously multiplied by its mania to return.

A meditation on historical circularity, then, *Imitations* begins with Achilles' manic joy in irrationality and violence and shows man repeating his madness. The Trojan War provides Lowell's main symbols — in the first and last poems, in Sappho ("Helen forgot her husband and dear children"), Villon ("Helen has paid this debt — no one who dies dies well"), Heine ("That fellow in Homer's book was quite right"), Valéry (the poem "Helen"), and Pasternak ("Summer . . . hears the god's Homeric laughter"). Troy, of course, merely represents man's ever-present mania for violence.

But equally strong and as omnipresent is man's impulse toward boredom. Indeed, though violence and ennui seem to be opposites, they are really, Lowell suggests, but the two faces of the single mania of the human condition, the alternating poles between which human activity runs. Sappho ("to have lived is better than to live!") and Montale ("even your ennui is a whirlwind") both hint at this relatedness, directly treated in Lowell's imitation of Baudelaire's "To the Reader": "Among the vermin, jackals, panthers, lice, / gorillas and tarantulas" driving man, his central impulse, Lowell writes, "makes no gestures, never beats its breast, / yet it would murder for a moment's rest, / and willingly annihilate the earth. / It's BOREDOM." Atrocity and ennui, the manias which Lowell orchestrates in his sequence, combine at the book's center in Rimbaud's "The Poet at Seven": "What he liked best were dark things: / . . . dizziness, mania, revulsions, pity!" Other recurrent themes, concerning the melancholy state of existence, old age and death, and endeavor and frustration, provide a dark background for these even darker main themes.

Certainly, what Lowell called "the dark . . . against the grain" stands out in *Imitations*; but blind mania is not the unabated concern of the book. In *Prometheus Bound* his hero declares that "Zeus has consented to let [man] live, miserable, dying, though equal to the gods in thought." This distinction between a blank, unremitting universe and man's consciousness runs through *Imitations*. The artist's confrontation of human atrocity in himself and others, and the self-consciousness which, in consequence, he may turn into art as a heritage for others — this alone prevents history from being merely a sequence of manias. The light against the grain in Lowell's series is the growth of sensibility. Lowell constructs a myth by using other poets and their poems as characters and themes; those he imitates as well as the contemporaries to whom he dedicates his imitations — Williams, Eliot, William Meredith, and Stanley Kunitz — are characters in this cultural myth. His poems are testaments of the consciousness which artists have achieved in the "troubled depths" of atrocity and indifference.

His imitations, Lowell said, were guided by his sense of "what my authors might have done if they were writing their poems now and in America." *The Old Glory*, his dramatic trilogy, is a forceful restoration, on native grounds, of Hawthorne and Melville, who perceived in the 1850s the development of national dilemmas which have culminated disastrously in the present. The mania for authority pervading American culture connects the separate plays of *The Old Glory*. Ideals are inevitably compromised by becoming institutionalized; their triumphs include the promise of their defeats; fearing, yet wishing, their own destruction, men hold power through oppression, even while knowing that this must bring their downfall. In Lowell's first play, *Endecott and the Red Cross*, two versions of authority collide through Blackstone and Morton. Blackstone argues for a hierarchical world in which "Our kingdom is a pyramid, / Charles Stuart stands at the top. Below him, / his sub-

jects descend uniformly and harmoniously / down to the lowest
farmer." "That's your theory," replies Morton, who represents
the commercial values of the merchant class. "I have mine for
this country. / Lords and college men are needed in England.
I'm needed here." Holding the power to establish either
Blackstone's political or Morton's commercial authoritarianism
on American soil, Endecott, the governor of Puritan Salem, in-
clines toward both; wavering, feeling himself a "suit of empty
armor," and knowing that he must betray one part of him-
self whatever he does, he determines to establish Puritan
Theocracy — the authority of God — and to expunge both
Blackstone and Morton.

The result is foreseeable. By the Revolutionary period, when
My Kinsman, Major Molineux takes place, Puritanism has become
decadent through power and Blackstone's and Morton's au-
thoritarianisms are once again in conflict. Molineux, representa-
tive of the king, a later Blackstone, has gained power; but he is
once again opposed by the commercial spirit of Morton, rep-
resented by the democratic Man in Periwig, who cries: "I
have / authority, authority!" When political power leads to op-
pression, democratic commercialism seems to promise freedom.
Molineux is ousted and his kinsman, Robin, the central figure
in the play, remains in the commercial town of Boston. "It's
strange / to be here on our own — and free," he says. But al-
ready sensing the impermanence of freedom, he also asks uneas-
ily: "Where will it take us to?" Inevitably, as *Benito Cereno* shows,
in democracy different forms of authority and oppression are
instituted. Convinced that in his "icy dignity" a captain is the
opposite of a slave, Captain Amasa Delano loves hierarchy of all
kinds and re-creates Blackstone's pyramidal world on his ship.
"*A good master deserves good servants!*" he declares. His name, he
thinks, has "some saving / Italian or Spanish virtue in it"; he tells
his mate: "We need inferiors, Perkins, / more manners, more
docility, no one has an inferior mind in America."

Delano is a later Endecott whose democracy is compromised
by his power. Lowell wrote *Benito Cereno*, he said, "to show my
horror of slavery and violence." Though Delano can kill Babu,

the trilogy shows that the exercise of power is the doom of
authority. "The future is with us," the slave cries before he is
killed; and Delano answers, as he shoots, "This is your future."
Their future — our own time — is different from what either
could envision, yet both are right: Endecott, the revelers of
Merry Mount, Robin, his brother, the citizens of Boston, Delano,
Perkins, and Babu are all innocents spun about by their in-
volvement in history. "America's is the Ahab story of having to
murder evil: and you may murder all the good with it if it gets
desperate enough to struggle," Lowell has written. "God help
me," Delano moans, "nothing's solid." What *is* solid, *The Old
Glory* shows, is the mania for power in history and the inevitabil-
ity of its corruption through the "occult connection" between
idealism and violence.

Lowell's poetic and dramatic imitations constituted only one of
the developments in his work in the fifties and sixties. For a time
after completing *The Mills of the Kavanaughs*, Lowell seemed un-
able to write original poems — his imagination seemed clogged.
Dissatisfied with his "distant, symbol-ridden, and willfully
difficult" manner, he felt that all his work had the same "stiff,
humorless and even impenetrable surface." A number of factors
were important in the unbinding of his imagination. His imita-
tions freed him from too narrow a concentration on America by
prodding him to discover in his own voice the equivalent to the
voices of earlier, non-American poets. Settling in Boston in 1954
with a view toward rediscovering some roots, he made a start on
a prose autobiography. He became interested in psychoanalysis,
particularly in Freud. Now, "Freud seemed the only religious
teacher" to him. He began giving poetry readings, and "more
and more [he says] I found that I was simplifying my poems. If I
had a Latin quotation I'd translate it into English. If adding a
couple of syllables in a line made it clearer I'd add them." His
readings loosened his tight, difficult forms; and his interest in
autobiography and self encouraged respect for prose ("less cut
off from life than poetry is") and diminished his interest in
highly rhetorical poetry. In short, he became interested in the
discovery, the invention, and the definition of his self; and he

attempted to incorporate into his work the contemporary forms, myths, and metaphors which describe the individual imagination.

The result was *Life Studies*. Believing that personal experience alone guarantees truth, many modern poets have written autobiography. But Lowell's confessional poetry derives less from alienation than from an understanding of the destiny of personality in culture. Terrorization of individual man, he knows, has been continuous in the history of society; but culture sometimes nourishes the best achievements of the self. Involved in both, he renders the interconnected realities of personality and culture without simplifying or distorting either. Modernizing Thoreau through Freud, Lowell writes letters from the distant land of self to kindred selves. Even his most painfully personal poems have public dimensions and (as confessions) imply a listener — the analytic faculty of the poet's imagination overhearing the secrets of his personality. The New Englander and the Viennese Jew are Lowell's distant kindred, and their sharply different cultures the mixed audience he assumes.

Lowell gave *Life Studies* coherence through carefully structuring his book into four parts. In the first poem, "Beyond the Alps," he describes his meditations during a train trip from Rome to Paris; concluding that he will leave "the City of God where it belongs" to take up citizenship in the City of Man, he announces the point of view from which the volume is organized. Through commentary on economics, politics, and militarism, the next three poems in Part One explore the societal context for human activity outside the City of God. The remaining three parts investigate the consolations given to the sensibility willingly exiled in the City of Man. Human responsiveness — to humor and guilt, memory and remorse, consciousness and conscience — in short, receptivity to experience, still remains. "91 Revere Street," an autobiographical prose fragment, shows Lowell in the process of revivifying his own responsiveness by remembering its origins in his youth. Reviving Henry James's concept of autobiography in *A Small Boy and Others*, he first gives an account of the solitary "small boy," then of the "others" through whom he further defines himself and grows to manhood. He implies that a childhood constituted as his was led him to the discovery of artistic sensibility and made it inevitable that he become a poet. Appropriately, then, "91 Revere Street" is followed by four poems exploring varieties of aesthetic impulses. "Ford Madox Ford," "For George Santayana," "To Delmore Schwartz," and "Words for Hart Crane" suggestively parallel the first four poems of the volume and explore what satisfaction art opens to men having to do without faith though "divorced" from the "whale-fat" of corrupted social life. These form a dramatic interlude equipping the man of experience with intimations about how to make experience meaningful, a substitute for the lost life of the City of God, through art.

The synthesis of experience and art is tested in the fifteen confessional poems of Part Four, "Life Studies." Section i of this part, consisting of eleven poems, continues the reminiscential materials of "91 Revere Street." But now the poems imply connections between the poet in the present and his accounts of his past. This is obvious by the ninth poem, "During Fever," when Lowell refers to his own child, his "daughter in fever." In the next two poems, "Waking in the Blue" and "Home after Three Months Away," Lowell defines his present dilemmas as the result of his heritage and writes about himself, "frizzled, stale and small." In contrast to his first three volumes, where experience grates against the perception of it, in *Life Studies* Lowell is unwilling and unable to locate value through the absolutes of the City of God and accepts the City of Man as the single context for the content of human experience.

This shift of context is stressed in "My Last Afternoon with Uncle Devereux Winslow," a poem designed to remind the reader of "In Memory of Arthur Winslow." Both are four-parted; and, as the earlier poem is followed in *Land of Unlikeness* by a coda ("Winter in Dunbarton"), "My Last Afternoon" precedes "Dunbarton," an account of the burial place of Devereux Winslow. As before, Lowell hints at the vacuity, spiritual hollowness, and pretensions of his ancestors. But he also adopts the perspective of the Jamesian small boy, to whom "Nowhere was anywhere after a summer / at my grandfather's farm"; the boy's puzzled and sympathetic point of view prevails. Certainly, as F. W. Dupee wrote of *Life Studies*, "The book abounds in second-class Lowells, in mothers who were unequal to their pretensions when alive and to their black and gold coffins when dead"; but the poems as critically observe the boy "who had chronic asthma, chronic truculence, and got himself expelled from the public gardens. Lowell's often merciless anatomy of his parents is matched by his merciless account of himself." Like his Victorian ancestors, whom he can now accept with their unmitigable faults, the poet is on a journey — toward the acceptance of his own faults, and so of himself as their inheritor. Thus in *Life Studies* there is no gritting between the poet and his experience. Both are criticized, understood, and accepted from the same perspective.

"My Last Afternoon" epitomizes Lowell's synthesis of material experience with art, its images paralleling the four basic elements with kinds of art. Section i combines images of earth ("One of my hands was cool on a pile / of black earth, the other warm / on a pile of lime") and the fertility of the earth ("oranges, lemons, mint, and peppermints") with images of literature ("A pastel-pale Huckleberry Finn"). Section ii develops this order by naming water ("Distorting drops of water") and expanding the plastic imagery of section i in references to sculpture: the boy speaks of the "Olympian / poise of my models" and sees himself as a "stuffed toucan." Moving upward in the elements in section iii, he looks "Up in the air," and also portrays his Great Aunt Sarah and the "soundless" music which she practices on a dummy piano. Deepening his perception of the connections between nature and art in this section, he summarizes his earlier images — of earthy fertility and literature ("troublesome snacks and Tauchnitz classics"), of water ("by the lakeview window," "a thirsty eye"), of statuary ("naked Greek statues draped with purple") and the bird ("risen like the phoenix").

All these are focused on section iv, as, combining nature with art, the poet prepares to face the otherwise meaningless early death of Devereux Winslow. While the fourth element of fire ("a barrage of smoke-clouds") is hinted at, and another form of art, posters and photographs, is introduced, the important movement of the imagery in section IV is its aesthetic synthesis of the boy's metaphoric experience; he has achieved perspectives whereby to view death as an aspect of natural and artistic order. His heightened sense of the connections between experience and art allows the poet to become simultaneous with his own childhood and assert "I wasn't a child at all." The child who experienced the death and the adult artist are united. At the end of the poem, he returns to the earth, meaningful in terms of the whole ordered cycle of creation:

> He was dying of the incurable Hodgkin's disease. . . .
> My hands were warm, then cool, on the piles
> of earth and lime,
> a black pile and a white pile. . . .
> Come winter,
> Uncle Devereux would blend to the one color.

The four poems in the second section of "Life Studies" unify the volume by closely paralleling the four which began it. Since secularism, economics, politics, militarism, and insanity — public and private madness — have assumed personal meaning through the revelations and identifications of the intervening poems, the poet renders them through his own experiences, rather than those of Marie de Medici, President Eisenhower, or a mad Negro soldier. Having delineated experience through symbols external to his own experience, Lowell made himself his central symbol and so passed (as he remarked of "Skunk Hour") "way beyond symbols into reality." "I want the reader of my poems to say, this is true," he declared in an interview. "I want him to believe he is getting the *real* Robert Lowell."

The authentic Lowell dominates "Skunk Hour," where he writes of the crisis of self which led to the mental derangements and hospitalization dramatized earlier in *Life Studies*. Here he investigates the principles by which the ill mind moves — tentatively, and through art — back to health. Hinting in his title at the formalized Chinese calendar, Lowell suggests that he too will have his hour of truth — new awareness. Stanzas 1–4 center on the paradoxical association of role-playing with death: in the aged "hermit / heiress"; in the gaily dressed summer millionaire who has either died or become bankrupt; and in the Maine landscape, whose ruddy autumn barely conceals the white death of approaching winter. Masks have less and less efficacy to hide the dead hollows beneath them. The portrait of the decorator in stanza 4 outrightly names him "our fairy"; and though he laments that "there is no money in his work, / he'd rather marry," the feminine rhyme (fairy / marry) strikes through the mask. Human corruption — through solitude, fraudulence, and trivialization — is vividly portrayed in this first half of the poem. The second half focuses on the poet, himself implicated in the masquerading "ill-spirit" he observes in others. How can he avoid the corruption that he sees? And if he responds intensely to it, how can he preserve himself from despondency and madness, the derangements in his heritage?

"We poets in our youth begin in sadness; / thereof in the end come despondency and madness," Lowell had given Delmore Schwartz to say in Part Three of *Life Studies*. Schwartz cannot be a Wordsworth to Lowell's Coleridge; though "resolution" and "independence" might preserve him at the end of "Skunk Hour," Lowell is obliged to write odes to dejection before lyrics of affirmation. He defines his emotional crisis, then, by references to a variety of familiar passages describing spiritual disaster: St. John of the Cross's Dark Night of the Soul ("One dark night"), Christ's crucifixion ("the hill's skull"), Lear's confusion on the heath ("My mind's not right"), and Satan's self-condemnation at the prospect of Eden in Book IV of *Paradise Lost* ("I myself am hell; / nobody's here"). His sense of tradition does not save him — it simply gives him a way of understanding (and so for a moment controlling) his personal crisis, an aspect of the general human madness.

That the leap which his mind takes toward restoration occurs in the sole run-on stanza conveys vividly the mental rush necessary to revivify the disordered mind before self-disgust extin-

guishes it. The available image ("only skunks") which he almost
hopelessly seizes upon for support turns out to possess extraor-
dinary power as a symbol for naturalness, passion ("eyes' red
fire"), fertility, and persistence — human qualities which the
poet must revive in himself. Not the literature of disaster, but
the primitive nature religion of the racial unconscious provides
his symbols — the column and the pail, the "wedge-head" and
the "cup" — reminders (from *The Golden Bough*) of continuing
fertility. "Skunk Hour," in short, describes a poet who has
moved from contemplation of the hermit-mother "in her dot-
age" to the skunk-mother in her prime, from a decadent human
world to individual revitalization. Lowell began *Life Studies* by
pointing to the journey he would take. In "Skunk Hour" he is
still traveling. He has gone beyond Paris, the City of Man, to
himself, in Maine. Often set adrift, and through the shipwreck
of his absolutes made "frizzled, stale and small," he ascends in
this last poem "the hill's skull" for one more crucifixion. But by
finding in the mother skunk a way to express the possibility of
vitality, he stands at the end "on top / of our back steps." The
steps of his own house are all the Alps or Golgotha he will have;
for he has shown through the volume that the City of Man — of
society and of self — will suffice. Now, like the skunk, he "will
not scare." Instead, as in a symposium Lowell said of his compo-
sition of this poem, he survives his "strange journey . . . cling-
ing to spars, enough floating matter to save [him], though
faithless."

After the completion of *Life Studies* Lowell felt emptied of self,
uninterested in individuality. "Something not to be said again
was said," he wrote to M. L. Rosenthal. "I feel drained, and
know nothing except that the next outpouring will have to be
unimaginably different — an altered style, more impersonal
matter, a new main artery of emphasis and inspiration." At
the Boston Arts Festival in 1960, Lowell remarked: "When
I finished *Life Studies* I was left hanging on a question mark.
. . . I don't know whether it is a death rope or a lifeline."
It remained for him to join the modes of *Imitations* and
Life Studies by investigating simultaneously the sense that self

makes out of the history it hoards and the culture that draws back the self which would be lost through fleeing it. The possibilities of this synthesis provide the "new main artery of emphasis and inspiration" of *For the Union Dead* and *Near the Ocean*.

In *For the Union Dead* old poems are revived, previous themes are reinvigorated, the vatic utterance of his earliest manner and the confessional tone of his most recent are recalled. It is not so much a coming to grips with a new poetry as a completion of all that was implied in the earlier. The parallels with previous volumes are innumerable: "Water" recalls "The Quaker Graveyard" and "The North Sea Undertaker's Complaint," and (in its scene and situation) "Skunk Hour." "The Old Flame" rewrites the marriage sequence of *The Mills of the Kavanaughs* in personal terms, and recalls such *Life Studies* poems as "Man and Wife" and "'To Speak of Woe That Is in Marriage.'" "Memories of West Street and Lepke" ("These are the tranquillized *Fifties*, / and I am forty") is updated by "Middle Age" ("At forty-five, / what next, what next?"). "Grandparents" of *Life Studies* ("They're all gone into a world of light") is generalized both in "The Scream" and in "Those before Us." "The Public Garden," "Beyond the Alps," and "Epigram" are revisions of poems which appeared first in *The Mills of the Kavanaughs*, *Life Studies*, and *Imitations*. "The Drinker" secularizes "The Drunken Fisherman." "Salem," which presented the half-unconscious meditations of an old seaman concerning the past glory and present decay of the port, had alluded to the "Custom House" section of *The Scarlet Letter*; in "Hawthorne" Lowell treats his source directly. As a description of Hawthorne himself he goes on to incorporate into the poem Hawthorne's portrait of Septimius Felton and to gloss it with his own comment on the imaginative mode he shares with Hawthorne, who, he says, broods on "the true / and insignificant." In "Jonathan Edwards in Western Massachusetts" and "Fall 1961" he repeats the same process, openly recalling two earlier poems, "Mr. Edwards and the Spider" and "After the Surprising Conversions." Most strikingly recollective is "Soft Wood," another in the series of Winslow elegies. Its opening metaphor ("Sometimes I have supposed

seals / must live as long as the Scholar Gypsy") alludes directly to
the stanzaic form of "In Memory of Arthur Winslow." But like
other recent work, the new poem relies on ironic balances and
self-identification with tragedy. "Soft Wood" is perhaps Lowell's
first poem in which the chief values are the mixed, but trium-
phant, human values of weakness, "a wincing of the will," a
bending to the wind "forever," mortality and compromise, sen-
sitivity, and endurance.

The Americans about whom Lowell writes in the title poem
gave up everything to serve the state. Resembling poems like
Tate's "Ode to the Confederate Dead" and James Russell
Lowell's "Ode Recited at the Harvard Commemoration," "For
the Union Dead" elegizes the war dead through a succession of
apparently unrelated "views" — the Old South Boston Aquar-
ium, the construction of a garage under Boston Common,
Augustus Saint-Gaudens's memorial relief of Colonel Robert
Gould Shaw leading his black regiment, and an advertisement in
a store window. Each becomes an apocalyptic analogue of the
other, each a monstrous emblem of man's self-destructiveness.
The central image of the poem derives from Albany's remark in
King Lear: "It will come. / Humanity must perforce prey on
itself, / Like monsters of the deep." The aquarium is closed and
its fish tanks are dry; breathing is cut off, life suffocated. The
steam shovels digging the garage resemble monstrous metal
fish, yellow dinosaurs; and the fence around the construction
site is a cage hardly protecting the city from these rough
apocalyptic beasts. The shaking Boston Statehouse is encircled
by girders, and the Shaw monument is unceremoniously
"propped by a plank splint against the garage's earthquake."
Compounding catastrophic signs, on Boylston Street, "a com-
mercial photograph / shows Hiroshima boiling / over a Mosler
Safe." The state demands servility; no longer confined to the
aquarium, its underworld is loosed upon the world: "Every-
where, / giant finned cars nose forward like fish; / a savage ser-
vility / slides by on grease." *For the Union Dead* seems destined
to conclude as *Lord Weary's Castle* did, with the poet declar-
ing himself "a red arrow on this graph / of Revelations," point-

ing a livid finger to the day of wrath, when man consumes himself through the inhumanity of the Leviathan state he has created to protect and nourish him.

But *Life Studies* had made a difference; even while terror accumulates about the emblems of final darkness, the poet's memory is not extinguished by the apocalypse of the state. He is in touch with the energy of true primitivity: "I often sigh still / for the dark downward and vegetating kingdom / of the fish and reptile." And he can restore, if not the Shaw monument, the more important recollection of what energies for human rights might still be symbolized by Shaw "and his bell-cheeked Negro infantry." Shaw can be a "compass-needle" pointing to a kind of human integrity which the state might extinguish, but whose importance it cannot alter. The millennial "ditch is nearer"; yet Shaw, who "waits / for the blessèd break" of the political bubble which drifts from the mouth of Leviathan, points to an alternative mode of political life. Enduring in the aquarium of memory, Shaw's monument reminds the poet of a life of service; his decision "to choose life and die" freed his life from the state. The poet, similarly, though hedged by apocalypse, can assert his own "blessèd break" with the state through a poetic career. This poem concludes a volume which summarizes that career by refocusing and revising the themes and emblems of his earlier work.

In *Near the Ocean* Lowell emphasizes invention over memory and makes striking combinations and juxtapositions of his central themes — the horrors and attractions of antiquity, of Western civilization, of nineteenth-century New England, and of his own age. Between Rome and America Lowell makes deft connections; both have the same imperial urge for dissipation and extinction. The sea extending from Europe to America is the ocean of his title, America is as near the ocean as Rome, and the Roman disease of power has washed over the American land. Juvenal's Romans know the terrors of night, where "each shadow hides a knife or spear"; while Lowell interrupts his night thoughts in "Central Park" to observe of the present: "We beg delinquents for our life. / Behind each bush, perhaps a knife."

Lowell's Romans are characterized (by way of Horace, Juvenal, Dante, and Gongora) as vain, envious, greedy, and lustful; their power is the fountain of their disgrace, their possessions the wellsprings of their unhappiness; their military triumphs the reason for their defeat; their desires reservoirs for the numbing of desire. From their greatness issues the chief horror — the insignificance of glory, the triumph of the quotidian: "what was firm has fled. What once / was fugitive maintains its permanence."

The same is true of the America described in "Waking Early Sunday Morning." Its subject is the degradation of the Pilgrim hopes for a Promised Land, and its form, consisting of eight-line stanzas of octosyllabic couplets, is that of a typical New England hymn. The poet stirs just before dawn; possessed by a sublime dream of freedom, he imagines himself a chinook salmon breaking loose from the sea to clear a waterfall — an Adamic man. But the dawn brings "blackout," domestic data that keep his mind from maintaining this imaginative intensity: the objects that possess his waking imagination are "serene in their neutrality." Lowell's reference to Wallace Stevens's "Sunday Morning" is self-deprecative; and fragments recalling romantic intensities available imaginatively to Wordsworth, Masefield, Whitman, and Homer mock the poet's inability to humanize nature or to naturalize the mind.

His meditation (stanzas 6–7) on the dream of the "City on a Hill" in America — as expressed in Puritanism ("they sing of peace, and preach despair") and in Transcendentalism ("Better dressed and stacking birch") — is interrupted by a recollection of Baudelaire's poem of despair "Anywhere Out of This World." Obliteration of the spirit is the only release in this post-Baudelairean world. Instead of going to church, then, the poet explores the woodshed of his imagination for "its dregs and dreck."

The "dregs and dreck" of the Puritan dream were revivified in America through the Federalist dream of the democratic republic. In stanzas 9–13 the poet extends his meditation to the contemporary consequences of that dream; recalling the decay of

Israel and Rome into militarism, he finds in America as well only "Hammering military splendor, / top-heavy Goliath in full armor," restlessness, excess, self-deception, and "ghost-written rhetoric." Again, he cries: "anywhere, but somewhere else." The Adamic dream of the individual, the Promised Land of America, and the dream of democracy have all been betrayed. Lowell's final stanza is a hymn whose theme is the poet's inability to sustain or create new hymns:

> Pity the planet, all joy gone
> from this sweet volcanic cone;
> peace to our children when they fall
> in small war on the heels of small
> war — until the end of time
> to police the earth, a ghost
> orbiting forever lost
> in our monotonous sublime.

What remains for the poet who has been made aware of the degradation of his democratic dogmas is his continuing ability to perceive (even to pity) the planet, to discover individual objects worth observing and naming, and to give them permanence through memory, and so preserve the self by its attachment to itself through things. The permanence of mind is the subject of "Fourth of July in Maine," another elegy on Harriet Winslow, where Lowell makes his cousin an emblem of the "genius" of memory. Although all the transcendental dreams — of personal freedom (she is "ten years paralyzed"), of religion ("not trusting in the afterlife"), and of politics (she dies in Washington, D.C.) — escaped her, she avoided the disasters which accompany them; she has the permanence of memory, of the transient, of the gentle. From writing poems in which his ancestors are emblems of all that is wrong with the past, Lowell found in her an emblem of what may be right about the future, and took Harriet Winslow as the genius for his own child, "mistress of / your tireless sedentary love."

In 1943 Lowell, "a fire-breathing Catholic C.O.," had been sentenced to a year and a day for refusing to serve in World War

II. After attempting to enlist earlier, he contended that now the Allies were fighting as ruthlessly as their opponents. In a published letter to President Roosevelt he reminded the President that he was "an American, whose family traditions, like your own, have always found their fulfillment in maintaining, through responsible participation in both civil and military services, our country's freedom and honor." From 1943 to the present, Lowell has been concerned with the relations between politics, society, and the individual. Active in civil-rights and antiwar protests, he refused an invitation from President Johnson in 1965 to appear at a White House arts festival, since "every serious artist knows that he cannot enjoy public celebration without making subtle public commitments." Somewhat later, introducing Soviet poet Andrei Voznesensky to a large Town Hall audience, he said: "This is indiscreet, but both our countries, I think, have really terrible governments. But we do the best we can with them."

Lowell's continuing concern with the relations between politics, society, and individual conscience is the subject of *Notebook 1967–68* (1969), a volume designed, he says, "as one poem, jagged in pattern." Its "plot" consists of the daily accumulations of memory, as chance events, which might drive the poet out of himself, instead bring his submerged thoughts, half-thoughts and unanswered puzzles into sharp focus and allow him, through meditation on them, to reach the partial answers and tentative solutions possible on that day. "Famished for human chances," he will not turn away from the daily dates of his culture — but he is also faithful to himself and asserts of events only what he can truly know or feel of and through them. As a man participating in culture, he experiencs its daily flux; as a poet so participating, he derives from the experience of culture and self the tentative, but objective, perception of value upon which a civilization can be based or an individual preserved. Through poetic form he saves the unsavable.

Notebook 1967–68 is unified through the development, restatement, and repetition of several themes and concerns: (1) growing, a theme embodied particularly in poems on Lowell's daughter, Harriet; (2) the relation between the past — what one grows from — and the present that one daily grows into (this theme leads Lowell to reflect on his childhood); (3) the contexts of growing: history (of Lowell's ancestors, of America, and of Europe), politics, and consciousness; (4) concern with the poet's personal history; (5) achievement of an uneasy, but joyful, acceptance of the dark side of history, politics, and modern life, so that even the apocalyptic poem "Dies Irae" can be subtitled "A Hope" (he ultimately asserts in "Mexico," 5: "I am learning to live in history"); (6) a willing involvement of himself with the tragedies of family, society, other persons, and self. What defenses are there against age and change and death, Lowell asks early in his poem (in "Long Summer," 11) — "Who can help us from our nothing to the all, / we aging downstream faster than a scepter can check?" His own right to involvement, hard-won in the book, provides the answer.

These themes develop within the general framework of the moving seasons. The poem begins in midsummer with "Harriet" and Lowell's reflection on growing. But the autumnal, Indian summer mood soon enters. Saying "we asked to linger on past fall in Eden," he moves from the innocence of growing to the state, "past fall," of experiencing other, adult concerns. Poems on "Aunt Sarah" and "My Grandfather," autumnal Victorians, and those, like "Munich, 1938" and "October and November," on modern degradation dominate this season's meditations. He recalls his own youth in "Harvard" and "In the Forties." The coming of winter inevitably leads him to pursue the theme of his growing to his present situation — as writer ("Writers"), as teacher ("Blizzard in Cambridge"), and as traveler ("Lines from Israel"). "Infirmity," he can at last declare (in "Mexico," 10) is "a food the flesh must swallow, / feeding our minds."

April and the approach of spring turns his mind to "shining remembrance" — of Harriet ("Words of a Young Girl"), who continues to grow, of women friends ("Mania"), and of historical personages whose power was more benevolent than others introduced earlier — Roland, Bishop Berkeley, and F. O. Matthiessen. Exhausted by winter, he finds a kind of rebirth in April and places his "New Year's Eve 1968" at this point, as the poem moves, through difficulty, upward. He affirms this restoration by revising, in the direction of acceptance, two poems from *For the Union Dead*, "Night-Sweat" and "Caligula," and one from *Near the Ocean*, "For Theodore Roethke: 1908–1963." Because he has experienced authentically the pain emphasized earlier, he can forcefully reject nihilism ("The Nihilist as Hero").

"Circles" introduces the expected return to summer. Several poems on Harriet and Lowell's wife appear as he moves toward passionate involvement with other people: his wife and child, his "family chronicle" ("Sound Mind, Sound Body"), and politics ("The Races"). Lowell has insisted, "It is harder to be a good man than a good poet." Understanding life as the supreme art, even in poems on writers (like Tate and Berryman) Lowell emphasizes their personal struggles. He has grown through art to life: instead of the book of a century ("Growth"), he writes the notebook of a year. "Summer" comes at last to complete the circle — of the seasons, and of his changing mind.. To express the new birth of energy which he has experienced, he writes of his possible reincarnations — as a seal ("If we must live again, not us; we might / go into seals") and again as a poet ("Some other August, / the easy seal might say, 'I could not sleep / last night; suddenly I could write my name'").

Affirming such imaginative energies, he can write a series of codas — "Close the Book," "Half a Century Gone," and "Obit" — ending in a vision of his personal death and his fierce continuance in eternal return, through involvement in life:

> I'm for and with myself in my otherness,
> in the eternal return of earth's fairer children,
> the lily, the rose, the sun on dusk and brick,
> the loved, the lover, and their fear of life,
> their unconquered flux, insensate oneness, their
>   painful "it was . . ."
> After loving you so much, can I forget
> you for eternity, and have no other choice?

His passionate involvement in what continues, continues him. This passion indeed, eventually carried *Notebook 1967–68* in

new directions, as Lowell almost literally lived in the imaginative
world of his book, watching and encouraging the development
of unforeseen shapes in it. Even as the first edition appeared,
Lowell was readying a revised second edition. Lowell admitted
that now he was revising his own published book "as if it were
manuscript," recast by him, reordered by time. By 1970, he had
revised almost a hundred of the poems in his sequence while
adding ninety new ones to it. Insisting upon its own ability to
expand and continue by edging out of the particular history of
1967–68 and projecting, instead, the continuance of the sensibil-
ity into the future, the volume now had to be retitled, simply,
Notebook (1970). Taking a hint from Norman Mailer, Lowell
gave his work up to process — history was poetry; poetry, his-
tory. "You've got to call your *Notebook, Book of the Century*," Har-
riet tells her father in "Growth." She and the book grow side by
side.

Notebook continued to exfoliate, and in two directions: toward
the poetry of the person understood through public history on
the one hand; and toward that of the self defined by its more
private affiliations, on the other. By 1973, with more than sixty
poems removed and eighty new ones added, *Notebook* became
History. Lowell at once strikes the note of the bumbling growth
of society in "History":

> History has to live with what was here,
> clutching and close to fumbling all we had —
> it is so dull and gruesome how we die,
> unlike writing, life never finishes.

As his work moves from the Garden of Eden and biblical time to
classical chronicle, Lowell allows for the gruesome and inconclu-
sive, the bulges and bumps in history, in attempting to account
for the strange shape his own being has achieved through his-
tory. History does not so much unfold as it tumbles forward,
helterskelter, just as the poet stumbles toward public under-
standing.

In *History*, Lowell meditates on well-known figures, poet-
friends, historical occasions, heroic recollections, and public pas-

sions. The faces of history determine the faces with which he will meet them. *For Lizzie and Harriet* (1973) is the book of his private angels and demons. This book was made of the personal poems dropped from *Notebook* for *History*; revised again and rearranged, they stress the character of Lowell as meditator, a self fostered by private devotions. More narrow in scope than *History*, *For Lizzie and Harriet* more intensely focuses upon the difficulties of the private self. "Our wars were simpler than our marriages," Lowell reminds us in "The Human Condition." Taken together, these two volumes follow the procedure devised by Henry James in his late autobiographies: the artist-person is seen by the "others" that claim some relation to it, others that are as distant as the ancient Greeks or as close as a wife and daughter.

A sequence of over 200 sonnets, *Notebook 1967–68* first appeared to insist upon Lowell's refusal to repeat himself as a poet, and to emphasize the need to develop new aesthetic forms. "Somehow [I] never wrote something to go back to," he says in "Reading Myself." But though he could not return to lost lives, lost poets, or lost faiths, he could still, the workings and reworkings of his *Notebook* show, preserve his own creations, his admirable fictions. Like Sidney or Samuel Johnson, he could learn to maintain that only invention survives history: only the created can endure, and only by changing. History breaks, but fiction lives by bending.

The last fiction of all is of course oneself, shattered by historical occasions but preserved by its imaginative encounters. For years Lowell had balanced between these in his work — coloring his fiction "with first-hand evidence," or marketing "as fiction" the truths that actual "letters and talk" contain. These phrases all come from the poem called "Heavy Breathing," which appears toward the end of Lowell's most recent volume, *The Dolphin* (1973). For many reasons this is a remarkable book. In it Lowell takes the loose sonnet which he invented as a form of chronicle for *Notebook 1967–68* and adapts it to a vigorously dense symbolic mode of poetic introspection. *The Dolphin* sums up the old

form and projects a new; it edges back toward *Life Studies* in its
concern for personal crisis, but only by projecting half-fictions,
in order that the sensibility, thus strengthened, might half-face
thereby its real actions in reality's mirror. Fiction and truth go by
halves as Lowell recounts the personal history of a new love,
Caroline, the partial, painful loss of Harriet and Lizzie, his re-
marriage, self-accusation, readjustments, and the new poems
that we see coming into being:

> The cardtable is black, the cards are played face down,
> black-backs on a black cloth; and soon by luck
> I draw a card I wished to leave unchosen,
> and discard the one card I had sworn to hold.
> . . . .
> Should revelation be sealed like private letters,
> till all the beneficiaries are dead,
> and our proper names become improper Lives?

The main metaphor of the book is that of the fisherman who has
set out his lines, as the poet does, and his nets, holding together
like poems, only to find a dolphin caught in the fisherman's nets
and a mermaid in the poet's. If the dolphin is "the only animal
man really loves," the mermaid is the poet's siren: both are as-
pects of the woman who is at the center of the book. He does not
seek compassion or forgiveness but only understanding; for he
insists that as man and poet he is caught in the very eel nets he
casts for the slippery creatures of experience. Old poet, old pa-
tient, old actor, old fisherman that he is, he concludes that to cast
his nets with care and craft, and with acceptance of what they
catch, is enough.

Robert Lowell has moved with his culture. Like earlier New
England poets, his sensibility first found itself in opposition; but
unlike them, he has been forced by the rapid changes in Ameri-
can life repeatedly to reconstitute his principles of opposition,
and thus always to define freshly his relation to his fellows. He
has developed three basic directions for his work: a critique of
public action and attitude in America; a critique of the state of
the individual ego; and a sense of the historical, religious,

mythological, and literary contexts which provide perspectives whereby to understand the possibilities of public or private life at any time. As his society has shifted during the last thirty years, Lowell has emphasized various combinations of these.

During the mid-forties, while Americans were confident, Lowell's poetry boiled with apocalyptic despair and condemnation of the diseases which infected Americans. During the late forties and early fifties, the era of the "silent generation," Lowell's poetry was rhetorical and extravagant. While Americans wished to consolidate minor triumphs, Lowell's verse suggested that success of an ordinary kind was impossible and undesirable.

By the late fifties, disillusioned with war and international involvements, Americans sought various escapes from self-consciousness and the powerhouse of history. In *Life Studies* and *Imitations* Lowell faced himself and America's European heritage directly. Increasingly, in the sixties, a sense of alienation and collective disaster darkened the American mind. Lowell well described the attitude: "We're burning, we're decaying, we're in mid-century. . . . Genocide has stunned us; we have a curious dread it will be repeated." Americans had arrived at his earlier despair. But in *The Old Glory, Prometheus Bound*, and *For the Union Dead* Lowell was emphasizing the continuities of culture and the inevitable involvement of the private self with public concerns.

While Americans in the late sixties began stressing immediate social reform without correcting the roots of social ills, Lowell stressed the values of contemplation, a quiet faith amid public clamor, and intelligence in *Near the Ocean* and *Notebook 1967–68*. Even justice, he showed, can become a dogma and murder itself. "We must bend, not break," he says. Where Americans have understood new moral incoherence, he has seen new moral possibilities. He has defined the four major contemporary problems as "how to join equality to excellence, how to join liberty to justice, how to avoid destroying or being destroyed by nuclear power, and how to complete the emancipation of the slaves." As a radical he has identified these, as a conservative declared them "almost insoluble"; as a liberal he has worked to solve them and written poems describing a state of widened consciousness which might encourage solutions; and as a traditionalist, he has identified similar dilemmas in Roman history and nineteenth-century America, in the careers of Plutarch's heroes and Abraham Lincoln. He has kept his mind flexible and contradictory, allowing the half-truths of any position to support and absorb its opposite. An account of his career is a history of how he has allowed his contradictions to seep into his poetry as the society to which he is responding changes.

His work, in short, has been a mirror to his culture, supplying society with elements for advance. He has criticized the poets of his generation whose "writings seem divorced from culture." Culture, he came to see, provides the necessary background for art: neither, without the other, can endure. Constantly updating old poems for inclusion in new volumes, he moves with culture and refuses to let society catch up with him. "One side of me," he has said, "is a conventional liberal, concerned with causes, agitated about peace and justice and equality. . . . My other side is deeply conservative, wanting to get at the roots of things, wanting to slow down the whole modern progress of mechanization and dehumanization, knowing that liberalism can be a form of death too." He has been able to combine these tendencies intricately and to employ his imaginative powers to locate and express permanent aspects of mind which his civilization has temporarily forgotten or rejected. "One feels," he said in criticism of Wallace Stevens, ". . . that a man is able to be an imagination and the imagination able to be disinterested and urbane only because it is supported by industrial slaves. Perhaps if there are platonists, there must always be slaves." Lowell has refused to be a platonist, an imagination, and has insisted on being a *man* of imagination. Serving and leading his culture by opening, through his work, the lines along which it might evolve, he has built a career like those of Jonson, Dryden, Goethe, Howells, and James. His power as a poet derives from his understanding that, like these writers, he can be a man of letters only insofar as he can remain a man among men.

PETER MEINKE

Howard Nemerov

There is an instructive passage in *Journal of the Fictive Life* in which Howard Nemerov speaks of the sources of poetic power: "I conceive this responsibility of [lyric] poetry to be to great primary human drama, which poets tend to lose sight of because of their privilege of taking close-ups of single moments on the rim of the wheel of the human story. The poet will improve his art who acknowledges the necessity of always returning to that source; he will fail who always writes another poem instead. Hence it has seemed to me that I must attempt to bring together the opposed elements of my character represented by poetry and fiction."

These "opposed elements" in Howard Nemerov's character are reflected in his life and work: in the tensions between his romantic and realistic visions, his belief and unbelief, his heart and mind; and in his alternating production of poetry and prose. It is somehow typical that this humanitarian who writes of war as madness ("Redeployment") enlisted in the Royal Canadian Air Force when he graduated from Harvard in 1941. It is also typical that this "Jewish Puritan of the middle class" who "Grins at the consolations of religion as at a child's / Frightened pretensions" is a deeply religious poet who, in his central poems (e.g., "Runes") looks into "the dark marrow and the splintery grain" and sees "nothing that was not wood, nothing / That was not God."

Journal of the Fictive Life documents, by analyzing his own dreams, the deeply divided personality already evident to readers of his poetry and fiction. Despite his growing "success," financial, familial, critical, and popular, Nemerov's dreams are "spectacularly pessimistic" (which he typically calls a "rude awakening"). My theme here is that this inner division, under the constant pressure of Nemerov's poetic discipline and intelligence, accounts for the power of this writer who has become, more than any other contemporary poet, the spokesman for the existential, science-oriented (or science-displaced), liberal mind of the twentieth century.

The quality that sets Nemerov's writings apart from other modern writers is its consistent intelligence, a breadth of wit in the eighteenth-century sense of the word, expanded to cover a very modern awareness of contemporary man's alienation and fragmentation. One of the primary divisions of Nemerov's mind is apparent in his ability to remind his readers of both Pope and Dostoevski at the same time, a split symbolized by poems like "The Salt Garden," where man is alternately proud of his "good house" and "garden green, / . . . Turnip and bean and violet / In a decent order set," and torn by a desire to abandon civilized life for "the wild waters" where "his salt dream lies."

Nemerov's own upbringing was an extremely civilized one, a privileged one, and this, coupled with his awareness of the miseries of this world, undoubtedly led to guilt feelings or at least a cynicism at life's capriciousness (he writes in the *Journal*, "I want the world to think me a nice fellow, while I know I am not").

He was born on March 1, 1920, in New York City, and this city dominated the imagery of his poems until he moved to Vermont in 1948. His wealthy and culture-minded parents sent him to the exclusive Fieldston School, where the young Nemerov was an outstanding student and a good athlete. Graduating in 1937, he then went to Harvard, receiving his A.B. just in time for World War II. Like many other modern poets (Jarrell, Ciardi, Dickey), he was romantically attracted to the air force, with the romance gradually turning to horror at the war's realities. Nemerov served first as a flying officer with the RAF Coastal Command, attacking German shipping over the North Sea, and then in 1944 switched to the Eighth United States Army Air Force, based in Lincolnshire. He married an English girl, to whom he's rather unfashionably still married, and in 1945 was discharged as a first lieutenant.

After the war, Nemerov and his wife lived in New York City for a year, during which he wrote *The Image and the Law*. Running short of money, in 1946 he accepted a position as instructor of English at Hamilton College, Clinton, New York; in 1948 he joined the faculty at Bennington College, with which he was associated until 1966, when he moved to Brandeis University in Massachusetts. The Nemerovs have three sons, David, Alexander, and Jeremy, the period just before Alexander's birth being the subject of Nemerov's "meditations" in *Journal of the Fictive Life*.

In 1958–59 he was a visiting lecturer in English at the University of Minnesota, and in 1962–63 was writer-in-residence at Hollins College in Virginia. He also served as consultant in poetry at the Library of Congress in 1963–64, succeeding Louis Untermeyer and preceding his friend Reed Whittemore, with whom he worked for several years on the delightful and irreverent magazine *Furioso* (predecessor of today's *Carleton Miscellany*). In 1969–70 he was writer-in-residence at Washington University, in Missouri.

As he notes in the *Journal*, his writing has slowly been attracting a widening audience. In 1966 he delivered the Joseph Warren Beach Lecture at the University of Minnesota to an appreciative standing-room-only crowd (the lecture was published in the *American Scholar*, summer 1967). He has received numerous awards, including a Guggenheim in 1968 and the Frank O'Hara Memorial Prize in 1971. In 1965 he was made a member of the National Institute of Arts and Letters, and in 1966 a fellow of the American Academy of Arts and Sciences.

Howard Nemerov, who never went to graduate school, finds teaching "a fairly agreeable way of making a dollar": it "makes possible a more or less quiet life." When asked to name the best contemporary American poet, he replied, "For me to do so would be not only immodest, but very possibly inaccurate as well." But in the opinion of a growing number of readers and critics, Nemerov is a major American writer, and certainly one of the best poets writing today. Versatile and prolific, he has published to date three novels (*The Melodramatists*; *Federigo, or, The Power of Love*; *The Homecoming Game*), two collections of short stories (*A Commodity of Dreams*; *Stories, Fables & Other Diversions*), two verse plays (*Cain, Endor*), eleven books of poetry (*The Image and the Law, Guide to the Ruins, The Salt Garden, Mirrors & Windows, New & Selected Poems, The Next Room of the Dream, The Blue Swallows, A Sequence of Seven With a Drawing by Ron Slaughter, Winter Lightning, The Painter Dreaming in the Scholar's House, Gnomes and Occasions*), two collections of essays and criticism (*Poetry and Fiction: Essays*; *Reflexions on Poetry and Poetics*), and the unclassifiable literary-psychoanalytical *Journal of the Fictive Life*. He also edited and introduced Longfellow's poems in the Laurel Poetry Series and is the editor of *Poets on Poetry* and *Poetry and Criticism*.

The twentieth century, perhaps every century, has been often derided as an unpoetic age, especially the second half of it: where is the successor to Frost, Eliot, Williams, Auden, Yeats? The fact is that there are plenty of successors, that excellent poetry is being written by many modern poets, and that no doubt a few of them will withstand "windy time / and the worm," and emerge as that strange and amorphous creature, the Major Poet. Of the "war generation" poets, Nemerov and Lowell are the two who have held up best, and the development of Nemerov is the most striking.

The sixty-seven poems contained in *The Blue Swallows* (1967), published exactly twenty years after Nemerov's first book, represent not so much a culmination of his efforts as another step along a clearly defined technical evolution, and another elucidation (another series of examples) of what might be called a philosophy of minimal affirmation. Like his gulls and swallows,

Nemerov circles around and around the things of this world, finding them insubstantial, frightening, illusory, beautiful, and strange. Nowhere is his divided view of man as both hopeless and indomitable better expressed than in the conclusion of "Beyond the Pleasure Principle":

> There, toward the end, when the left-handed wish
> Is satisfied as it is given up, when the hero
> Endures his cancer and more obstinately than ever
> Grins at the consolations of religion as at a child's
> Frightened pretensions, and when his great courage
> Becomes a wish to die, there appears, so obscurely,
> Pathetically, out of the wounded torment and the play,
> A something primitive and appealing, and still dangerous,
> That crawls on bleeding hands and knees over the floor
> Toward him, and whispers as if to confess: *again, again.*

In *The Blue Swallows* the polarities of Nemerov's thought are typically symbolized by physics and theology ("This, That & the Other"), reality and imagination ("The Companions"), pain and significance ("Creation of Anguish"). He has come a long way from his first slim volume, *The Image and the Law* (1947), but there is continuity as well as development.

The title of his first book refers to the two ways man has of looking at things, realistically through the eye (image) and imaginatively through the mind (law), and what Nemerov looks at is, in a word, death. Poem after poem revolves around his war-given realization of the casual, callous, accidental, and inevitable fact of death.

> You watch the night for images of death,
> Which sleep in camera prints upon the eye.
> Fires go out, and power fails, and breath
> Goes coldly out: dawn is a time to die.

and

> You try to fix your mind upon his death,
> Which seemed it might, somehow, be relevant
> To something you once thought, or did, or might
> Imagine yourself thinking, doing. When?

Along with death, war and the city are Nemerov's main subjects, often in the same poem (e.g., "The Frozen City"). Two other major aspects of this early work should be mentioned because they carry over to his later poetry: religion and wit. Poetry and religion both attempt to carve meaning out of chaos — poetry by form, religion by faith. But Nemerov's poetry is often *specifically* religious, by vocabulary, by reference, by subject. Saints and angels abound in his poetry; references to Christ, God, St. Augustine, Aquinas, and the like are also frequent. It is clear that the Old Testament, especially, is influential (as in his later plays, *Cain* and *Endor*). A representative poem in *The Image and the Law* is "Lot's Wife," in which Nemerov uses the woman as a symbol for a world in tears, trapped between lust and faith, unwilling and unable to commit itself fully to either.

> I have become a gate
> To the ruined city, dry,
> Indestructible by fire.
> A pillar of salt, a white
> Salt boundary stone
> On the edge of destruction.
>
> A hard lesson to learn,
> A swift punishment; and many
> Now seek to escape
> But look back, or to escape
> By looking back: and they
> Too become monuments.
>
> Remember me, Lot's wife,
> Standing at the furthest
> Commark of lust's county.
> Unwilling to enjoy,
> Unable to escape, I make
> Salt the rain of the world.

The satirical turn of Nemerov's mind which dominates his novels is also evident in his poetry. His wit ranges from "Rump-Trumpet, the Critic / . . . Who would have to rise above himself / In order to talk through his hat," to the more subtle debunking in "History of a Literary Movement."

Nemerov has said "the serious and the funny are one"; the same dark viewpoint underlies both his "witty" and his "serious" poems, and often these elements are fused (e.g., "The Truth of the Matter"). This is as true of *The Blue Swallows* as of *The Image and the Law*. These poems, with their ironic detachment, are not "cold" poems, but their voice "is that of a man thinking," as Nemerov has said about Wallace Stevens.

In *The Image and the Law* and *Guide to the Ruins* (1950) Nemerov is "writing the war out of his system," as they say; he is also, more important, writing Eliot, Yeats, and Stevens out of his system.

ELIOT   Descending and moving closer
          I saw the sad patience of
          The people awaiting death
          (They crossed their bony legs,
          Their eyes stared, hostile and
          Bright as broken glass).

YEATS   But I, except in bed,
          Wore hair-cloth next the skin,
          And nursed more than my child
          That grudge against my side.
          Now, spirit & flesh assoil'd,
          I lace my pride in,
          Crying out odd and even
             Alas! that ever I did sin,
             It is full merry in heaven.

STEVENS   What, Amicus, constitutes mastery?
          The perdurable fire of a style?

The early poems in general have an abstract, literary quality, an esoteric vocabulary, many allusions. One marked tendency in Nemerov's technical development has been a growing direct-ness, not toward the "country" simplicity of Robert Frost but toward the simplicity of a highly educated man trying to convey the substance of his meditations clearly. Compare, for example, these two descriptions of October, the first early, the second late (1962):

A) An old desperation of the flesh.
   Mortification and revivification

> Of the spirit. There are those
> Who work outdoors, and others
> Who pull down blinds against the sun.

B) Now I can see certain simplicities
> In the darkening rust and tarnish of the time,
> And say over the certain simplicities,
> The running water and the standing stone,
> The yellow haze of the willow and the black
> Smoke of the elm, the silver, silent light
> Where suddenly, readying toward nightfall,
> The sumac's candelabrum darkly flames.

In both poems the subject is the same, October being used as a metaphor for death, but the qualities Nemerov has gained are evident: a greater subtlety of rhythm, more visual imagery, a feeling of control that communicates itself as part of the "message."

Guide to the Ruins, however, represents a considerable advance in Nemerov's growth as a poet, leading directly toward *The Salt Garden*, where he reaches his poetic maturity. Such poems as "The Lives of Gulls and Children," "Elegy of Last Resort," and "Fables of the Moscow Subway" indicate that Nemerov has found his most characteristic voice: a quiet intelligent voice brooding lyrically on the strange beauty and tragic loneliness of life.

> But they knew the Atlantic kind he was,
> And for this moment saw him swaying
> In the grey dark above the cold sea miles,
> Wingtips ticking the spray of the slow waves,
> Leaning on the unhavening air the dangerous
> Sustaining of his own breastbone; they knew
> The indifference of time dragging him down.
> And when after silence they turned away,
> "No one has ever been here before,"
> They cried, "no one, no one, no one."
> Their mournful word went out, no one,
> Along the shore, now that they turned for home
> Bearing the lonely pride of those who die,
> And paced by the sweet shrieking of the quick.

Guide to the Ruins is filled with a great variety of styles: epigrams, fragments, ballads, lyrics, fables, sonnets, elegies, madrigals, even a carol. Its greatest advance over *The Image and the Law* is a lessening of the Audenesque flatness of the first book: a line like "Swinging over the wash and rush of the sea" is an almost onomatopoeic example of the marriage of rhythm and image which marks Nemerov's later poetry — for example, these lines from *The Blue Swallows*:

> See now, the ships depart through the dark harbor
> And past the breakwater rocks where the first
> White-riding wave hits at the hull and washes on.
> Rhythm of voyages, going out and coming back,
> Beat of the sea, procession of times and seasons,
> Command of variables, calculus of fluxions
> *Cuius Nomen est Oriens* . . .

Guide to the Ruins, though much broader in scope than *The Image and the Law*, is still very much concerned with war. The "ruins" (also "runes") are the ruins of civilization after World War II, and the war is not really over, as seen in such poems as "Redeployment," "A Fable of the War," "The Bacterial War," and "To a Friend." Nemerov's double vision, his sense of being trapped between art-faith and science-reality is much in evidence, as in the raging lines "And when the Germans bled the babies white / Where was the *skepsis* of the sculptor's art / The question is of science not to doubt / The point of faith is that you sweat it out." Nemerov's religion, like Dostoevski's, is not one of easy acceptance; it involves constant doubting and agony of spirit. The doubting is, paradoxically, a positive value in Nemerov's poetry: it prevents him from preaching. His religious position, to judge from his writing, is that of a nonpracticing Jew engaged in a continual dialogue with Christianity, searching for its meaning, testing its relevance in the modern world. Unlike Bernard Malamud, his former colleague at Bennington, Nemerov does not write very often specifically about "Jewishness" (though in a letter he has said, "I was frightened by the Old Testament when a child, and have never got over it"). In the *Journal* he notes that at Harvard he was almost converted to

Catholicism on "foolish" aesthetic grounds, but he has always
drawn back to affirm his essential Jewishness. Perhaps his
clearest statement on this theme is in "Debate with the Rabbi"; in
the first three stanzas the Rabbi chides the protagonist for losing
his religion. Then the poem concludes:

> Stubborn and stiff-necked man! the Rabbi cried.
> The pain you give me, said I.
> Instead of bowing down, said he,
> You go on in your obstinacy.
> We Jews are that way, I replied.

The union in several poems of religion and war marks a de-
velopment in Nemerov's pessimism that will become more
noticeable in later writings: the celebration of life despite the
horror of the surroundings, perhaps *because* of the horror: "I
stretch myself on joy as on the rack, / And bear the hunch of
glory on my back." The book as a whole is undoubtedly too
much under the influence of the later Yeats, but a certain Yeat-
sian toughness of spirit has stayed with Nemerov as he forged
his own style. His use of gulls, for example, inevitably reminds
one of Yeats's swans (or Stevens's pigeons, Keats's nightingales):
they symbolize the grace and rather arrogant pride of nature,
the "Atlantic" beauty which holds heaven and earth together.
These birds appear in many of the best of Nemerov's later
poems ("The Gulls," "The Salt Garden," "The Town Dump"),
but even this early, in individual poems like "The Lives of Gulls
and Children," he has mastered the Yeats influence and speaks
in his own manner.

There is, in the lines "They would have reached out hands to
him / To comfort him in that human kind / They just were
learning," a slight hint of another influence, later to become
stronger: the quiet conversational tone of Robert Frost (Frost
would have written "They were just learning"). Nemerov is one
of the few poets to learn something from Frost, to assimilate the
Frostian narrative technique, as seen in Nemerov's story poem
"The Pond" (from *The Salt Garden* and appended to *Journal of the
Fictive Life*).

Guide to the Ruins was sensibly criticized as lacking "a center of gravity or of force, the sense of a strong controlling sensibility." It is in *The Salt Garden* (1955) that Nemerov first unifies his talent. "The Goose Fish," "The Scales of the Eyes," "The Sanctuary," "The Quarry," "I Only Am Escaped Alone to Tell Thee," "The Salt Garden," "The Pond," "Deep Woods" are just a few which have already become much anthologized. This book, praised by virtually all critics, had the misfortune to run up against *The Collected Poems of Wallace Stevens*, which swept the literary awards of 1955.

The Salt Garden is unified by Nemerov's growing interest in nature. The typical adjective describing nature is "brutal," and the link between brutal nature and "decent" bumbling man is found in the liquids, ocean and blood, which fuse into man's "salt dream," the submerged and subconscious call of the wild. The title poem, for example, begins with the speaker admiring his "good house," and the garden and lawn "In a decent order set"; he is proud that he has reclaimed the land from what was once "the ocean floor." But the "salt wind," the memory of "the ocean's wrinkled green" — unlike his smooth green garden — and finally "the great gull," which contemptuously surveys the speaker's "poor province," humble him, as he imagines the "wild sea lanes he wandered by / And the wild waters where he slept / Still as a candle in the crypt." Written in short-lined unevenly rhymed verse, this poem encompasses the main theme of the book: man's divided nature. A clear and "easy" poem of rational man rationally musing on his estate, "The Salt Garden" has as its counterpart the long and "difficult" "The Scales of the Eyes," which is a nighttime fantasy, a Freudian dream sequence, on the same subject. One can detect in "Scales" the influence of Theodore Roethke's poetry (e.g., the surreal "The Shape of the Fire"), which, as Nemerov himself has noted, is also partly "a result of the Freudian discoveries" — as are many of Nemerov's analyses in *Journal of the Fictive Life*. This series of eighteen short "dream songs" (like Berryman's later ones) traces a man's inward journey from despair (winter) to hope (spring). It presents a stream-of-consciousness nightmare vision of New York as graveyard ("Dead men in their stone towns") and offers a general vision of modern civilization as inferno ("From Coney Island to Phlegethon / Is no great way by ferris wheel").

"The Scales of the Eyes" (a title with Joycean possibilities) not only holds together as a sequence, but also many of the individual sections are effective lyrics by themselves, eerie scenes of some dreamland out of an Arthur Davies painting.

> The low sky was mute and white
> And the sun a white hole in the sky
> That morning when it came on to snow;
> The hushed flakes fell all day.
>
> The hills were hidden in a white air
> And every bearing went away,
> Landmarks being but white and white
> For anyone going anywhere.
>
> All lines were lost, a noon bell
> I heard sunk in a sullen pool
> Miles off. And yet this patient snow,
> When later I walked out in it,
>
> Had lodged itself in tips of grass
> And made its mantle bridging so
> It lay upon the air and not the earth
> So light it hardly bent a blade.

The poem which strikes one most strongly at first is "I Only Am Escaped Alone to Tell Thee," a tour de force describing the underlying agony of a superficially prosperous nineteenth-century woman. Nemerov takes the reader by degrees from a description of the lady to the "black flukes of agony." First he compares the mirror, "the long inaccurate glass," to "troubled water," and the "immense" shadow to a "giant crab." Having established the sea and giant motif, Nemerov goes on to describe her "strict" corsets and the "huge arrangements of her hair" as "no rig for dallying," and finishes with a simile comparing the lady to "a great ship," not unlike Milton's description of Delilah in *Samson Agonistes.* Then Nemerov pushes the metaphor to the furthest step, and his packed conclusion refers back to the corsets, the sea, the mirror, and the light referred to earlier:

> I know
> We need not draw this figure out.
> But all that whalebone came from whales.
> And all the whales lived in the sea,
> In calm beneath the troubled glass,
> Until the needle drew their blood.
>
> I see her standing in the hall,
> Where the mirror's lashed to blood and foam,
> And the black flukes of agony
> Beat at the air till the light blows out.

In *The Salt Garden*, Nemerov's fascination with the workings of the human mind first becomes clear (his poetry is filled with images of reflections, mirrors, cameras, dreams in dreams, etc.), a fascination that is still stronger in the *Journal* and *The Blue Swallows*; also, Nemerov has clearly been influenced by Owen Barfield's ideas on perception in Barfield's *Poetic Diction: A Study in Meaning* (for second edition of which Nemerov wrote an introduction). In the *Journal* Nemerov states: "I hate intelligence, and have nothing else." Poem after poem fastens on man's mind, its loneliness, its limitations, its appeal: the joys of meditation which turn in on themselves and make nothing happen. One of the central poems on this subject in *The Salt Garden* is "The Sanctuary," written in a blank verse whose meditative rhythms and intelligent voice mark it as Nemerov's own:

> Over a ground of slate and light gravel,
> Clear water, so shallow that one can see
> The numerous springs moving their mouths of sand;
> And the dark trout are clearly to be seen,
> Swimming this water which is color of air
> So that the fish appear suspended nowhere and
> In nothing. With a delicate bend and reflex
> Of their tails the trout slowly glide
> From the shadowy side into the light, so clear,
> And back again into the shadows; slow

And so definite, like thoughts emerging
Into a clear place in the mind, then going back,
Exchanging shape for shade. Now and again
One fish slides into the center of the pool
And hangs between the surface and the slate
For several minutes without moving, like
A silence in a dream; and when I stand
At such a time, observing this, my life
Seems to have been suddenly moved a great
Distance away on every side, as though
The quietest thought of all stood in the pale
Watery light alone, and was no more
My own than the speckled trout I stare upon
All but unseeing. Even at such times
The mind goes on transposing and revising
The elements of its long allegory
In which the anagoge is always death;
And while this vision blurs with empty tears,
I visit, in the cold pool of the skull,
A sanctuary where the slender trout
Feed on my drowned eyes. . . . Until this trout
Pokes through the fabric of the surface to
Snap up a fly. As if a man's own eyes
Raised welts upon the mirror whence they stared,
I find this world again in focus, and
This fish, a shadow dammed in artifice,
Swims to the furthest shadows out of sight
Though not, in time's ruining stream, out of mind.

The anagoge is always death: but it is not war-death that Nemerov now addresses, but death as part of nature, "time's ruining stream." Meditations all lead to the reality of death, the unreality of life, culminating in several poems in *The Blue Swallows*, like "In the Black Museum," which ends "Or as two mirrors vacuum-locked together / Exclude, along with all the world, / A light to see it by. Reflect on that."

The concluding poem of *The Salt Garden* is "Deep Woods," in which Nemerov expresses his feeling about the hugeness and permanence of nature as against small impermanent man. Walking through these deep New England woods is like a "dream of being lost" — a dream Nemerov frequently has. Like Frost,

Nemerov is a realist, and does not romanticize nature (which does not, after all, need it).

> Line, leaf, and light; darkness invades our day;
> No meaning in it, but indifference
> Which does not flatter with profundity.
> Nor is it drama. Even the giant oak,
> Stricken a hundred years ago or yesterday,
> Has not found room to fall as heroes should. . . .

Insisting on the reality, Nemerov goes through the list of enchanted forests, the "Black Forest where the wizard lived," the Chinese forest "with bridge, pagoda, fog," the forests "invented by Watteau or Fragonard," and, in modern times, by Disney. But the real "deep woods" is so primitive, so virginal, so untouched by man that it is like the Garden of Eden before the Fall:

> Most probably
> Nothing will happen. Even the Fall of Man
> Is waiting, here, for someone to grow apples;
> And the snake, speckled as sunlight on the rock
> In the deep woods, still sleeps with a whole head
> And has not begun to grow a manly smile.

Mirrors & Windows (1958) continues with the elements already noted, plus a new one: Nemerov's quiet confidence in himself as a poet, a feeling that he can control internal despair with external craftsmanship. A great many of these poems (e.g., "Holding the Mirror Up to Nature," "Painting a Mountain Stream," "Writing," "To Lu Chi") are about Nemerov writing poetry, a subject continued in later books: "Maestria" in *New & Selected Poems*; "Vermeer" and "Lion & Honeycomb" in *The Next Room of the Dream*; "The May Day Dancing," "Projection," and "Style" in *The Blue Swallows*. The trend toward nature begun in *The Salt Garden* continues in *Mirrors & Windows*, the difference being that in the later book he is consciously aware that he is a *poet* looking at nature, trying to capture it in his poems: "Study this rhythm, not this thing / The brush's tip streams from the wrist / of a living man, a dying man. / The running water is the wrist." The claims made for art — as for everything else — are minimal; he never claims for poetry powers not to be found in it. On the contrary, he is typically deprecating about his "modest art" which makes him — like Keats's poet — "appear a trifle colorless." Nemerov's honesty leads him to admit that even art is not permanent.

> Miraculous. It is as though the world
> were a great writing. Having said so much,
> let us allow there is more to the world
> than writing; continental faults are not
> bare convoluted fissures in the brain.
> Not only must the skaters soon go home;
> also the hard inscription of their skates
> is scored across the open water, which long
> remembers nothing, neither wind nor wake.

Art and beauty (e.g., the birds in "The Town Dump") are what make life bearable, but nothing makes life understandable, nothing makes death meaningful. In *Mirrors & Windows* Nemerov's philosophy of minimal affirmation can be clearly seen.

"A Day on the Big Branch" is a good example of Nemerov's attitude, which might be called realistic romanticism. That is, the poems seem to be composed by a romantic sensibility which is at the same time too analytical and too honest to see things other than as they really are. In "A Day on the Big Branch" a group of, one would guess, college teachers have had an all-night poker party and, "still half drunk," they drive "to a stream in the high hills" with a vaguely formed "purgatorial idea," "the old standard appeal to the wilderness." And the wilderness *is* beautiful, "a paradise / for ruined poker players, win or lose," and they lie back on the rocks waiting for something to happen. "The silence . . . / grew pregnant; but nothing else did." Nemerov's rocks are "hard as rocks." Nevertheless, something is learned, something "concerning patience / and enduring what had to be endured . . . / weathering in whatever weather." The men talk of the war and of life, and the majestic beauty of nature forces them into "poetry and truth," which may be the same thing:

> so that at last one said, "I shall play cards
> until the day I die," and another said,
> "in bourbon whiskey are all the vitamins

and minerals needed to sustain man's life,"
and still another, "I shall live on smoke
until my spirit has been cured of flesh."

Then the men climb downstream again, noting how the stream
("time's ruining stream") during a recent flood had smashed
three bridges "practically back to nature," drive home,
and resume their card game. Written in Nemerov's flexible and
disciplined blank verse, "A Day on the Big Branch" is a mature
achievement: one senses that Nemerov's irony (rocks as "hard as
rocks") has been subdued to greater uses than in his earlier
poetry.

The poems in this book are life-reflecting mirrors, and win-
dows through which we see with the poet's "infinitely penetrant"
eye. Consequently, the poems are extremely visual, and espe-
cially concerned with the movement of light: ". . . within the
ledges / the water, fast and still, pouring its yellow light, / and
green . . . falling in a foam / of crystal to a calm where the
waterlight / dappled the ledges as they leaned / against the sun."
The last poem of the book, "Holding the Mirror Up to Nature,"
is typical, and sums up Nemerov's dark view of the universe. His
use of mirrors reminds one of Hart Crane's lines which
Nemerov used as an epigraph to *Federigo*: "As silent as a mirror
is believed / Realities plunge in silence by. . . ." The object of
poetry is to catch as in a mirror the beauty and terror in life, not
to make life prettier, not to make it easier for us, not even to
help us understand it. Poetry can, if it is truthful, show us some
aspect of real life by stopping it in a frame (the poet's discipline)
and one can simply say, "How beautiful. How terrible." "Hold-
ing the Mirror" concludes:

> I know
> a truth that cannot be told, although
> I try to tell you, "We are alone,
> we know nothing, nothing, we shall die
> frightened in our freedom, the one
> who survives will change his name
> to evade the vengeance for love. . . ."
> Meanwhile the clouds go on clowning

over our heads in the floodlight of
a moon who is known to be Artemis
and Cynthia but sails away anyhow
beyond the serious poets with their
crazy ladies and cloudy histories,
their heroes in whose idiot dreams
the buzzard circles like a clock.

Mirrors & Windows is the work of a confident poet. M. L. Rosenthal, in his review, said that in "a good poet a fine mind is one of God's greatest blessings." Sense and sensibility are abundant in this book, and it should have made clear to the critics that Nemerov is not the "cold" writer he has often been accused of being. (His writing is more endangered by sentiment than cerebration.) Perhaps under the not-very-softening influence of nature, his feelings — always present — are more in evidence in these poems permeated by a humanitarian and stoic outlook.

New & Selected Poems (1960) contains fifty-eight poems, only fifteen of them new. Actually, the best part of this book is section II, which includes thirty-five poems from *The Salt Garden* and *Mirrors & Windows*, a sustained performance hard to match anywhere. The new note in *New & Selected Poems*, suitable for the maturing poet, is an even more overriding concern with his "deare times waste." Time and the loss of innocence, of friends, of hope, are the themes of the new poems. "I cried because life is hopeless and beautiful," he writes, and the beauty teaches him to "endure and grow." Nemerov's pessimism, dark as ever, is nevertheless not an empty nihilism: he affirms "the stillness in moving things" while attacking the emptiness of modern life.

The central poem here is "Runes," Nemerov's longest poem, symmetrically consisting of fifteen fifteen-line stanzas. Like "The Scales of the Eyes," "Runes" is a sort of dream fantasy, but it is more tightly organized, the fifteen stanzas being meditations clustered around the images of water and seed, "where time to come has tensed / Itself." (In Engle and Langland's *Poet's Choice*, 1962, Nemerov chooses "Runes" as his favorite among his own poems.) The run-on blank verse lines consistently match rhythm and content: a "liquid sense trembles in his lines."

The basic theme of "Runes" (ruins) is mutability, and the dominant tone is religious, sometimes pantheistically Wordsworthian or transcendentally Emersonian. By watching water, "Water of dirt, water of death, dark water," the poet tries to find the secret of the universe, of life. Water is a "many-veined bloodstream," an "echoing pulse," "a mirror of / The taste of human blood." Sometimes lyrically, sometimes satirically, Nemerov turns his theme over and over in the many-prismed glass of his verse. Typical of his impeccable style is stanza XII:

> Consider how the seed lost by a bird
> Will harbor in its branches most remote
> Descendants of the bird; while everywhere
> And unobserved, the soft green stalks and tubes
> Of water are hardening into wood, whose hide,
> Gnarled, knotted, flowing, and its hidden grain,
> Remember how the water is streaming still.
> Now does the seed asleep, as in a dream
> Where time is compacted under pressures of
> Another order, crack open like stone
> From whose division pours a stream, between
> The raindrop and the sea, running in one
> Direction, down, and gathering in its course
> That bitter salt which spices us the food
> We sweat for, and the blood and tears we shed.

The water streaming in the seed streams through our world, our bodies, holding everything together in its always-changing permanence. The subtle rhythms support the imagery in a fusion of form and content; run-ons, alliteration, repetition, all playing important roles in the structure. The "s" sound in "soft green stalks and tubes," the "d" sound in "hardening into wood, whose hide, / Gnarled, knotted" reinforce the meaning; the rhythm, stopped by "whose hide, / Gnarled, knotted," flows forward again with "flowing, and its hidden grain." The end of the first sentence holds the paradox of permanent impermanence in the ambiguous "streaming still." The onomatopoeic "crack" splits the second sentence, whose alliteration and longer phrases ("gathering in its course / That bitter salt which spices us the food / We sweat for") underline the stanza's conclusion.

Satirically, still working with water, Nemerov speaks of our "dehydrated time"; one perhaps thinks of Eliot's *Waste Land*, but this is clearly Nemerov, not Eliot; he has by this time mastered his influences. Some of his satire is tough indeed: "The plastic and cosmetic arts / Unbreakably record the last word and / The least word, till sometimes even the Muse, / In her transparent raincoat, resembles a condom." How to act in this kind of world, *which* sailor — the Homeric or the Dantean Ulysses — to emulate? Watching the water, symbol of eternal regeneration, Nemerov prepares us for death, "the pit where zero's eye is closed"; the secret, found in "small freshets / Leaping and limping down the tilted field / In April's light," is — to keep the secret "hidden from yourself." Working, like the metaphysical poets, with paradox, Nemerov implies that to prepare for life one should study nature, at the same time keeping the secret (nature is death) hidden from oneself.

Perhaps because of certain satirical poems (e.g., "Life Cycle of Common Man," "Boom!"), some critics wondered that Nemerov could be, as one put it, "strangely light-hearted about the whole enterprise" (the harshness of life); surely this is a mistaken reading of Nemerov. There is sometimes the tough gaiety of Yeats and sometimes the serene acceptance of Wordsworth, but Nemerov is never really lighthearted. The typical tone is one of quiet anguish (often based on personal experience, such as his father's death).

> Only he died
> that day. "Unlucky boy," my father said,
> who then was dying himself without a word
> to anyone, the crab's claw tightening
> inside the bowel that year to the next
> in a dead silence. I do not know if things
> that happen can be said to come to pass,
> or only happen, but when I remember
> my father's house, I imagine sometimes
> a dry, ruined spinster at my rainy window
> trying to tally on dumb fingers a world's
> incredible damage — nothing can stand it! — and
> watching the red shirt patched against the sky,
> so far and small in the webbed hand of the elm.

Nothing can stand it, nothing will yield: there is no lighthearted-
edness here.

"Mrs. Mandrill" (another Joycean title) is Nemerov's equiva-
lent of Wallace Stevens's "Sunday Morning," where the dying
Mrs. Mandrill muses on God, death, and nature (of which she is
about to become a part). Some of the lines are memorable for
their surreal power: "I was a little thing, before my face / broke
like a cheese"; "hearing this creature cry / before her wet heart
spills and goes to seed." Nature is really "unintelligible" to man,
though we can learn from it by analogy (in "The Companions"
in *The Blue Swallows* he says, "That's but interpretation, the deep
folly of man / To think that things can squeak at him more than
things can"). But when we die we become a part of nature and
the natural process — "they mean me now," thinks Mrs. Man-
drill. One thinks of Thomas Wolfe's "And the strange and
buried man will come again, in flower and leaf the strange and
buried man will come again. . . ."

One last poem in *New & Selected Poems* that should be men-
tioned is "Maestria," because it leads directly to Nemerov's two
best poems on "poetics" — "Vermeer" and "Lion & Hon-
eycomb" in *The Next Room of the Dream*. In "Maestria" Nemerov
points out that it is not the *meaning* of a poem that is important:
"you need not agree with its views / About money or the mean-
ing of numbers" (e.g., Pound, Dante). It would no doubt "be
better to be always right," but a good poem outstrips the errors
and "mortality of its maker, / Who has the skill of his art, and a
trembling hand."

> There remains
> A singular lucidity and sweetness, a way
> Of relating the light and the shade,
> The light spilling from fountains, the shade
> Shaken among the leaves.

In his introduction to Barfield's *Poetic Diction*, Nemerov
writes: "But when the poet is older, if he has continued to write,
it is at least probable that he will reach a point, either a stopping
point or a turning point, at which he finds it necessary to inquire

into the sense of what he has been doing, and now the question of poetic diction becomes for him supremely important, nothing less than the question of primary perception, of imagination itself, of how thought ever emerged (if it did) out of a world of things. There is some evidence that poets reaching this point — I think for example of Yeats, Valéry, Stevens — may feel acutely their want of formal philosophical training, so that they either abandon poetry and turn to study for a time, or else direct their poetry itself toward this study."

There is some evidence that Nemerov himself has reached this point in *The Next Room of the Dream* (1962): "The time came / He had to ask himself, what did he want? / What did he want when he began / That idiot fiddling with the sound of things." The subject matter of this book indicates his decision to stay close to "great primary human drama." Besides the two one-act verse plays, *Cain* (1959) and *Endor* (1961) — more successful as verse than as drama — poem after poem shows Nemerov's humanitarianism, notably "The Iron Characters," where he pities (more precisely: Nemerov *presents*; *we* pity) important men, governors, executives, who have broken under their responsibilities; but he concludes, pushing sympathy to its furthest limit, "Let the orphan, the pauper, the thief, the derelict drunk / And all those of no fixed address, shed tears of rejoicing / For the broken minds of the strong, the torn flesh of the just." It is, Nemerov implies, common helplessness that unites us.

In *Next Room of the Dream* the poems continue to simplify, emphasizing natural description and precise observation. In "Human Things," describing the effects of a sunset on a barn: "even / Nail holes look deep enough to swallow / Whatever light has left to give." Describing goldfish, he writes "The bearded goldfish move about the bowl / Waving disheveled rags of elegant fin / Languidly in the light."

The poem which best summarizes the general philosophy of the book is one called "Nothing Will Yield." Art smashes on the rocks of reality:

> Nothing will yield. The pretty poems are dead,
> And the mad poets in their periwigs,
> Bemused upon a frontispiece before
> The ruined Temple of Art, and supervised
> By the Goddess of Reason leaning from a cloud,
> In reality died insane. Alas, for the grave
> And gaudy forms! Lord Hi and Lady Ho,
> Those brazen effigies upon a plinth
> Of pink granite, seem immutable,
> But seem.

And yet there is still beauty, though beauty is always sad: "Lachrymae Christi is / A beautiful sound, a Neapolitan wine, / The Tears of Christ. And yet nothing will yield." In spite of this, poets will always speak their "holy language," in the teeth of despair. Nemerov concludes: "It takes great courage to go on the stage."

Seemingly effortlessly, Nemerov writes in blank verse, quatrains, triplets, sonnets, and a great variety of complex rhyme schemes; one senses immediately a poet with complete control of the tools of his trade, a poet for whom discipline means inspiration rather than restriction. Consistently simple, clear, direct, he time and again cuts open our experience to the anguished bone. In "Somewhere," Nemerov speaks of all the tragic events happening *exactly now*: "A girl this evening regrets her surrender with tears," errant schoolboys, vicious fathers, gluttons waiting to vomit, unfaithful wives:

> The stones of the city have been here for centuries,
> The tides have been washing backwards and forwards
> In sunlight, in starlight, since before the beginning.
> Down in the swamp a red fox runs quietly, quietly
> Under the owl's observation, those yellow eyes
> That eat through the darkness. Hear the shrew cry!

The rocking rhythm of "In sunlight, in starlight," the repetition of "quietly, quietly," are precise meaningful technical devices, and the poem ends with the nice irony of people listening to stories somewhere, stories of lust and violence, enraptured by "the sweet seductions / Punishable by death, with the song's word: long ago."

"Vermeer" expresses Nemerov's view on the relation between nature and poetry: "Taking what is, and seeing it as it is, / Pretending to no heroic stances or gestures, / Keeping it simple; being in love with light / And the marvelous things that light is able to do, / How beautiful!" The job of the poet is to present these things to the audience "and make it stick." Like Wilbur's "Juggler" ("who has won for once over the world's weight"), Nemerov's artist can make people "for one moment happy / In the great reckoning of those little rooms / Where the weight of life has been lifted and made light." But the capstone of *The Next Room of the Dream* is "Lion & Honeycomb," the closest thing to Nemerov's *ars poetica*, which begins "He didn't want to do it with skill, / He'd had enough of skill," and concludes:

> So there he was, this forty-year-old teen-ager
> Dreaming preposterous mergers and divisions
> Of vowels like water, consonants like rock
> (While everybody kept discussing values
> And the need for values), for words that would
> Enter the silence and be there as a light.
> So much coffee and so many cigarettes
> Gone down the drain, gone up in smoke,
> Just for the sake of getting something right
> Once in a while, something that could stand
> On its own flat feet to keep out windy time
> And the worm, something that might simply be,
> Not as the monument in the smoky rain
> Grimly endures, but that would be
> Only a moment's inviolable presence,
> The moment before disaster, before the storm,
> In its peculiar silence, an integer
> Fixed in the middle of the fall of things,
> Perfected and casual as to a child's eye
> Soap bubbles are, and skipping stones.

"Out of the eater came forth meat, and out of the strong came forth sweetness." Nemerov in this poem presents Samson's riddle as a parable of poetry. Poetry is the honey in the carcass of a lion; the poet manufactures this honey from the decaying grandeur surrounding him. In "Lion & Honeycomb" Nemerov both defines and exemplifies what he is trying to do. The rhythms of the poem are "Perfected and casual": note, for example, the placement of "Grimly," the balance of "So . . . so / Gone . . . gone." Unpretentious and simple, like "Soap bubbles" and "skipping stones," this poem shows Nemerov to be at a peak in his poetic powers.

But while *The Next Room of the Dream* seems to record a crisis and resolution in Nemerov's poetry, *Journal of the Fictive Life* (1965), records an unresolved crisis in Nemerov's fiction: an inability to complete another novel. This might be a good place to look back at Nemerov's novels, and see their relation to his poetry. Nemerov's fiction is in some danger of slipping undeservedly into oblivion: his novels and short stories are out of print, despite a generally good critical reception on their first appearance. One reason for this neglect is that his stories are uncompromising in their intellectual and moral implications, and unromantic in their presentation. In fact, one of his major themes is the disaster incurred when romantic people ("melodramatists") clash with reality. Reality, to Nemerov, is infinitely complex; the simplest act (speeding in a car, taking a bath) can, to a subtle mind, have enormous and far-reaching consequences. These books do not duck these complexities, and thus, despite much high humor, would have to be lucky to capture the popular imagination.

Like his poems, they are basically pessimistic. The condition of man is not an enviable one: we act foolishly and understand imperfectly. Nemerov's dark viewpoint, which in his poetry is redeemed by beauty (e.g., the wild birds in "The Town Dump"), in his fiction is redeemed by humor. There is in Nemerov much of the attitude of the "Absurd" playwrights: life may be meaningless, but at least we can laugh at it, and with laughter comes acceptance. Wallace Stevens wrote that poetry makes our completely inexplicable lives acceptable; humor has this function in Nemerov's novels. It involves looking at life honestly and not giving in to the modish despair Nemerov satirizes in his poem "To the Bleeding Hearts Association of American Novelists." For example, the death of Susan Boyne in *The Melodramatists* is tragic and unexpected, and yet ludicrous; it has a lot in common with the death of Jerry in Albee's *Zoo Story*. Both are semi-suicides which take the action out of the realm of dialectic: death, at least, is real. Unsentimental, without illusions, Nemerov's comic viewpoint presents man as hopelessly inept and at the same time unquenchably enduring.

There has been some development in Nemerov's prose, though not so striking as in his poetry, but even in his first novel his salient qualities are apparent: humor, intellectual precision, fantasy, and a smooth, "classical" prose style. *The Melodramatists* (1949) is a wild first novel. Stylistically it is an odd but appealing mixture: a Trollope bitten by a Heller, perhaps, or vice versa, combining a slow, old-fashioned elegance of prose with comic, almost surrealistic events. It switches from Socratic dialogue to drunken orgy, from dialectic to destruction, without missing a beat. The action takes place among an old Boston "Brahmin" family, and the tone is consistently satirical. Though compared by reviewers to Waugh and Huxley, Nemerov seems stylistically closer to more leisurely writers — Trollope, as mentioned above, or Henry James, in his elegance of phrasing and (like his poetry) precision of observation: "When her mother wept, as she did now, all the jewels on her fingers and at her throat winked in sparkling connivance as at a joke which, they seemed to say, you too might appreciate, were you as detached as a stone — cold as this sapphire, hard and cutting as this diamond. Mrs. Boyne's tears fell heedlessly where they might, into her coffee, over the bright little spoons and dessert knives, stained the damask cloth. . . ." A perhaps more profitable comparison can be made with a novelist greatly admired by Nemerov: Thomas Mann (Nemerov has two essays on Mann in *Poetry and Fiction: Essays*). If there is any real similarity between *The Melodramatists* and another novel, it would be with Mann's *Magic Mountain*. Just as Herren Settembrini and Naphta tirelessly engage in a religious, philosophical, and scientific debate for the soul of Hans Castorp, so in *The Melodramatists* Dr. Einman and Father Meretruce debate for the souls of Susan and Claire, debates which are never resolved, but which culminate in disaster.

The action in *The Melodramatists* proceeds from sanity to madness, in several ways. The thin line between madness and sanity is one of Nemerov's chief themes — it shows up in *Federigo*, in *The Homecoming Game*, and in several of his short stories ("A Secret Society," "The Web of Life"), as well as in poems like "The Iron Characters" and "The Rope's End." The plot here, as in most of his fiction, is a bizarre and often grotesque vehicle for his satire. The two main targets are psychiatry, in the person of Dr. Einman, and religion, in the persons of Father Meretruce and the Hungarian nuns. The religion Meretruce represents is a false one, and, indeed, religion as a panacea for society's ills turns out very badly in this book. The only real religious experience in it is incurred by Claire and described as a spiritual rape; and even prayer is described repulsively: "The Hungarian nuns were praying at an almost breathless speed. They were knelt down near to and facing a wall to which they addressed a continuous muttering. They rocked slightly back and forth, and swayed a little from side to side; the flow of their words was interrupted only occasionally for a brief instant in which one of them would gulp back from the corners of her mouth an excess of saliva, or swiftly wipe her lips at the wrist of her garment." It is no wonder Claire eventually loses her faith.

The major theme in *The Melodramatists* is the inability of these characters to cope with reality. The only character who is *not* a romanticist is Mother Fosker, and this grotesque old madam caters to the romanticism of society in general by basing her "entertainments" on illusion — the illusion of love, of pursuit, of youth, of gaiety. And time after time Nemerov digresses in his learned and amusing way on the nature of romanticism: "It is easy to imagine the other worlds that might be. One, for example, of a delicious lubricity, indiscriminate and always pleasant copulation *à la Thélème*, and every nymphomaniac there remains sixteen for always and always but is an intelligent conversationalist, charmed by poetry and good music, who can repeat to you word for word the entire *Book of the Courtier*. There on Urbino's windy hill, where blows Castiglione's wise and sexual beard, the sun varies in color from a bloody incandescence in the morning to a dusk of lavender, heliotrope, pale rose, and a few ruins by Piranesi delicately accent the small cumulus clouds artistically piled at one corner of a sky which is not too large."

There are weaknesses in the book. It is longer than it need be — the part played by Roger, though often amusing, seems unnecessary. Some of the discussions seem too long; some scenes are a little like a bad play; some of the humor strains too hard to be clever ("we know where our breed is bettered"). But in general *The Melodramatists* is a highly successful first novel, a book by an erudite and witty young man who presents his criticism of society without writing the usual disguised autobiography. The Boyne mansion stands at the end of the book as an apt symbol of society: science and religion (Einman and Meretruce) are prisoners upstairs, while lust and lechery reign below. But, as in the final stanza of many of his poems, in the final passage of the book all is not hopeless. In a "minimal affirmation," Claire reacts to this debacle not by breaking down, but by turning to music: "Claire got up, and, without looking at Hogan or John or the priest, went to the harpsichord. She sat down and began to play, inattentively at first but presently with more care, a little piece in fugue. The instrument was out of tune and not only that, but broken glass tinkled on some of the strings, but it seemed not to matter. The morning light seemed to clear the room as the voices in a minor key steadily moved to and from one another, showing an inexorable confidence in their not quite harmonious world." The house (the world) is a catastrophe, but it endures, and begins again.

Nemerov's second novel, *Federigo, or, The Power of Love* (1954), is, among other things, a sex farce, a sort of rococo updating of a story from, perhaps, Boccaccio's *Decameron*. While Nemerov is not coy, and will use on occasion the suitable four-letter words, his handling of sexual scenes is basically psychological, not detailed or graphic. Concentrating on *style*, on good writing, rather than on titillation or easy shock, Nemerov bypasses contemporary vogues to write a novel that is consistently in good taste (in this way, and others, often reminding one of Vladimir Nabokov). *Federigo* is Nemerov's best novel, a tour de force whose intricate plot unravels with the inevitable logic of

Chaucer's "Miller's Tale"; crammed with wit and wisdom, it begins with a lovely sentence: "Young men in our country are brought up to believe that they have a destiny, a guiding idea shaped like a star; most of them pass their lives in unawareness that this destiny is gradually becoming the sum of everything that has happened to them, and need not have been represented by a star in the first place, being perhaps more like the false beacon set up by smugglers to direct a vessel toward a convenient disaster. Disaster, *dés*, from, *astre*, a star."

The plot, really an elaborate joke, is the line on which Nemerov hangs his criticism of society and his psychological insights into existential man. But he compounds the "unreality" of this novel by introducing an element of high fantasy, an element very prominent in his short stories (e.g., "Yore," "The Sorcerer's Eye"). Fantasy in *Federigo* centers around the character of Federigo himself. Actually, there are three Federigos: the invented Federigo (the one used by Julian and Marius in their letters); the real Federigo (Federigo Schwartz, a shadowy figure who looks like Julian and whom Elaine has met); and the apparition Federigo, who appears throughout the book to Julian, walking through walls, recalling scenes of Julian's childhood, predicting the future, disappearing and appearing at will. This Federigo, literarily speaking, has much in common with the devils which appear in Mann's *Doctor Faustus* and Dostoevski's *The Brothers Karamazov*: he is a taunting intellectual sort of fellow, and Julian is never quite clear whether he actually sees him or just imagines him. One reason *Federigo* is successful is that it seems to mirror the "opposed elements" already noted in Nemerov's poetry.

Federigo is used by Nemerov to develop Julian's character, and consequently we understand more about Julian than we did about any of the characters in *The Melodramatists*. Federigo is indeed the devil, but he is also Julian's second self — the devil in every man which is usually suppressed. Through Federigo we know the worst of Julian Ghent: a hint of homosexuality, a yearning for the death of his wife, an emptiness of spirit. "To make me leave you alone," says Federigo, "you must be other than you are." When Julian, at the end, discovers he is not cut out to be unfaithful, Federigo disappears.

The problem Federigo causes Julian is the problem of sanity. If Federigo "is the Devil," Julian thinks, then "I am insane." But Nemerov's point is that it is not Julian who is insane, but life in general: "But Julian considered that all these fine ladies and gentlemen gathered here, listening to the fine talk, kept in their hearts the secret of lust, that their inmost thoughts were concentrated on sex, that madness thinly veiled possessed them all, the madness which all the forces of society seemed designed at once to provoke and restrain but never to allay."

Julian (Jay) Ghent is — like Fitzgerald's Jay Gatsby — a romanticist who bangs hard against reality, though, this being a comedy, he survives. The power of love (the ironic subtitle) is really not very powerful in a world where people are not sure whom they love, or in what way. Julian tries to become a great lover, and fails except by mistake with his wife. The animals in the zoo seem to Julian to be neater and more dignified than humans; and toward the end of the book when Marius and Elaine walk along the shore the huge head of a dead fish grins up at them (the same fish as in Nemerov's most anthologized poem, "The Goose Fish"). Human love, Nemerov realizes, has "pitched his mansion in / The place of excrement"; more than that, there are no lights in this mansion and one needs luck to stumble into someone's arms.

Federigo is as smoothly written as *The Melodramatists*, but sharper, more epigrammatic: "The future is in the lap of the gods, and they are standing up to see what is going to happen." It is not only the epigrams, however, which strike the reader of Nemerov's prose. His sentences have a fine balance, an almost Baconian resonance, marked by impeccable grammar and a rising and falling rhythm: "Julian and Sylvia Ghent are still together, without being altogether certain why; though it is true that there was born to them a child, whose creation could have been dated to that night. This child was a boy, whom they named Peter." This balance is often achieved by rhythmically matched clauses and phrases, frequently joined by the semico-

lon: "They had, she believed, a modern marriage; this was, how-
ever, the expression people typically used. . . ." The colon, too,
is frequently used by Nemerov to set up parallel lists and de-
scriptions: "The furniture too rebuked them, entering into the
spirit of the silence: the clean-lined, slender legs of the low,
modern tables, the alert appearance of the couch with its square
corners and straight back, the inquisitive curve of a lamp which
bent its bell-head heavily from a corner; all these smart imper-
sonal objects, as coldly reasonable here as they had been in the
shops whence they came, all at once achieved the identity of
unhappiness: if we thought you would be like this, they seemed
to say, we would not have come here."

To sum up (as Nemerov typically says in his critical reviews),
Federigo can be best explained in the words of Marius when
Sylvia tells him about the letters. "How very funny," he says. "Yet
how very serious, too." Of course, the same could be said about
The Blue Swallows or *The Next Room of the Dream*.

The Homecoming Game (1957), a humorous takeoff on a sort of
Rover Boy plot, is his last and least ambitious novel, its en-
thusiastic reception at least partly caused by Nemerov's growing
reputation. Ironically, this book made Nemerov the most
money, being turned into a vapid Broadway comedy by Lindsay
and Crouse, and a ridiculous Hollywood movie starring Jane
Fonda. "All one winter and spring," writes Nemerov in *Journal of
the Fictive Life*, "my shoulder ached from carting those checks to
the bank." This "capriciousness in the relation between work
and pay" is one of the reasons he has not written another novel:
"how easy it would be to become a writer who worked for the
money."

The Homecoming Game is set at a small old eastern coeduca-
tional college (physically reminding one of Hamilton); Charles
Osman, the protagonist, is a history teacher who has just flunked
the star quarterback. Nemerov turns this cliché into a tremen-
dously complicated situation, a moral and philosophical tangle
almost impossible to unravel. The second half of *The Homecom-
ing Game* redeems what begins as a weak performance. Even
Nemerov's style falters a bit in the beginning, occasionally ap-

proaching uncomfortably close to the old "Tom Swifties," as on pages 30–31:

> Charles laughed rather hopelessly. . . .
> "Yes," she said earnestly. . . .
> "You speak delightfully of 'us,'" Charles said glumly. . . .
> "Where in all this is Blent?" Charles asked angrily. . . .

Also, the improbability of the given situation, before Nemerov ingeniously works it out, tends to keep the reader uninvolved. One can accept a student athlete being offered a bribe — that happens all the time — and one can gleefully accept wild events such as the student falling into the pep-rally bonfire and getting burned to death: a macabre symbol of a pagan ritual; but it is harder to accept the student council threatening the professor, the quarterback and the professor being in love with the beautiful daughter of trustee Herman Sayre, the quarterback being from the home town of Senator Stamp, Stamp and Sayre both being such primitive types, the president being such a servile and contemptible coward: these touches in toto do not succeed the way *Federigo* succeeds.

Nemerov uses football as a multivalent symbol of society, life, and death. Charles, like Nemerov, has a metaphysical turn of mind (also like Julian Ghent in *Federigo*, who compares at great length his bathroom to a church); football, to Charles, is like society because it consists of "orderly violence," reminding him of all the products of civilization, from war to cities to symphonies. It is like death because it ends so abruptly; it seems so real, and then is gone. It is like life because of its ebb and flow, and because it is, somehow, deceptive: "Football is unreal, if you care to say so; but as you grow older many things become unreal, and football stands out somehow as an image. And there under the shadow of the stone, empty stadium, after the captains and the kings depart, after all the others too depart, in that last lonely and cold air, you may, if you care for games, experience something of what is meant by vanished glory. Symbolical — perhaps. But it is commonly allowed that you may more easily call the things of this world symbolical than say what they are symbolical of."

In no other book has football, that national phenomenon, been so subtly analyzed as in *The Homecoming Game*. Despite a lack of memorable characters, the madness that grips the students (which, Nemerov points out, has disturbing similarities to the madness of Nazi Germany), the ridiculous but real tension . on the campus, the pressures on faculty members who have star athletes in their classes, the power plays of alumni and trustees, and even the beauty of the actual game itself (and even when the beautiful game is beautifully fixed), are all unforgettably presented in this novel.

Nemerov's three novels, plus his books of short stories (*A Commodity of Dreams*, 1959, *Stories, Fables and Other Diversions*, 1971), are remarkable in their consistency of superior writing. Too intellectual, perhaps, for real popularity, they nevertheless should not be out of print. One charge that has been made against all of them (similar to one made against his poetry) is that Nemerov treats his characters coldly. The real problem is that readers do not know how to take Nemerov: Is he being funny, or what? Is he kidding us?

The point is that Nemerov, like the "Absurd" playwrights, is humorous and serious at the same time. One should not confuse seriousness with solemnity; Nemerov is never solemn but is always, even at his funniest, serious. When Julian and Sylvia sit up in bed and recognize each other, this is funny; but it also underlines Nemerov's thesis: we think we know what we are doing, but we do not; we think we are in control of the situation, but we are not. "Reality," observes Mr. le Mesurier in "Yore," "is always improbable," and man's understanding of reality is always incomplete and distorted. Because Nemerov's major prose mode is satire and comedy (while his major poetic mode is lyric), this "coldness" is necessary; if a figure is to be comic, he must be fallible and weak (Falstaff, Pangloss, Don Quixote, Humbert Humbert). Because Nemerov looks on fate as inexorable, enigmatic, and accidental, and sees man as a victim of this fate, his writing must be either tragic or comic; it cannot be heroic or sentimental. Basically speaking, Nemerov's prose is comic;

Nemerov's poetry is tragic: both come from the same fatalistic philosophy, representing the two ways that the "opposed elements" of his character show their responsibility to the human drama.

In *Journal of the Fictive Life* Nemerov attempts to fuse these elements by plunging into confession and self-analysis written in a cross between poetry and prose. Proceeding by epigram ("The novel is marriage. Poetry is infidelity") and association, Nemerov analyzes his inability to write a fourth novel by analyzing his dreams, his relationship with his parents and wife, his taboos and prejudices, in a Dostoevskian manner: "As though to say: Yes, I am a loathsome fellow, but beautifully composed! And all through these so intimate, so personal, observations runs the thought that I shall one day publish them, in a gesture of confessional defiance or proud self-contempt. For I am trying to tell the truth, and it is a trouble to me."

Anyone interested in the link between the subconscious mind and creativity will find riches in this book. There is much also that helps one understand particular poems, parts of the novels, and various influences such as Nabokov and Empson. The most surprising aspect of the book, however, is its sexual frankness, an area in which Nemerov has previously been reticent.

Journal of the Fictive Life is the record of a disturbed man who turns the rather awesome battery of his intelligence inward on his own mind, seeking the source of his disturbance. But the source is, simply, his humanness; here also is the source of reconciliation, as the *Journal* ends with the birth of Nemerov's son and a hopeful pointing toward the "magical poetry" of Shakespeare's Last Plays.

Nemerov's next work, *The Blue Swallows* (1967), is a worthy successor. It has the variety, wit, and technical skill we have come to expect; it is also full of wisdom and gentleness.

> . . . even the water
> Flowing away beneath those birds
> Will fail to reflect their flying forms,
> And the eyes that see become as stones
> Whence never tears shall fall again.

O swallows, swallows, poems are not
The point. Finding again the world,
That is the point, where loveliness
Adorns intelligible things
Because the mind's eye lit the sun.

Without basically changing his dark philosophy, or losing his satirical edge, Nemerov has progressed steadily in his poetry to a broader, more tolerant view, less bitter and more sad. While the themes and images are often specifically contemporary (Auschwitz, burning monks, a Negro cemetery, cybernetics), Nemerov is mainly concerned with finding timeless metaphors for the human condition, "relation's spindrift web." In poem after poem we are likened (without his saying so explicitly) to cherries picked off trees, snowflakes falling in black water, lobsters waiting in a tank, days falling to darkness, planted rows dwindling to wilderness, fields becoming shadows. These poems are used more or less contrapuntally with tremendously effective satire on the Great Society ("Money," "On the Platform," "To the Governor & Legislature of Massachusetts"). A typical example (not best, but chosen for brevity) is "Keeping Informed in D.C.":

Each morning when I break my buttered toast
Across the columns of the *Morning Post*,
I am astounded by the ways in which
Mankind has managed once again to bitch
Things up to a degree that yesterday
Had looked impossible. Not far away
From dreams of mine, I read this dream of theirs,
And think: It's true, we *are* the bankrupt heirs
Of all the ages, history *is* the bunk.
If you do not believe in all this junk,
If you're not glad things are not as they are,
You can wipe your arse on the *Evening Star*.

Nature, still treated unromantically, permeates these poems; in "The Companions," which is a sort of modern "Immortality Ode," Nemerov describes the pull toward nature that, for example, Frost writes about in "Directive." Nemerov refuses to see "messages" there, and yet "there came those voices up out of the ground / And got into my head, until articulate sound / Might speak them to themselves." A fascination with light, "Firelight in sunlight, silver pale," still plays over his pages, and indeed each of these poems can be thought of as a "small flame" like that which concludes the book's final poem:

> So warm, so clear at the line of corded velvet
> The marvelous flesh, its faster rise and fall,
> Sigh in the throat, the mouth fallen open,
> The knees fallen open, the heavy flag of the skirt
> Urgently gathered together, quick, so quick,
> Black lacquer, bronze, blue velvet, gleam
> Of pewter in a tarnishing light, the book
> Of the body lying open at the last leaf,
> Where the spirit and the bride say, Come,
> As from deep mirrors on the hinted wall
> Beyond these shadows, a small flame sprouts.

One reason why Nemerov speaks effectively to this age is that his poetry attempts to come to terms with science: not just psychology, as in the *Journal*, but "hard" science. Light years and nebulae, the speed of light, electrodes, a heterodyne hum, physicists and particles are typical subjects for him. His general position seems to be that science is "true," but never quite accounts for our lives (though it tries): science lacks "blood" and "mystery"; it misses the essential.

> For "nothing in the universe can travel at the speed
> Of light," they say, forgetful of the shadow's speed.

While Nemerov's typical form is still the loose blank-verse line, in *The Blue Swallows* he uses more short-lined poems, trimeter and dimeter, than in his earlier work, keeping with his trend toward simplicity. In this form, too, his rhythms are varied and subtle, as in the first stanza of "Celestial Globe":

> This is the world
> Without the world.
> I hold it in my hand
> A hollow sphere
> Of childlike blue
> With magnitudes of stars.

> There in its utter dark
> The singing planets go,
> And the sun, great source,
> Is blazing forth his fires
> Over the many-oceaned
> And river-shining earth
> Whereon I stand
> Balancing this ball
> Upon my hand.

The Blue Swallows is the work of a poet who is a master of his craft; rhythm, image, sound fuse in poem after poem. And the poetry speaks to us, as poems should. There is no certainty, much agony, our minds bow down "Among the shadows / Of shadowy things, / Itself a shadow / Less sure than they." Nemerov's general intelligence and craftsmanship perhaps seem old-fashioned today, when blood-and-guts, a confessional softness, and a sort of sloppiness are thought to be more "honest" or "spontaneous"; he is perhaps closer in this to, say, Pope, who is also out of favor (nevertheless the eighteenth century is called the Age of Pope). And underneath the darkness, fragmented and dying, Nemerov continually strikes the existential spark, as in the conclusion of his poem describing an oil slick polluting a stream:

> The curve and glitter of it as it goes
> The maze of its pursuit, reflect the water
> In agony under the alien, brilliant skin
> It struggles to throw off and finally does
> Throw off, on its frivolous purgatorial fall
> Down to the sea and away, dancing and singing
> Perpetual intercession for this filth —
> Leaping and dancing and singing, forgiving everything.

SELECTED BIBLIOGRAPHIES

Selected Bibliographies

ARCHIBALD MacLEISH

Works

POETRY

Songs for a Summer's Day (A Sonnet-Cycle). New Haven, Conn.: Yale University Press, 1915.

Tower of Ivory, with a Foreword by Lawrence Mason. New Haven, Conn.: Yale University Press, 1917.

The Happy Marriage, and Other Poems. Boston and New York: Houghton Mifflin, 1924.

The Pot of Earth. Boston and New York: Houghton Mifflin, 1925.

Streets in the Moon. Boston and New York: Houghton Mifflin, 1926.

The Hamlet of A. MacLeish. Boston and New York: Houghton Mifflin, 1928.

New Found Land: Fourteen Poems. Boston and New York: Houghton Mifflin, 1930.

Conquistador. Boston and New York: Houghton Mifflin, 1932.

Frescoes for Mr. Rockefeller's City. New York: John Day, 1933.

Poems, 1924–1933. Boston and New York: Houghton Mifflin, 1933.

Public Speech: Poems. New York: Farrar and Rinehart, 1936.

Land of the Free — U.S.A. New York: Harcourt, Brace, 1938.

America Was Promises. New York: Duell, Sloan and Pearce, 1939.

Actfive and Other Poems. New York: Random House, 1948.

Collected Poems. Boston: Houghton Mifflin, 1952; enlarged ed., 1962.

Songs for Eve. Boston: Houghton Mifflin, 1954.

The Wild Old Wicked Man, and Other Poems. Boston: Houghton Mifflin, 1968.

The Human Season: Selected Poems, 1926–1972. Boston: Houghton Mifflin, 1972.

PLAYS

Nobodaddy: A Play. Cambridge, Mass.: Dunster House, 1926.

289

Union Pacific — A Ballet. Produced 1934; published in Gerald Goode, ed., *The Book of Ballets.* New York: Crown, 1939.

Panic: A Play in Verse. Boston and New York: Houghton Mifflin, 1935.

The Fall of the City: A Verse Play for Radio. New York and Toronto: Farrar and Rinehart, 1937.

Air Raid: A Verse Play for Radio. New York: Harcourt, Brace, 1938.

The States Talking. In *The Free Company Presents . . . A Collection of Plays about the Meaning of America.* New York: Dodd, Mead, 1941.

The American Story: Ten Broadcasts. New York: Duell, Sloan and Pearce, 1944.

The Trojan Horse: A Play. Boston: Houghton Mifflin, 1952.

This Music Crept by Me upon the Waters. Cambridge, Mass.: Harvard University Press, 1953.

J. B.: A Play in Verse. Boston: Houghton Mifflin, 1958.

Three Short Plays: The Secret of Freedom, Air Raid, The Fall of the City. New York: Dramatists Play Service, 1961.

Herakles: A Play in Verse. Boston: Houghton Mifflin, 1967.

Scratch. Suggested by Stephen Vincent Benét's short story "The Devil and Daniel Webster." Boston: Houghton Mifflin, 1971.

MISCELLANEOUS PROSE WORKS

Housing America, by the Editors of *Fortune.* New York: Harcourt, Brace, 1932. (Written by MacLeish.)

Jews in America, by the Editors of *Fortune.* New York: Random House, 1936. (Written by MacLeish.)

Background of War, by the Editors of *Fortune.* New York: Knopf, 1937. (Of the six articles in this collection, all but the third were written by MacLeish.)

The Irresponsibles: A Declaration. New York: Duell, Sloan and Pearce, 1940.

The American Cause. New York: Duell, Sloan and Pearce, 1941.

A Time to Speak: The Selected Prose of Archibald MacLeish. Boston: Houghton Mifflin, 1941.

American Opinion and the War. Cambridge: The University Press, 1942.

A Time to Act: Selected Addresses. Boston: Houghton Mifflin, 1943.

Poetry and Opinion; The Pisan Cantos of Ezra Pound: A Dialog on the Role of Poetry. Urbana: University of Illinois Press, 1950.

Freedom Is the Right to Choose: An Inquiry into the Battle for the American Future. Boston: Beacon Press, 1951.

Poetry and Experience. Boston: Houghton Mifflin, 1961.

The Eleanor Roosevelt Story. Boston: Houghton Mifflin, 1965.

A Continuing Journey. Boston: Houghton Mifflin, 1968.

Champion of a Cause: Essays and Addresses on Librarianship. Compiled and with an Introduction by Eva M. Goldschmidt. Chicago: American Library Association, 1971.

Bibliography

Mizener, Arthur. *A Catalogue of the First Editions of Archibald MacLeish.* New Haven, Conn.: Yale University Press, 1938.

Autobiography and Criticism

Bush, Warren V., ed. *The Dialogues of Archibald MacLeish and Mark Van Doren.* New York: Dutton, 1964.

Falk, Signi Lenea. *Archibald MacLeish.* New York: Twayne, 1965.

RICHARD EBERHART

Works

POETRY

A Bravery of Earth. New York: Jonathan Cape and Harrison Smith, 1930.
Reading the Spirit. New York: Oxford University Press, 1937.
Song and Idea. New York: Oxford University Press, 1942.
Poems, New and Selected. Norfolk, Conn.: New Directions, 1944.
Burr Oaks. New York: Oxford University Press, 1947.
Brotherhood of Man. Pawlet, Vt.: Banyan Press, 1949.
An Herb Basket. Cummington, Mass.: Cummington Press, 1950.
Selected Poems. New York: Oxford University Press, 1951.
Undercliff: Poems 1946–1953. New York: Oxford University Press, 1953.
Great Praises. New York: Oxford University Press, 1957.
Collected Poems 1930–1960. New York: Oxford University Press, 1960.
The Quarry: New Poems. New York: Oxford University Press, 1964.
Selected Poems 1930–1965. New York: New Directions, 1965.
Thirty-One Sonnets. New York: The Eakins Press, 1967.
Shifts of Being. New York: Oxford University Press, 1968.
Fields of Grace. New York: Oxford University Press, 1972.

PLAYS

Collected Verse Plays. Chapel Hill: University of North Carolina Press, 1962.

PROSE

"Empson's Poetry," in *Accent Anthology*, edited by Kerker Quinn and Charles Shattuck. New York: Harcourt, Brace, 1946. Pp. 571–88.
"Notes on Poetry," in *Mid-Century American Poets*, edited by John Ciardi. New York: Twayne, 1950. Pp. 225–29.
"The Stevens Prose," *Accent*, 12:122–25 (Spring 1952).
"Will and Psyche in Poetry," in *The Moment of Poetry*, edited by Don Cameron Allen. Baltimore: Johns Hopkins Press, 1962. Pp. 48–72.
"Tragedy as Limitation: Comedy as Control and Resolution," *Tulane Drama Review*, 6:3–14 (Summer 1962).
"Emerson and Wallace Stevens," *Literary Review*, 7:51–71 (Autumn 1963).
"On Theodore Roethke's Poetry," *Southern Review*, 1:612–20 (Summer 1965).
"How I Write Poetry," in *Poets on Poetry*, edited by Howard Nemerov. New York: Basic Books, 1966. Pp. 17–39.
"Introduction," in *Paradise Lost, Paradise Regained, and Samson Agonistes*, by John Milton. New York: Doubleday–The Literary Guild, 1969.
"Pure Poetry and the Idea of Value," in *Quality in the Arts*. New York: Atheneum, 1969.

EDITED ANTHOLOGY OF POETRY

War and the Poet (with Selden Rodman). New York: Devin-Adair, 1945.

Biography

Roache, Joel. *Richard Eberhart: The Progress of an American Poet*. New York: Oxford University Press, 1971.

Critical Studies

Booth, Philip. "The Varieties of Poetic Experience," *Shenandoah*, 15:62–69 (Summer 1964).

Dickey, James. "Richard Eberhart," in *The Suspect in Poetry*. Madison, Minn.: The Sixties Press, 1964. Pp. 95–96.

Donoghue, Denis. *The Third Voice*. Princeton, N.J.: Princeton University Press, 1959. Pp. 194–95, 223–35.

———. "An Interview with Richard Eberhart," *Shenandoah*, 15:7–29 (Summer 1964).

Engel, Bernard F. *The Achievement of Richard Eberhart*. Glenview, Ill.: Scott, Foresman, 1968.

———. *Richard Eberhart*. New York: Twayne, 1971.

Hall, Donald. "Method in Poetic Composition," *Paris Review*, 3:113–19 (Autumn 1953).

Hall, James. "Richard Eberhart: The Sociable Naturalist," *Western Review*, 18:315–21 (Summer 1954).

Hoffman, Daniel. "Hunting a Master Image: The Poetry of Richard Eberhart," *Hollins Critic*, 4:1–12 (October 1964).

Mills, Ralph J., Jr. "Richard Eberhart," in *Contemporary American Poetry*. New York: Random House, 1965. Pp. 9–31.

"On Richard Eberhart's 'Am I My Neighbor's Keeper?'" in *The Contemporary Poet as Artist and Critic*, edited by Anthony Ostroff. Boston: Little, Brown, 1964. Pp. 141–66. (This includes short essays by Louise Bogan, Philip Booth, and William Stafford, and Eberhart's reply.)

Rodman, Selden. "The Poetry of Richard Eberhart," *Perspectives U.S.A.*, 10:32–42 (Winter 1955).

Rosenthal, M. L. *The Modern Poets: A Critical Introduction*. New York: Oxford University Press, 1960. Pp. 246–48.

Thorslev, Peter L., Jr. "The Poetry of Richard Eberhart," in *Poets in Progress*, edited by Edward B. Hungerford. Evanston, Ill.: Northwestern University Press, 1962. Pp. 73–91.

THEODORE ROETHKE

Works

POETRY

Open House. New York: Knopf, 1941.

The Lost Son and Other Poems. Garden City, N.Y.: Doubleday, 1948.

Praise to the End! Garden City, N.Y.: Doubleday, 1951.

The Waking: Poems 1933–1953. Garden City, N.Y.: Doubleday, 1953.

Words for the Wind: The Collected Verse of Theodore Roethke. Garden City, N.Y.: Doubleday, 1958.

I Am! Says the Lamb. Garden City, N.Y.: Doubleday, 1961.

Sequence, Sometimes Metaphysical. Iowa City: Stonewall Press, 1963.

The Far Field. Garden City, N.Y.: Doubleday, 1964.

The Collected Poems of Theodore Roethke. Garden City, N.Y.: Doubleday, 1966.

PROSE

On the Poet and His Craft: Selected Prose of Theodore Roethke, edited by Ralph J. Mills, Jr. Seattle: University of Washington Press, 1965.

Selected Letters of Theodore Roethke, edited by Ralph J. Mills, Jr. Seattle: University of Washington Press, 1968.

MISCELLANEOUS

Straw for the Fire: Selections from Theodore Roethke's Notebooks 1943–1961, edited by David Wagoner. Garden City, N.Y.: Doubleday, 1972.

Bibliography

McLeod, James R. *Theodore Roethke: A Manuscript Cheklist.* Kent, Ohio: Kent State University Press, 1971.
———. *Theodore Roethke: A Bibliography.* Kent, Ohio: Kent State University Press, 1972.
Matheson, John William. "Theodore Roethke: A Bibliography." University of Washington, Master of Librarianship thesis, 1958.

Concordance

A Concordance to the Poems of Theodore Roethke, edited by Gary Lane, programmed by Roland Dedekind. Metuchen, N.J.: Scarecrow Press, 1972.

Biography

Seager, Allan. *The Glass House: The Life of Theodore Roethke.* New York: McGraw-Hill, 1968.

Critical Studies

Arnett, Carroll. "Minimal to Maximal: Theodore Roethke's Dialectic," *College English*, 18:414–16 (May 1957).
Blessing, Richard Allen. *Theodore Roethke's Dynamic Vision.* Bloomington: University of Indiana Press, 1974.
Bogan, Louise. "Stitched in Bone," in *Trial Balances*, edited by Ann Winslow. New York: Macmillan, 1935. Pp. 138–39.
Burke, Kenneth. "The Vegetal Radicalism of Theodore Roethke," *Sewanee Review*, 58:68–108 (Winter 1950).
Dickey, James. "Theodore Roethke," in *Babel to Byzantium: Poets and Poetry Now.* New York: Noonday Press, 1968. Pp. 147–52.
Gross, Harvey. *Sound and Form in Modern Poetry.* Ann Arbor: University of Michigan Press, 1964. Pp. 282–90.
Heyen, William. *Profile of Theodore Roethke.* Columbus, Ohio: Charles E. Merrill, 1971.
Kramer, Hilton. "The Poetry of Theodore Roethke," *Western Review*, 18:131–46 (Winter 1954).
Kunitz, Stanley. "News of the Root," *Poetry*, 73:222–25 (January 1949).
———. "Theodore Roethke," *New York Review of Books*, 1:22 (October 17, 1963).
———. "Roethke: Poet of Transformations," *New Republic*, 152:23–29 (January 23, 1965).
Lee, Charlotte I. "The Line as Rhythmic Unit in the Poetry of Theodore Roethke," *Speech Monographs*, 30:15–22 (March 1963).
McClatchy, J. D. "Sweating the Light from a Stone: Identifying Theodore Roethke," *Modern Poetry Studies*, 3:1–24 (1972).

McMichael, James. "The Poetry of Theodore Roethke," *Southern Review*, n.s., 5:4–25 (Winter 1969).

Malkoff, Karl. *Theodore Roethke: An Introduction to the Poetry*. New York: Columbia University Press, 1966.

Martz, William J. *The Achievement of Theodore Roethke*. Glenview, Ill.: Scott, Foresman, 1966.

Mills, Ralph J., Jr. "Roethke's Garden," *Poetry*, 100:54–59 (April 1962).

———. "Theodore Roethke," in *Contemporary American Poetry*. New York: Random House, 1965. Pp. 48–71.

———. *Creation's Very Self: On the Personal Element in Recent American Poetry*. Fort Worth: Texas Christian University Press, 1969. Pp. 8–13.

Northwest Review, 11 (Summer 1971). Special issue on Theodore Roethke.

Ostroff, Anthony, ed. *The Contemporary Poet as Artist and Critic*. Boston: Little, Brown, 1964. (This includes essays on Roethke's "In a Dark Time" by John Crowe Ransom, Babette Deutsch, and Stanley Kunitz, with a reply by the poet.) Pp. 23–53.

Ramsey, Jarold. "Roethke in the Greenhouse," *Western Humanities Review*, 26:36–47 (Winter 1972).

Rosenthal, M. L. *The Modern Poets: A Critical Introduction*. New York: Oxford University Press, 1960. Pp. 240–44.

———. *The New Poets: American and British Poetry since World War II*. New York: Oxford University Press, 1967. Pp. 112–18.

Schwartz, Delmore. "The Cunning and Craft of the Unconscious and the Preconscious," *Poetry*, 94:203–5. (June 1959).

Scott, Nathan A., Jr. *The Wild Prayer of Longing*. New Haven, Conn.: Yale University Press, 1971.

Southworth, James G. "The Poetry of Theodore Roethke," *College English*, 21:326–38 (March 1960).

Spender, Stephen. "Words for the Wind," *New Republic*, 141:21–22 (August 10, 1959).

Staples, Hugh B. "The Rose in the Sea-Wind: A Reading of Theodore Roethke's 'North American Sequence,'" *American Literature*, 6:189–203 (May 1964).

Stein, Arnold, ed. *Theodore Roethke: Essays on the Poetry*. Seattle: University of Washington Press, 1965.

Tate, Allen. "In Memoriam — Theodore Roethke, 1908–1963," *Encounter*, 21:68 (October 1963).

Vernon, John. "Theodore Roethke's *Praise to the End!* Poems," *Iowa Review*, 2:60–79 (Fall 1971).

Waggoner, Hyatt H. *American Poets from the Puritans to the Present*. Boston: Houghton Mifflin, 1968. Pp. 564–77.

Winters, Yvor. "The Poems of Theodore Roethke," *Kenyon Review*, 3:514–16 (Autumn 1941).

JOHN BERRYMAN

Works

POETRY

Twenty poems in *Five Young American Poets*. Norfolk, Conn.: New Directions, 1940.

Poems. Norfolk, Conn.: New Directions, 1942.
The Dispossessed. New York: William Sloane Associates, 1948.
Homage to Mistress Bradstreet. New York: Farrar, Straus and Giroux, 1956.
His Thought Made Pockets & the Plane Buckt. Pawlet, Vt.: C. Fredericks, 1958.
77 Dream Songs. New York: Farrar, Straus and Giroux, 1964.
Berryman's Sonnets. New York: Farrar, Straus and Giroux, 1967.
Short Poems. New York: Farrar, Straus and Giroux, 1967.
His Toy, His Dream, His Rest. New York: Farrar, Straus and Giroux, 1968.
Love and Fame. New York: Farrar, Straus and Giroux, 1970.
Delusions, Etc. New York: Farrar, Straus and Giroux, 1972.

PROSE

"The Imaginary Jew," *Kenyon Review,* 7:529–39 (Autumn 1945).
"The Lovers," *Kenyon Review,* 7:1–11 (Winter 1945). Also in *The Best American Short Stories 1946,* edited by Martha Foley. Boston: Houghton Mifflin, 1946.
"Young Poets Dead," *Sewanee Review,* 55:504–14 (July–September 1947).
"The Poetry of Ezra Pound," *Partisan Review,* 16:377–94 (April 1949).
Stephen Crane. New York: William Sloane Associates, 1950.
"Shakespeare at Thirty," *Hudson Review,* 6:175–203 (Summer 1953).
"The Long Way to MacDiarmid," *Poetry,* 88:52–61 (April 1956).
"Spender: The Poet as Critic," *New Republic,* 148:19–20 (June 29, 1963).
"Despondency and Madness" (on Robert Lowell's "Skunk Hour"), in *The Contemporary Poet as Artist and Critic,* edited by Anthony Ostroff. Boston: Little, Brown, 1964. Pp. 99–106.
"One Answer to a Question," *Shenandoah,* 17:67–76 (Autumn 1965).
Recovery. New York: Farrar, Straus and Giroux, 1973.

Bibliography

Kelly, Richard J. *John Berryman: A Checklist.* Metuchen, N.J.: Scarecrow Press, 1972.

Reviews and Critical Studies

Bellow, Saul. "John Berryman, Friend," *New York Times Book Review,* May 27, 1973, pp. 1–2.
Blum, Morgan. "Berryman as Biographer, Stephen Crane as Poet," *Poetry,* 78:298–307 (August 1951).
Bogan, Louise. "Verse," *New Yorker,* 40:242–43 (November 7, 1964).
Brinnin, John Malcolm. Review of *77 Dream Songs, New York Times Book Review,* August 23, 1964, p. 5.
Carruth, Hayden. "Love, Art, and Money," *Nation,* 211:437–38 (November 2, 1970).
Ciardi, John. "The Researched Mistress," *Saturday Review,* 40:36–37 (March 23, 1957).
Connelly, Kenneth. "Henry Pussycat, He Come Home Good," *Yale Review,* 58:419–27 (Spring 1969).
Cott, Jonathan. "Theodore Roethke and John Berryman: Two Dream Poets," in *On Contemporary Literature,* edited by Richard Kostelanetz. New York: Avon Books, 1964. Pp. 520–31.
Eberhart, Richard. "Song of the Nerves," *Poetry,* 73:43–45 (October 1948).
Evans, Arthur, and Catherine Evans. "Pieter Bruegel and John Berryman: Two

Winter Landscapes," *Texas Studies in Literature and Language*, 5:310–18 (Autumn 1963).

Fitts, Dudley. Review of *The Dispossessed, New York Times Book Review*, June 20, 1948, p. 4.

Holmes, John. Review of *Homage to Mistress Bradstreet, New York Times Book Review*, September 30, 1956, p. 18.

Howard, Jane. "Whiskey and Ink, Whiskey and Ink," *Life*, 63:67–76 (July 21, 1967).

Jarrell, Randall. Review of *The Dispossessed, Nation*, 167:80–81 (July 17, 1948).

Kessler, Jascha. "The Caged Sybil," *Saturday Review*, 51:34–35 (December 14, 1968).

Kunitz, Stanley. "No Middle Flight," *Poetry*, 90:244–49 (July 1957).

Meredith, William. "Henry Tasting All the Secret Bits of Life: Berryman's 'Dream Songs,'" *Wisconsin Studies in Contemporary Literature*, 6:27–33 (Winter–Spring 1965).

————. "Swan Songs," *Poetry*, 122:98–103 (May 1973).

Rosenthal, M. L. "The Couch and Poetic Insight," *Reporter*, 32:53–54 (March 25, 1965).

————. *The New Poets: American and British Poetry since World War II*. New York: Oxford University Press, 1967. Pp. 118–30.

Schorer, Mark. "The Lonely Calm," *Atlantic*, 232:92–94 (August 1973).

Seidel, Frederick. "Berryman's Dream Songs," *Poetry*, 105:257–59 (January 1965).

Shapiro, Karl. "Major Poets of the Ex-English Language," *Washington Post Book World*, January 26, 1969, p. 4.

Stitt, Peter A. "The Art of Poetry XVI — John Berryman 1914–72," *Paris Review*, 14:177–207 (Winter 1972).

RANDALL JARRELL

Works

POETRY·

The Rage for the Lost Penny. In *Five Young American Poets*. Norfolk, Conn.: New Directions, 1940.

Blood for a Stranger. New York: Harcourt, Brace, 1942.

Little Friend, Little Friend. New York: Dial, 1945.

Losses. New York: Harcourt, Brace, 1948.

The Seven-League Crutches. New York: Harcourt, Brace, 1951.

Selected Poems. 1st edition, New York: Knopf, 1955. 2nd edition, including *The Woman at the Washington Zoo*, New York: Atheneum, 1964.

The Woman at the Washington Zoo. New York: Atheneum, 1960.

The Lost World. New York: Macmillan, 1965. (Paperback reprint with Robert Lowell's essay "Randall Jarrell, 1914–1965: An Appreciation" appended. New York: Collier, 1966.)

The Complete Poems. New York: Farrar, Straus and Giroux, 1969. (Includes *Selected Poems*, poems omitted from *Selected Poems*, and sections of "Uncollected Poems (1934–1965)" and "Unpublished Poems (1935–1965).")

FICTION

Pictures from an Institution, a Comedy. New York: Knopf, 1954.

CRITICISM

Poetry and the Age. New York: Knopf, 1953.
A Sad Heart at the Supermarket. New York: Atheneum, 1962.
The Third Book of Criticism. New York: Farrar, Straus and Giroux, 1965.

Bibliographies

Adams, Charles M. *Randall Jarrell: A Bibliography.* Chapel Hill: University of North Carolina Press, 1958. (A supplement to this bibliography appears in *Analects*, 1:49–56 (Spring 1961).)

Gillikin, Dure J. "A Check-List of Criticism on Randall Jarrell, 1941–1970, with an Introduction and a List of His Major Works," *Bulletin of the New York Public Library*, 74:176–94 (April 1971).

Kisslinger, Margaret V. "A Bibliography of Randall Jarrell," *Bulletin of Bibliography*, 24:243–47 (May–August 1966).

Shapiro, Karl. *Randall Jarrell.* Washington, D.C.: Library of Congress, 1967. (Includes a bibliography of primary works and a list of Jarrell materials in the collections of the Library of Congress: manuscripts, phonodiscs, magnetic tapes, and motion pictures as well as books and uncollected poems and prose.)

Critical and Biographical Studies

Fein, Richard. "Major American Poetry of World War II." Doctoral dissertation, New York University, 1960.

Lowell, Robert, Peter Taylor, and Robert Penn Warren, eds. *Randall Jarrell, 1914–1965.* New York: Farrar, Straus and Giroux, 1967. (Essays by Hannah Arendt, John Berryman, Elizabeth Bishop, Philip Booth, Cleanth Brooks, James Dickey, Denis Donoghue, Leslie A. Fiedler, Robert Fitzgerald, R. W. Flint, Alfred Kazin, Stanley Kunitz, Robert Lowell, William Meredith, Marianne Moore, Robert Phelps, Sister M. Bernetta Quinn, John Crowe Ransom, Adrienne Rich, Delmore Schwartz, Maurice Sendak, Karl Shapiro, Allen Tate, Eleanor Ross Taylor, Peter Taylor, P. L. Travers, Robert Watson, and Mrs. Randall Jarrell. Pages xi–xii list all of Jarrell's books, including editions in preparation, as of the volume's date of publication.)

Mazzaro, Jerome. "Between Two Worlds: The Post-Modernism of Randall Jarrell," *Salmagundi*, Fall 1971, pp. 93–113.

Rideout, Walter B. "'To Change! to Change!'" in Edward Hungerford, ed., *Poets in Progress.* Evanston, Ill.: Northwestern University Press, 1967.

Rosenthal, M. L. *The Modern Poets: A Critical Introduction.* New York: Oxford University Press, 1960.

ROBERT LOWELL

Works

POETRY

Land of Unlikeness. Cummington, Mass.: Cummington Press, 1944.

Lord Weary's Castle. New York: Harcourt, Brace, 1946.
The Mills of the Kavanaughs. New York: Harcourt, Brace, 1951.
Life Studies. New York: Farrar, Straus and Cudahy, 1959.
Imitations. New York: Farrar, Straus and Cudahy, 1961.
For the Union Dead. New York: Farrar, Straus and Giroux, 1964.
Near the Ocean. New York: Farrar, Straus and Giroux, 1967.
The Voyage and Other Versions of Poems by Baudelaire. New York: Farrar, Straus and
    Giroux, 1968.
Notebook 1967–68. New York: Farrar, Straus and Giroux, 1969. 2nd printing,
    revised, New York: Farrar, Straus and Giroux, 1969. 3rd edition, revised and
    expanded, and retitled *Notebook*. New York: Farrar, Straus and Giroux, 1970.
For Lizzie and Harriet. New York: Farrar, Straus and Giroux, 1973.
History. New York: Farrar, Straus and Giroux, 1973.
The Dolphin. New York: Farrar, Straus and Giroux, 1973.

PLAYS

Phaedra, in *Phaedra and Figaro*, translated by Robert Lowell and Jacques Barzun.
    New York: Farrar, Straus and Cudahy, 1961.
The Old Glory. New York: Farrar, Straus and Giroux, 1965; revised edition, 1968.
Prometheus Bound. New York: Farrar, Straus and Giroux, 1969.

PROSE

"Four Quartets," *Sewanee Review*, 51:432–35 (1943).
"A Note" [on Hopkins], *Kenyon Review*, 6:583–86 (1944).
"The Verses of Thomas Merton," *Commonweal*, 42:240–42 (1945).
"Imagination and Reality," *Nation*, 164:400–2 (1947).
"Thomas, Bishop, and Williams," *Sewanee Review*, 55:493–503 (1947).
"Paterson II," *Nation*, 166:692–94 (1948).
"John Ransom's Conversation," *Sewanee Review*, 56:374–77 (1948).
"Prose Genius in Verse," *Kenyon Review*, 15:619–25 (1953).
"Visiting the Tates," *Sewanee Review*, 67:557–59 (1959).
"I. A. Richards as a Poet," *Encounter*, 14:77–78 (February 1960).
"Yvor Winters: A Tribute," *Poetry*, 98:40–42 (April 1961).
"William Carlos Williams," *Hudson Review*, 14:530–36 (1961–62).
"Randall Jarrell," in Robert Lowell, Peter Taylor, and Robert Penn Warren, eds.,
    Randall Jarrell 1914–1965. New York: Farrar, Straus and Giroux, 1967.

Critical Studies

Alvarez, A. "A Talk with Robert Lowell," *Encounter*, 24:39–43 (February 1965).
Cambon, Glauco. "Robert Lowell: History as Eschatology," in *The Inclusive Flame:
    Studies in American Poetry*. Bloomington: Indiana University Press, 1963.
Cooper, Philip. *The Autobiographical Myth of Robert Lowell*. Chapel Hill: University
    of North Carolina Press, 1970.
Cosgrave, Philip. *The Public Poetry of Robert Lowell*. London: Victor Gollancz,
    1970.
Eberhart, Richard. "Four Poets," *Sewanee Review*, 60:327–31 (1947).
Ehrenpreis, Irvin. "The Age of Lowell," in *American Poetry*. New York: St.
    Martin's Press, 1965.
Fein, Richard J. *Robert Lowell*. New York: Twayne, 1970.
Hochman, Baruch. "Robert Lowell's *The Old Glory*," *Tulane Drama Review*,
    11:127–38 (Summer 1967).

Kunitz, Stanley. "Talk with Robert Lowell," *New York Times Book Review*, October 4, 1964, pp. 34–36, 38–39.

Martz, William J. *The Achievement of Robert Lowell*. Glenview, Ill.: Scott, Foresman, 1966.

Mazzaro, Jerome. *The Poetic Themes of Robert Lowell*. Ann Arbor: University of Michigan Press, 1965.

Meiners, R. K. *Everything to Be Endured: An Essay on Robert Lowell and Modern Poetry*. Columbia: University of Missouri Press, 1970.

Mills, Ralph J., Jr. *Contemporary American Poetry*. New York: Random House, 1965.

Parkinson, Thomas, ed. *Robert Lowell: A Collection of Critical Essays*. Englewood Cliffs, N.J.: Prentice-Hall, 1968.

Perloff, Marjorie. "Death by Water: The Winslow Elegies of Robert Lowell," *ELH*, 34:116–40 (1967).

———. *The Poetic Art of Robert Lowell*. Ithaca, N.Y.: Cornell University Press, 1973.

Price, Jonathan ed. *Critics on Robert Lowell: Readings in Literary Criticism*. Coral Gables, Fla: University of Miami Press, 1972.

Ricks, Christopher. "The Three Lives of Robert Lowell," *New Statesman*, 69:496–97 (March 26, 1965).

Rosenthal, M. L. *The New Poets: American and British Poetry since World War II*. New York: Oxford University Press, 1967.

Seidel, Frederick. "An Interview," *The Paris Review Interviews, Second Series*, edited by Malcolm Cowley. New York: Viking Press, 1963.

Staples, H. B. *Robert Lowell*. New York: Farrar, Straus and Cudahy, 1962.

Waggoner, Hyatt H. *American Poets from the Puritans to the Present*. Boston: Houghton Mifflin, 1968.

Wilbur, Richard, *et al.* "On Robert Lowell's 'Skunk Hour,'" in Anthony Ostroff, ed., *The Contemporary Poet as Artist and Critic*. Boston: Little, Brown, 1964.

Woodson, Thomas. "Robert Lowell's 'Hawthorne,' Yvor Winters and the American Literary Tradition," *American Quarterly*, 19:575–82 (1967).

HOWARD NEMEROV

Works

POETRY

The Image and the Law. New York: Henry Holt, 1947.
Guide to the Ruins. New York: Random House, 1950.
The Salt Garden. Boston: Little, Brown, 1955.
Small Moment. Los Angeles: Ward Ritchie, 1957. (Broadside.)
Mirrors & Windows: Poems. Chicago: University of Chicago Press, 1958.
New & Selected Poems. Chicago: University of Chicago Press, 1960.
Endor. New York: Abingdon, 1961.
The Next Room of the Dream. Chicago: University of Chicago Press, 1962.
The Blue Swallows. Chicago: University of Chicago Press, 1967.
A Sequence of Seven with a Drawing by Ron Slaughter. Detroit: Tinker Press, 1967.
Winter Lightning. London: Rapp and Whiting, 1968.
The Painter Dreaming in the Scholar's House. New York: Phoenix Book Shop, 1968.
Gnomes and Occasions. Chicago: University of Chicago Press, 1972.

FICTION

The Melodramatists. New York: Random House, 1949.
Federigo, or, The Power of Love. Boston: Little, Brown, 1954.
The Homecoming Game. New York: Simon and Schuster, 1957.
A Commodity of Dreams & Other Stories. New York: Simon and Schuster, 1959.
Stories, Fables and Other Diversions. Brookline, Mass.: David R. Godine, 1971.

OTHER PROSE

Poetry and Fiction: Essays. New Brunswick, N.J.: Rutgers University Press, 1963.
Journal of the Fictive Life. New Brunswick, N.J.: Rutgers University Press, 1965.
Reflexions on Poetry and Poetics. New Brunswick, N.J.: Rutgers University Press, 1972.

EDITED VOLUMES

Longfellow. New York: Dell, 1959.
Poets on Poetry. New York: Basic Books, 1965.
Poetry and Criticism. Cambridge, Mass.: Adams House and Lowell House Printers, 1965.

Critical Studies and Reviews

Arrowsmith, William. "Recent Verse," *Hudson Review*, 1:98–105 (Spring 1948).
Bartholomay, Julia. *The Shield of Perseus.* Gainesville: University of Florida Press, 1972.
Berryman, John. "Waiting for the End Boys," *Partisan Review*, 15:254–67 (February 1948).
Bogan, Louise. "Verse," *New Yorker*, 37:129–31 (April 1, 1961).
Boyle, Kay. "Saluting Kings and Presidents," *Nation*, 214:184–87 (February 7, 1972).
Burke, Kenneth. "Comments on 18 Poems by Howard Nemerov," *Kenyon Review*, 60:117–31 (Winter 1952).
Carruth, Hayden. "The Errors of Excellence," *Nation*, 192:63–64 (January 21, 1961).
Ciardi, John. "Dry and Bitter Dust," *Saturday Review*, 44:66 (February 11, 1961).
Daiches, David. "Some Recent Poetry," *Yale Review*, 40:352–57 (Winter 1951).
Dickey, James. *Babel to Byzantium.* New York: Farrar, Straus and Giroux, 1968. Pp. 35–41.
Duncan, Bowie, ed. *The Critical Reception of Howard Nemerov.* Metuchen, N.J.: Scarecrow Press, 1971.
Eberhart, Richard. "Five Poets," *Kenyon Review*, 14:168–76 (Winter 1952).
Elliott, George P. "Fiction Chronicle," *Hudson Review*, 10:288–95 (Summer 1957).
Fitts, Dudley. "Poetry Chronicle," *Partisan Review*, 22:542–48 (Fall 1955).
Flint, R. W. "Poetry," *New York Review of Books*, 1:26–27 (Special Issue 1963).
Foster, Richard. "Neither Noble nor Savage, but Nice," *Minnesota Review*, 1:109–13 (Fall 1960).
Gerstenberger, Donna. "An Interview with Howard Nemerov," *Trace*, 35:22–25 (January–February 1960).
Harvey, Robert D. "A Prophet Armed: An Introduction to the Poetry of Howard Nemerov," in *Poets in Progress*, edited by E. B. Hungerford. Evanston, Ill.: Northwestern University Press, 1962. Pp. 116–33.

Howe, Irving. "A Cultivated Mind Willing to Bend to the Work at Hand," *New York Times Book Review*, March 29, 1964, p. 5.

Jarrell, Randall. "Recent Poetry," *Yale Review*, 45:122–32 (September 1955).

Jerome, Judson. "For Summer, a Wave of New Verse," *Saturday Review*, 46:30–32 (July 6, 1963).

Johnson, W. R. "Review," *Carleton Miscellany*, 4:120–24 (Spring 1963).

Kizer, Carolyn. "The Middle of the Journey," *Poetry*, 92:178–81 (December 1958).

Knock, Stanley F., Jr. "Renewal of Illusion," *Christian Century*, 80:84–85 (March 20, 1963).

Kunitz, Stanley. "Many Exertions, Some Excellencies," *New York Times Book Review*, July 21, 1963, p. 4.

Mizener, Arthur. "Spring Fiction," *Kenyon Review*, 19:484–93 (Summer 1957).

Rosenthal, M. L. "'False Wentletrap! Avaunt,'" *Nation*, 187:27–28 (August 16, 1958).

———. "Something That Might Simply Be," *Reporter*, 29:54–58 (September 12, 1963).

Waggoner, Hyatt H. *American Poets from the Puritans to the Present*. Boston: Houghton Mifflin, 1968. Pp. 610–14.

Whittemore, Reed. "Observation of an Alien," *New Republic*, 138:27–28 (June 23, 1958).

Wright, James. "Some Recent Poetry," *Sewanee Review*, 66:657–68 (October–December 1958).

ABOUT THE AUTHORS

About the Authors

GROVER SMITH, professor of English at Duke University, is the author of *T. S. Eliot's Poetry and Plays: A Study in Sources and Meaning* and of *Ford Madox Ford*. He has edited *Josiah Royce's Seminar, 1913–1914, as Recorded in the Notebooks of Harry T. Costello* and *Letters of Aldous Huxley*.

RALPH J. MILLS, JR., is the author of *Contemporary American Poetry*, *Cry of the Human* (essays), and *Door to the Sun* (poems), and editor of *On the Poet and His Craft: Selected Prose of Theodore Roethke* and *Selected Letters of Theodore Roethke*. He teaches English at the University of Illinois at Chicago Circle.

M. L. ROSENTHAL, poet, critic, and professor of English at New York University, is the author or editor of many books, among them *The New Poets: American and British Poetry since World War II*, *The View from the Peacock's Tail: Poems*, and *Poetry and the Common Life*.

WILLIAM J. MARTZ is editor of *The Distinctive Voice*, a collection of twentieth-century American poetry, and general editor of the Modern Poets Series, as well as the author of *Shakespeare's Universe of Comedy*. He is a professor of English at Ripon College.

JAY MARTIN is the author of *Conrad Aiken: A Life of His Art*, *Harvests of Change: American Literature 1865–1914*, and *Nathanael West: The Art of His Life*. He is a professor of English and comparative literature at the University of California, Irvine.

PETER MEINKE is director of the Writing Workshop at Eckerd College. He has published poetry, reviews, and articles in the *New Republic* and other magazines; his latest book is *Lines from Neuchâtel*.

305

INDEX

Index

309